BIBLIOGRAPHY OF LANGUAGE ARTS MATERIALS

FOR NATIVE NORTH AMERICANS

Bilingual, English as a Second Language and

Native Language Materials 1965-1974

G. Edward Evans, Principal Investigator
Karin Abbey, Research Director
Dennis Reed, Research Assistant

Los Angeles
1977

$4.00

Send checks payable to:
Regents of the University of California

University of California
American Indian Studies Center
Room 3220 Campbell Hall
405 Hilgard Avenue
Los Angeles, California 90024

Partially supported by Ford Foundation
Grant #710-0370
and
The Graduate school of
Library and Information Science,
UCLA

ACKNOWLEDGEMENT

We wish to express our thanks to a number of people who have contributed their time and knowledge to this project. Although we (Edward Evans and Karin Abbey) have degrees in Anthropology, neither of us is a trained linguist. Without Dr. William O. Bright's (Department of Linguistics, UCLA) selfless assistance, this project could never have been completed effectively. Professor Bright gave generously of his time and expertise in American Indian languages. We would also like to thank William Leap of the Center for Applied Linguistics for his encouragement and continued moral support.

The research project was partially funded by a grant from the Ford Foundation #710-0370 through the Institute of American Cultures and the American Indian Studies Center. It was also supported by the Graduate School of Library and Information Science through funding of research assistants and release time for Dr. Evans.

Finally, we wish to thank the staff of both the Indian Center and the Library School. In particular, we would like to express our gratitude to Dr. Charlotte Heth, Director of the Center, and Dr. Robert M. Hayes, Dean of the Library School.

TABLE OF CONTENTS

INTRODUCTION

I. INTRODUCTION

A new era of Federal recognition of Indian culture and language began with the passage by Congress of the Economic Opportunity Act of 1964 (P.L. 88-452, 78 Stat. 508) and the Elementary and Secondary Education Act of 1965 (P.L. 89-10, 79 Stat. 27). These acts gave Indians the right to exercise local control over the education being offered to them. To a limited extent there has been progress toward this goal during the years since the passage of these acts.

Many individuals view this legislation as the most important step the United States government has taken toward self-determination for Indians. From the first contact up to 1965, white society has tried to destroy Indian culture. Despite these efforts Indian cultures have managed to survive. When physical annihilation of Indians appeared to be unworkable and unnecessary, assimilation--cultural annihilation--became the goal. There were many reasons for the failure of assimilation, among them the continued existence of reservations and the "separate" societies on them. The "Indian Problem" remained and nothing seemed to solve it. It is to be hoped the laws passed in the last twelve years mean that the dominant culture finally recognizes the rights of other cultures to exist side by side with it. Certainly the idea that Indian peoples, among others, have a right to self-determination is overdue.

Self-determination means, among other things, the right to maintain one's own language. The teaching of and in the native language is a means to that end. Prior to the passage of the above acts, Federal policy was against such teaching. As an example of this policy, the rules for Bureau of Indian Affairs Schools stated, in part:

> All instruction must be in the English Language.
> Pupils must be compelled to converse with each
> other in English, and should be properly rebuked

1

or punished for persistent violation of this rule.
Every effort should be made to encourage them to
abandon their tribal language. To facilitate this
work it is essential that all school employees
be able to speak English fluently, and that they
speak English exclusively to the pupils, and also
to each other in the presence of the pupils.

> Report of the Commissioner
> of Indian Affairs. T. J.
> Morgan. September 5, 1890.
> (Washburn 1973:493)

Most of the American government programs aimed at American Indians
did not have the desired effect--acculturation. After more than two
hundred years of effort by the United States government, many Indians
still speak only their native language. The majority of Americans are
not aware of this fact; they simply assume that everyone born in this
country speaks English.

> Congress and the American people generally find
> it hard to sympathize with educational programs
> designed to teach English as a second language to
> Indian school children. Their assumption often
> is that the Indian should long since have been
> utilizing English as his principal language.
> Perhaps the urban riots of the late 1960's and
> emphasis upon teaching English as a second
> language to Negro youth will have a sobering
> effect on those who long believed that both
> Negro and Indian needed merely to be prodded
> to cause them to "catch up" with the dominant
> whites. (Washburn 1971:220)

2

All of us who are involved in teaching, regardless of level, share to some degree the belief that formal education is a benevolent means of affecting social change and "progress." That is, those of us who have been brought up through a system modeled after the Western European educational pattern. Certainly most of the American government educational policy toward Indians has had that concept as one of its keystones.

In general, education is a formalized portion of the enculturation process which begins when a person is born. But when children of a cultural background different from the dominant culture are the focus of the educational process, severe problems can arise. In this case, formal education is no longer just a means of transmitting knowledge and social values with which the child already has some degree of familiarity. Instead, education becomes the focal point of intense struggle for the mind of the child. If the curriculum reflects solely the dominant culture, the struggle is clear cut and evident to all. A more complex situation arises when "elements" of both the child's culture and the dominant culture are incorporated into the educational program. For the child, this situation may be more difficult to handle than a straight acculturation curriculum.

Bilingual education is essentially a compromise between the self-determinist's view that the native language should form the basis of formal education, and the established view that English should be this basis. Depending upon the degree to which elements of either culture and language are involved in the curriculum, it is possible for persons from each culture to assume that the objective of the program is to support that particular culture.

For Indians, everyone acknowledges the impossibility of returning to the "old ways." Both the physical environment of the contemporary world, and a lack of comprehensive knowledge of what the "old ways" are, combine to create this situation. On the other hand, the American government is now finally willing to concede that acculturation/assimilation programs have failed to transform Indians into west Europeans, in so far as values and attitudes are concerned. Therefore, bilingual/bicultural education is at least minimally acceptable to both sides of the argument. Unless there is a real effort to create a bicultural and bilingual program, there is little likelihood that there will be any agreement as to the value of the educational process for native Americans.

Since language is an important part of culture, bicultural education will not succeed unless there is also bilingual education. Our research effort was directed toward identifying bilingual educational materials developed for natives of America north of Mexico in the period between 1965 and 1974. These materials include native language and English as a Second Language (ESL) publications. One very important result of our endeavor has been to provide a comprehensive listing of contemporary materials, that is, as comprehensive as it is possible to make when one must rely upon the voluntary cooperation of field workers and language specialists. We received excellent cooperation and wish to thank everyone who took time to send us data. In order to have true bilingual/bicultural education, materials of the type we have identified are an absolute essential.

Before we discuss the results of our search, we feel it would be useful to give a brief review of Indian education programs as supported by the American government, in order to establish what makes our list of materials so important for anyone concerned with Indian education.

II. HISTORY

Prior to the American Revolution there were several schools or
"colleges" for Indian students that were supported by private charities.
Although none were very successful, they did set the basic American
philosophy aimed at "civilizing" the Indians. One such school was
established at William and Mary College in Williamsburg, Virginia, with
funds allocated in 1697. The students were often unwilling "hostages
for the peace," the sons of hostile or formerly hostile Indian leaders.
They were instructed in English, reading, writing, and the Christian
religion. Many died, but most returned to their tribes at the end of
their schooling, and, to the dismay of their educators, resumed tribal
customs almost as if there had been no interruption. The few successes
of this institution were the young Indians who remained in "civilized"
Virginia; maintained as servants in colonial homes. (William and Mary
College, 1870:37-38)

Many New England homes also had Indian servants or apprentices,
and their employers were required by law to instruct the Indians in the
Puritan faith. John Eliot's famous Indian Bible was a direct result of
these laws. Another school for Indians was established at Harvard.
Called the Indian College, in its eleven years of operation, 1654 to 1665,
only one student was graduated with a bachelor of arts degree, and he
unfortunately died of tuberculosis within a year of leaving school. After
1665, no more Indian students came to the school, and the building was
used to house the first American university press. It was on this press
that John Eliot's Indian Bible was printed. (Morison 1936:36-39)

A few years later Eleazer Wheelock in Connecticut was approaching
education from a different point of view--boarding school. He established
such a school at his home in Lebanon, Connecticut, and later moved it to
Hanover, New Hampshire, where it was first called Moor's Charity School,
and later Dartmouth. (Berry 1972:33) His idea was to train missionaries

5

who would then set up missions with the Indian tribes. At first he took only Indians into the schools but soon displaced most of the Indian students with whites. Because of the strong mission orientation Wheelock received considerable financial support and was successful in hiring competent teachers and providing sound training.

The colonial period established the basic elements of Indian education which have been more or less followed up to the present time. First there was an emphasis on isolating the Indian from his native culture. Second, the content of the curriculum was the same as the white students'-- reading, writing, mathematics, logic, philosophy, English, Greek, and Latin. Although he was taught white culture, the Indian student was kept apart from local white society, making it very difficult for him to enter that society.

Had either the French or Spanish prevailed in controlling North America the course of Indian education would have been very different. Indians were an essential element in the economy as established under French and Spanish rule. Unfortunately, under the English system, the best one can say is the Indian was an incidental element. In many cases the Indian represented an environmental element that had to be removed before the British/American economic system could be fully operative. Thus the major emphasis was on "solving the Indian Problem" rather than on helping Indian peoples adjust and survive in a rapidly changing environment.

From 1789 to 1819 the funding of Indian education was haphazard at best. Responsibility for Indian education was left almost exclusively to the missionaries. In 1794 the first Indian treaty which mentioned education was concluded with the Oneida, Tuscarora and Stockbridge Indians living in the Oneida territory. Article III of the treaty stated that the United States would provide funds "to instruct some young men of the three nations in the arts of miller and sawyer . . ." (Washburn 1973:2293)

The second U.S. treaty to deal with Indian education was directed more toward a "liberal arts" education than the technical education supported above, but it was through a missionary intermediary. This treaty, signed with the Kaskaskia Indians of Illinois, stated that one hundred dollars would be supplied annually for seven years for the support of a priest, who would, among his other duties, "instruct as many of their children as possible in the rudiments of literature." (Ibid: 2310)

Generally, treaties were little concerned with educating Indians. Conditions of hostility between whites and Indians generally meant that treaties, when they were signed, dealt almost exclusively with the major issues of land, removal and compensation. Nevertheless, there was the feeling, among many Americans of good will, that if the Indian could be educated to agriculture, he would find himself happier, healthier and more adaptable to the culture of the United States. Experiments along these lines were generally unsuccessful, however.

In 1840 "manual labor" boarding schools were being established by the missionaries on the western reservations. The shift in emphasis to practical manual skills, an important change, did not change the emphasis upon isolating the child from the native culture. Isolation was thought to help affect changes in the child and through those changes change the native culture when the individual returned home. Although the following quotation is from a later period the concept was firmly established long before 1840. The purpose of the boarding school was "to free the children from the language and habits of their untutored and oftentimes savage parents." (U.S. Department of Interior 1886: 23) In addition, the manual labor performed--farming, animal husbandry, carpentry, masonry, weaving, sewing, etc.--helped reduce the cost of operating the school. A few teachers had the hope that this more practical training (no more Latin and Greek) would be more meaningful to the students.

The involvement of independent church groups in the educational system was beginning to show some strain after the Civil War. A triangular arrangement was in operation, each side of which pulled in a different direction. On one side the tribes, at least on paper, viewed as independent foreign nations, were not all that anxious to benefit from white education. Members of the tribe had widely divergent opinions about the value of white society and the ways and needs of maintaining the native society. On the second side was the Federal Government slowly developing an Indian policy of assimilation. On the third side were the missionaries who had a primary goal: convert the "heathen" to the true belief. Because they did receive government funds there was some expectation the missionaries would support the Bureau of Indian Affairs' policy, but not all the missionaries thought the assimilation policy was right.

Thus a situation existed in which one group wanted Indian children to be raised as Indian children with their own religion. Another group wanted Indian children raised as white children, regardless of religious belief. Finally, there was a group who wanted Indian children raised as Christians, regardless of whether their culture was Indian or white. Needless to say the students found this to be highly confusing.

President Grant strongly criticized the missionaries for their continued use of native languages in Indian education, in 1870. (Adams 1946:50) As the government became more and more unhappy about the failure of missionary schools to support official policy, more and more Bureau Schools were established. No matter who offically controlled the school two basic ideas were firmly established by 1870. One was the boarding school and the other was use to student labor to reduce operating costs. For most tribes this would be the pattern for the next sixty years.

There was a notable expection to this situation. A few tribes were able to create a school system largely, if not completely, under their own control. Most tribes did not gain this right for another 100 years. The Cherokees and Choctaws had flourishing school systems as early as 1821.

By 1852 the Cherokees had 21 schools, 2 academies, and an enrollment of 1100 students. The Choctaws were only slightly behind the Cherokees, and the Creeks, Chickasaws and Seminoles also were able to establish their own systems before the Civil War started. (Berry 1972:36) Although the schools were supervised by the tribes and in some cases (Cherokees and Choctaws) funded by the tribe, the curriculum was that of the white society. There was little or no instruction in native culture or language. One interesting feature of the Choctaw program was the inclusion of a separate project to provide a basic education for adults. It is unfortunate that these programs were not considered as models for Indian education.

Although the words used to describe Federal Indian policy after 1870 were softer sounding--"peace policy," "civilization and citizenship,"-- the basic objective remained unchanged: eradicate Indian culture. Even if such a policy was ethical the manner of implementation ensured its failure. By failing to know or recognize an essential principle of culture change the program of rapid training in white cultural values and skills was doomed to failure. Cultural change is a long term process in which the individual and the culture assess the worth of new traits and slowly accommodate new traits as they seem valuable.

Throughout the period 1869-1933, there was some effort to revive bilingual education. A few of the missionary societies and many individual missionaries from all denominations felt that bilingual education was or would be valuable. However, government policy stated that only English could be studied. Nevertheless, interest in translating the Bible into native languages stayed alive. After all, the missionaries' prime goal was not to make the Indian a good member of Western society, but to make him a good Christian; and it was felt that this would be easier if the Christian texts were presented in a language comprehensible to him. Obviously, producing a translated Bible was of little value unless the people could read it. This in turn meant giving instructing in reading the native language--a direct violation of government policy. In 1879 two missionary societies were told to stop this process or lose their Federal aid. (Adams 1946:50)

In 1887 the expenditure for Indian education was $20,000, which went to establish 48 small boarding schools and 102 day schools with 3,598 pupils. The annual expenditure jumped in 1899 to $2,638,390, which went to the support of 148 boarding schools, and 295 day schools supporting 24,004 pupils. (Dawes 1899:281) In fact a total of $29,352,344 was spent between the years of 1877 and 1899 in an effort to assimilate the Indian via white men's educational means. However intense the assimilation program might have been, it was nevertheless a failure. In an article published in 1899 Dawes lamely tried to defend the barbarous governmental policy by stating:

> It was plain that if he (the Indian) were left
> alone he must of necessity become a tramp and
> beggar with all the evil passions of a savage, a
> homeless and lawless poacher upon civilization,
> and a terror to the peaceful citizen. It was
> this condition which forced on the nation its
> present Indian policy. It was born of sheer
> necessity. (Ibid)

The first Indian students were enrolled in public school systems near their homes in 1890. Generally this experiment was a failure for several reasons. First the local non-Indian population disliked the Indian population and often expressed the dislike physically. A second factor was that the public school curriculum was geared to a white audience with a white background. It is true that the reservation and off reservation Indian schools had a white oriented curriculum in terms of vocational education; however, the teachers did realize all their students came from a different cultural background. A third factor was that most of the Indian children's environment was not geared to academic training and formal education. The Indian child therefore started public school with a great disadvantage, which tended to be magnified as time went on.

10

Most of the missionary schools still in operation in 1890 were "contract" schools, if they received Federal funds. In 1897 the contract system was abolished by law; however, by 1905 a few contract schools were reestablished. They were reestablished because of tribal and missionary society pressure. Only a few of the pre-1897 schools were reopened but those that were had and still have an excellent reputation.

By 1920, things were at a very low point, as described by Evelyn Adams:

> The record was drab at the end of a half century
> of full government responsibility in Indian Affairs.
> Most of the Indians had been kept peaceful, many
> of them had been kept idle, and too many students
> had been kept ignorant of techniques that would
> make them vocationally adept. Large amounts of
> government money had been spent for schools that
> were lost in their own machinery.
>
> Student labor in its institutional setting com-
> prised the washing of tons of dishes, the making
> of acres of beds, the laundering of mountains of
> clothing, the cleaning of countless huge dormi-
> tories, and many other regimented duties on a
> wholesale scale equally remote from the student's
> miserable home on a barren reservation which he
> presumably was being taught to improve.
>
> Indian education closely trailed the development
> of the public school system, with slight relation-
> ship to Indian needs. The difficulty lay in the
> slavish imitation of the white school. The empty,
> expensive, time-consuming education program for the
> Indian did not bring to him economic betterment,
> nor did it destroy his native way of life as it

so woefully intended, because his school followed
a sterile path and made only a tip of the wing
contact with his tribal experience and his actual
reservation surroundings. (Adams 1971:64)

During the Coolidge Administration a survey of reservation conditions
was conducted at the direction of Herbert Work, Secretary of the Interior.
Dr. Lewis Merriam was in charge of the survey. Experts in the field of
health, education and law visited Indian communities throughout the United
States.

The Merriam Report focused on education as the solution to the
"problems of the Indian wards." It pointed out many problems in Indian
education which are still extant today. Among the recommendations of this
report was the suggestion that boarding schools be changed to day schools
wherever conditions of transport made this possible, and that schools which
continued to board students be improved. The period from 1928 to World
War II was a relatively enlightened era of Bureau of Indian Affairs policy.
The Rhoads-Scattergood administration put into effect several of the
recommendations of the Merriam Report. Congress allocated more money for
the improvement of schools and the hiring of better personnel. The number
of Indian children enrolled in public schools rose from 38,000 in 1929-30
to 48,000 in 1931-32. (MacLean 1973:8) This was regarded as progress,
although, as has been noted, there was considerable reason to question the
advisability of sending Indian children to public schools.

John Collier became head of the BIA in 1933. He was an able administrator, committed to making Indian education relevant to the Indian way of
life. He was also responsible for hiring more Indians to work within the
BIA. The Indian Reorganization Act of 1934 strengthened the tribes' rights
of self-government and reawakened official interest in native languages.
At the Indian Service Summer School, started in 1936, classes were offered
in both Sioux and Navajo. (Liebowitz 1971:5) However, John Collier was

disliked by Congress and he and the policies he sponsored also met strong opposition from entrenched BIA officials in the field. He resigned his office in 1944.

The House Select Committee on Indian Affairs made recommendations for "the final solution of the Indian problem"--a phrase with an appropriately ominous ring--in 1944. The committee criticized the new day schools for adapting to the Indian way of life, and advocated a return to the boarding school system. It stated: "The goal of Indian education should be to make the Indian child a better American rather than to equip him simply to be a better Indian." (U.S. Congress Senate 1969:13)

World War II had occasioned cutbacks in funding for Indian Education, and the end of the war marked the beginning of the "termination" policy and more cutbacks. By the early 1950's the termination policy was in full operation. In 1952 the BIA closed all Federal schools in Idaho, Michigan, Washington, and Wisconsin. The following year many boarding and day schools in other states closed, forcing the Indian students to transfer to public schools. Assimilation was again attempted by removing the children from their home environment--Navajo children were sent to school in Oregon, children from the Northwest Coast were shipped to Oklahoma. (U.S. Congress Senate 1969:14) House Concurrent Resolution 108 of 1953 called for the end of all federal services to Indians, including education. (Leibowitz, ibid)

But by the end of the fifties, it was clear that termination was not a success. Tribes which had been terminated found themselves in much worse condition culturally and economically than they had been before losing their reservations. The Kennedy Administration set up a task force under Secretary of the Interior Stewart Udall to study Indian Affairs. Their report in July 1961 suggested, among other things, greater involvement of the Indian community in the education of their children. (U.S. Congress Senate 1969:15) This recommendation was implemented by the Economic

13

Opportunity Act of 1964, which also designated that English must be taught
as a Second Language to children for whom English was not a native language,
and that Indian schools should help transmit Indian culture. The Elementary and Secondary Education Act of 1965 went on to fund 90,000 teacher
aides, bilingual in the children's native language, to expand schools and
to enroll 475,000 minority children, including Indians, in pre-school
classes. These two pieces of legislation have had a greater impact on
Indian education than almost anything since Eliot and Wheelock started
their missionary boarding schools.

Bilingual education has always been an idea underlying at least some
portion of Indian education. There was, as we have seen, a brief moment
during colonial times (Eliot, Wheelock et al.) when there was active use
of native languages, at least in religious instruction. The first offi-
cially sanctioned instruction in native languages did not take place until
the 1930's however, and this effort faded with the onset of World War II.
Finally, in the mid-60's, there is legislation which gives legal sanction
and financial support to bilingual education for "minority" children in
American schools.

III.   EDUCATIONAL/CULTURAL PROBLEMS IN THE LANGUAGE
        EDUCATION OF THE AMERICAN INDIAN CHILD

We are currently in a transition period in the attitude shown by
established educational institutions, including the Bureau of Indian
Affairs, toward their Indian and Eskimo students. The Federal Government
has recognized from the beginning that the Native American child comes to
school with attitudes, background and beliefs different from Anglo students,
and that one of the most apparent differences lies in language. The current
transition in attitude is from one of wishing to eradicate these differences
to one of wishing to help preserve them. The early efforts to eradicate
those things, particularly language, which set the Indian apart from the
mainstream of American life were fully consistent with the "melting pot"
view of American society. But these efforts failed. Current educators,
influenced by the new view of America as a land where cultural pluralism
is not only acceptable but desirable, also recognize the distinct status
of the Indian student, and beyond this, the distinct status of each of the
several tribes and bands of Indians, Eskimos, and Aleuts. They wish not
to destroy these distinctions, but to encourage pride in them, while
exposing the student to the culture and language of the majority of
Americans. This new attitude is expressed in a recent government report
as follows: "Essentially the goals (of American Indian Education) are to
enlarge the area of choice of Indian people and to help them maintain
their dignity." (Havighurst 1970:3)

There are several aspects of a language which must be understood if
that language is to be taught in an academic setting, and if speakers of
that language are to be taught English effectively. These include the
basic concepts inherent in the grammar and syntax of the language and the
sound system employed in the phonology of that language.

A few well known examples of syntactic and grammatical characteristics
of native North American languages may serve here to illustrate this point.

In Hopi, plurals and cardinal numbers can only be used for things which can be seen together as objective groups. In Wintu, the following are recognized as fundamental categories of speech: subjectivity vs. objectivity, knowledge vs. belief, and freedom vs. actual necessity; thus the English sentence, "Harry is chopping wood" must be translated into Wintu in one of five ways, depending on whether the person who is speaking knows this by observation, hearsay, or by inference in three distinct degrees of plausibility. In Navajo it is not possible to say simply, "He goes." The speaker must specify whether "he" goes on foot, on horseback, in a wagon, car, train, airplane, or boat; and further if by horse, at what gait the horse is traveling, and if by boat, how that boat is powered. (Kluckhohn 1963:140-143)

Each language has its own sound system, choosing from among the wide range of sounds possible for the human vocal system to produce those particular sounds it will use, and which distinctions among sounds it will recognize as meaningful. Any English speaker who learns a foreign language is introduced to sounds that he has never before produced. In order to teach any second language, the differences in the sound systems of the two languages in question must be compared. Do the languages distinguish between "d" and "t;" do they regard "p" "b" "v" as three sounds, two, or one? Added to the questions of production of sound is that of whether the languages import meaning through stress, tone, pitch or a combination of these elements.

Examples of syntactical, grammatical and phonological difficulties encountered by the Navajo speaker in learning English as a Second Language are presented briefly by Yvonne J. Weaver, in her article "A Closer Look at TESL on the Reservation," (1967) and in greater detail by Mary Jane Cook and Margaret Amy Sharp in their "Problems of Navajo Speakers in Learning English" (1966). In a partial list of grammatical problems likely to be encountered by the Navajo student of English, Weaver includes: (1) distinction of number, (2) expression of possession, (3) application of adjectives to nouns, (4) distinction of gender, (5) usage of subject and object, (6) usage of definite and indefinite articles, (7) usage of definite and indefinite pronouns, (8) usage of correct verb inflections, and (9) usage of negative question. (op. cit. 28)

So far, we have spoken largely of the problems involved in teaching a second language, English, to speakers of native North American languages. However, the mandate for bilingual education also demands that native languages be included in the curriculum. In regard to education in the native language, it is interesting to note a study made by Patrick E. Graham and Judson H. Taylor of seventy-three American Indian high school students involved in an Arizona Upward Bound program. The students came from the Apache, Hopi, Hualapai, Mohave, Navajo, Papago, and Pima tribes. In answer to questions about language preference 86% said that they spoke their tribal language, but 92% said that they would want their children to learn the tribal language. The students' interest in having their unborn children speak the native language cannot be explained as a simple desire that these children be able to communicate with their grandparents, since 94% of the students' parents could read and write English. (Graham and Taylor 1969:19-26)

There is a demand, then, for native language instruction. Introduction of the native language into the curriculum is a relatively new phenomenon, however, and there are many problems associated with it. In some cases, the native language is used only in oral form, and a curriculum designer unfamiliar with the native language will simply say to a teacher: "You may translate this lesson into the native language." In these situations the teacher or the aide will translate the material according to personal ability and the translation and instructional language will vary widely from class to class. This is especially true when the subject taught is one for which the native language does not have an established terminology, such as science or mathematics.

Oral use of the native language is not enough. Native languages must be included in written form as well, not only for the sake of uniformity of instruction, but for the psychological and material benefits a people receives from having its language available in written form. The rationale for native literacy programs is outlined forcefully by Willard Walker (1969:148). Among the reasons he puts forth for the development of literacy in native languages are the following:

--native language literacy can form a first step toward second language literacy for children who do not speak the second language when they enter school;

--through mutual control of reading and writing skills, and the increased communication this affords, native peoples can strengthen their sense of identity with their culture;

--possession of a written language can counteract the sense of inferiority so common among speakers of languages not previously written, since it demonstrates that the language is in fact a valid and complex means of expression;

--introduction of native language literacy can improve the relevance of the school curriculum to the native community.

Most native North American languages have not, historically, been written, although most have been recorded in written form by linguists at one time or another. Adequate orthographies for these languages must be developed--systems of writing which represent accurately the morphophonemic system of the language and which are readily recognizable to speakers of the language. Such orthographies are currently being developed for many, but not all of the languages in question. Since most languages lend themselves to adequate representation in alphabets, and since the Roman alphabet is employed by English speakers, most native American languages are being written in standard Roman orthography with the use of some invented letters to represent sounds not used in English, e.g., ł and ŋ .

18

In some cases, however, the Roman alphabet has been avoided altogether. The most well known such case is, of course, the Cherokee syllabary developed by Sequoyah over a twelve year period and finally accepted by the tribal council in 1819. Sequoyah's syllabary employed some characters resembling Roman letters, others similar to Greek or Cyrillic script, and others unique to his system. In all there are 85 symbols, each representing a single syllable in Cherokee. (Note: there is no correspondence between the English sounds of the Roman-like letters used and the sounds they represent in Cherokee, e.g., "A" in the Cherokee syllabary represents the sound "n" or "nho.") Sequoyah met a great deal of resistance in his attempts to get his syllabary accepted; however, once acceptance was achieved, native language literacy spread throughout the Cherokee nation with remarkable speed. Cherokees exchanged letters, kept accounts, and wrote down sacred rituals using the syllabary. A Cherokee national press was established by 1828 and produced, among other things, a weekly newspaper, many Biblical passages and an entire New Testament, hymn books, laws of the National Council, primers, and spelling books. There was a hiatus in publication during the Civil War, and another from 1906 until relatively recently, but currently the press is active, and materials are again being printed in the Cherokee syllabary. (Walker 1969:148-151)

Perhaps less well known is the non-Roman letter orthography currently employed in Canada for a variety of native languages. It was originally developed in 1840 by James Evans, a Methodist missionary to the Cree. The syllabary was accepted by both the Indian population and the Canadian administration and was used to produce religious texts. It is still widely used in Canada for secular as well as religious purposes, and has been adapted to various Cree, Ojibwa, Chipewyan, Slave and Innuit dialects. The syllabary consists of fourteen characters which are written in four different orientations, according to which of four vowel sounds are used. Thus in Moose Cree ∨ = pe, ∧ = pi, > = po, and < = pa. (Ibid:152-3, 159-160)

19

Languages such as Cherokee and Innuit lend themselves particularly
well to syllabic rather than alphabetic representation. On the other hand,
for a language which employs a wide variety of vowels and consonants, a
syllabary is impractical. Even where a syllabary is phonetically practical,
there are arguments against its use--the lack of cross-over benefits with
English language literacy, the necessity to produce special type faces for
printing the material, and the cost of producing typewriters using the
syllabary. Nevertheless, it would not seem wise to advocate abandoning
established syllabaries which have proven their effectiveness. The
ambiguity of reaction to this question is reflected by the fact that, at
this point, both syllabics and Roman letter transcription are being used
by the Cherokee and the native peoples of Canada, often side by side in
the same publication.

Navajo orthography has perhaps the longest history of any Roman letter
orthography, and has been used in a wide variety of publications. Despite
the wide use, the orthography is not completely settled. As early as 1940
an alphabet limited to the keys of a standard typewriter was developed for
Navajo and elementary readers were printed using it. These included
Little Man's Family and the Little Herder series. Adult materials were also
prepared, dealing with such subjects as soil conservation, health care,
employment opportunities and livestock management. (Bauer 1971:29)

In 1969, the Center for Applied Linguistics held a conference on
Navajo Orthography with the aim of developing a standard alphabet for use
in BIA schools. The alphabet recommended consisted of 36 letters or letter
combinations, and three "prosodic markers" to augment these letters.
Length is indicated by double letters, high tone by an acute accent above
the letter, and nazalization by a hook under the letter. (Ohanessian
1969:5-7) This orthography was developed from the viewpoint of the native
speaker of Navajo, which is a particularly important point. Most early
orthographies were developed by linguists and/or anthropologists to reflect
as accurately as possible the phonology of languages with which they were

not fully familiar. However, phonological changes are not always meaning-
ful--they may occur simply because of the juxtaposition of words and/or
sounds, and these morphologically insignificant phonological differences
should not be reflected in a language written for speakers of that
language. There are some Navajos who argue that prosodic markers are
unnecessary and even detrimental to the reading speed of a native speaker
of the language.

We have not yet discussed the non-linguistic cultural problems
confronting the American Indian child in school. One problem in education
for American Indians is the need to recognize that this child cannot be
expected to come to school with the same cultural equipment as the Anglo
child. This is self-evident to those readers who are American Indian, who
have had contact with American Indians, or who are by training and education aware of the wide variety of human cultures. It is often not evident,
however, to the teacher who gets a job in a BIA school, or a public or
private school attended by American Indian children. These teachers need
advance preparation in order to be able to cope with the problems they and
their students will face. This situation is aggravated by the high
turnover rate among teachers in Indian schools. The BIA estimates that
40% of all BIA teachers leave after only one year of teaching. (MacLean
1973:85)

It is difficult for any of us to realize how deep our own ethno-
centrism runs. It is perhaps particularly difficult for teachers, who
have the official task of enculturating young people, to recognize that
their reactions to students from a different culture are not the result
of those students' backwardness, but of their own biases. Too often
teachers, lacking awareness of the impact of the students' culture on them,
believe the students to be slow, mentally deficient, or purposefully
ignorant. When these teachers communicate such beliefs, they may be
accepted by the Indian students as valid, thereby becoming self-fulfilling
prophecies. There are many examples in the literature of this problem--an

educationally induced negative self-image.

Edward Dozier has pointed out many of the general differences between the American Indian cultures and the dominant culture--the importance to the former of the extended family, the permissive techniques of child rearing employed by most American Indian cultures, the absence of extensive trade and the values associated with it. Dr. Dozier points out that, regardless of how much information teachers have about cultural differences, they

> must have respect for the dignity of the individual,
> regardless of the student's particular family,
> ethnic, or cultural background. Here would be
> included certain peculiarities of dress, hair
> style, etc., whether idiosyncracies of the indivi-
> dual or the product of his particular cultural
> background. . . Secondly, a teacher must recognize
> that identity with one's specific heritage is
> natural, and is usually a cherished possession and
> hence cannot be demeaned, discredited or devalued.
> Here may be listed such things as language, reli-
> gion, values and so on, even though these cultural
> possessions are different from those held by the
> teacher. (Dozier 1972:21)

Miles Zintz lists six values which the dominant culture stresses and to which the Native American child must become acclimated:

1. He must climb the ladder of success, and in order to do this, he must place a high value on competitive achievement.

2. He must learn time orientation that will be precise to the hour and minute, and he must also learn to place a high value on looking to the future.

3. He must accept the teacher's reiteration that there is a scientific explanation for all natural phenomena.

4. He must become accustomed to change and must anticipate change. (The dominant culture teaches that "change" in and of itself is good and desirable!)

5. He must trade his shy, quiet, reserved, and anonymous behavior for socially approved aggressive, competitive behavior.

6. He must somehow be brought to understand that he can, with some independence, shape his own destiny, as opposed to the tradition of remaining an anonymous member of his society. (Zintz 1971:39)

Many publications note general differences between Native American cultures and the dominant Anglo culture, and most include some of those mentioned by Dozier and Zintz, particularly the different attitudes toward competition and property values. However, the teacher of Indians, Eskimos or Aleuts must not rely too heavily on lists of general differences. Each specific tribe has its own culture, with its own unique interfaces with the dominant culture.

Eleanor Provance, in her MA thesis, mentions that she had in her secondary school classroom both Eskimo and Tlingit Indian students. The Eskimo, according to Provance, were non-competitive, accustomed to permissive treatment, strongly aware of individual rights, and resentful of pressure or insistence. The Tlingit on the other hand, were competitive, had a strong sense of property ownership, and were accustomed to harsh discipline. (Berry 1968:76)

The Indian or Eskimo child's cultural conflicts are not limited to the school personnel and classroom situation. They also lie in the materials from which the child is supposed to learn. When the Anglo child enters first grade, he is expected to learn to read and write. The Native

23

American child is expected to learn a new language, to learn to read and write in that language, and, all too often, to read about concepts and situations totally foreign to him. Traditional primers are directed toward middle-class urban or suburban white American children; they are not relevant nor even comprehensible to the young Native American.

The Scott Foresman Basic Readers featuring the adventures of Dick and Jane are perhaps the most widely used beginning readers, and educators working with two widely separated groups of Native American children have pointed out the difficulties these populations have in using these books. The differences, as they are reported by these authors, follow:

Lee H. Salisbury points out that Eskimo children are confused by the stories of Dick and Jane on several grounds. Some points of confusion are:

Dick and Jane play together.	but	Eskimo boys and girls do not play together or share toys.
The children's dog, Spot, is a pet and a playmate.	but	Eskimo dogs are work animals.
"Father" leaves for the "office" every day and comes home at night without any food.	but	The Eskimo man's work and its products are immediately visible to the children. He leaves home to hunt or fish.
The children's grandparents live far away in the country.	but	Eskimo families live together, and regard any separation as unfortunate.

In addition, the Eskimo child must deal with such foreign items as automobiles, paved streets, policemen, cookies, farm, cows, chickens, and horses. (Salisbury 1967:5)

Evelyn Evvard and George C. Mitchell present a similar picture of the

conceptual confusion of the Navajo child who reads about Dick and Jane.
The list they present of some of the areas of conflict follows in amended
form:

DICK AND JANE	NAVAJO
Animals are pets, and have human-like personalities.	Animals are not treated as pets.
Life is child-centered.	Life is adult-centered.
Adults join in children's activities.	Children participate in adult activities.
Germ theory is implicitly expressed.	Good health results from harmony with nature.
Children and parents are masters of their environment.	Children accept their environment and live with it.
Children are energetic, outgoing, and obviously happy.	Children are passive and unexpressive.
Many toys and much clothing is an accepted value.	Children can only hope for much clothing and toys.
Life is easy, safe, and bland.	Life is hard and dangerous.

(Evvard & Mithcell 1966:5)

Craig Mayfield, in his Ph.D. dissertation, reported on reading readiness among Navajo students. He surveyed six widely used reading series and selected 165 concepts with which the editors presumably assumed their readers would be familiar. These included such things as train conductors, thermos bottles, and dog collars. Using pictures of the items and five word cards per picture, he asked Navajo youths at the Intermountain School at Brigham City, Utah, to match the correct word with the picture. The failure rate of the students ranged as high as 133--clearly showing the lack of familiarity with the cultural context of the readers of at least some of the students. (Berry 1968:69).

25

There are, of course, two ways of dealing with this problem. One is to give the students a crash course in the concepts used in the available readers. Another is to produce new readers which will not confuse the children. Our bibliography contains many examples of such ESL readers, using controlled vocabulary and situations and localities familiar to the children for whom the readers were developed. It is not necessary, however, that ESL texts for Native American children be limited in content to the cultural environment of the group addressed, as are almost all the materials cited here. The Eskimo, Aleut and American Indian children are no less able to understand or be interested in other cultures, people and places than Anglo children. What is essential is that the ESL texts for these children be written from the cultural context of the target populations. Books written for Navajo readers may be about Eskimos, Tahitians, natives of New York City or any other people, but they must treat as foreign such cultural traits and artifacts of these peoples as are, in fact, foreign to Navajo children. Existing texts could readily be rewritten, preferably by members of the target population, with this in view.

Obviously, if we are to have true bilingual education, there is a great need for materials in the native languages and suitable ESL materials. In the former category we need both texts which use the native language as subject matter, i.e., readers, spelling books, grammars; and texts which use the native language as the medium of instruction in other subjects. While books about native languages are now being produced, there are very few available texts in native languages about other subjects. In the category of ESL we need texts written with the linguistic and cultural background of the American Native in mind; both texts whose subject matter is within the cultural context of the Native North American, and texts which introduce him to concepts and cultures outside that context. Again, there are beginning to be a number of examples of the former, but very few of the latter.

IV. BILINGUAL/BICULTURAL EDUCATION AS IT NOW STANDS

Language and culture are not one and the same thing. One language can span several very different cultures. Nevertheless, a language is an important part of its culture. It is a recognizable difference among peoples; it carries with it a way of thinking, of seeing, and of expressing ideas. When a language dies, an irretrievable part of culture is lost. Young people who cannot speak their ancestral language are not able to share fully in the way of life of their elders.

That there are many distinct languages among the native peoples of North America is without question, but the exact number depends upon the enumerator's definition of a language--as opposed to a dialect. This is not the place to get into this discussion which has absorbed linguists for decades. Using William O. Bright's classification (1974:209) we can count 153 separate historically extant languages. Adding the four languages of the Far North--Aleut, Innuit, Siberian Yupik, and Yupik, we get a total of 157 languages, of which only 108 are still known to be spoken by more than ten people. Forty-nine languages, then, often whole language families, are extinct or nearly so. Of the remaining languages, twenty-one are spoken by fewer than one hundred people. The continued existence of these languages is therefore in considerable doubt.

Again using Bright's figures, with the addition of figures for the Far North (Krauss 1973) there are at least 357,190 people who speak one of the 108 extant languages, as opposed to the over 814,295 people who are identified as belonging to the cultures of which those languages are an important part (figures here from Murdock 1975, Bright 1974, and Krauss 1973). While the discrepancy between "tribal" membership and native language competency varies considerably from group to group, there is obviously a large number of native people who do not speak the langauge of their fathers. For example, the best figures available indicate that while there are 41,815 members of the six Iroquois nations (Seneca,

Mohawk, Cayuga, Oneida, Onondaga and Tuscarora) only approximately 4,000 speak their native language--less than 10%. The Athabaskan (Tanana, Koyukon, Tanaina and Kutchin) and Eskimo (Innuit and the two Yupik groups) of the Far North, on the other hand, are almost all fluent in their ancestral language.

Bilingual eduacation is, in part, an attempt to help native people restore and preserve their languages. However, of the one hundred and eight extant languages, we were able to locate language arts materials developed in the ten years, 1965-1974, for only forty-eight languages.

In this section, we will consider numerically, by type category the materials cited in this bibliography. A gross count like this is not, of course, an entirely satisfactory way of viewing the material. It does not take into account the quality of the individual items, their length, their breadth of applicability. Such a count does, however, allow us to see clearly where the major gaps in available language arts materials occur. The annotations in the bibliography itself will, we hope, point out the quality--often very high indeed, of the individual materials. This numerical survey will give us a clearer overview of the current language arts situation in regard to Indians, Eskimos, and Aleuts.

For a schematic view of extant languages, number of speakers, tribal population, and the types of materials collected here, see the chart on pages 30-37. In considering the chart and the following discussion, however, one must remember that the materials represented were limited to those produced from 1965 to 1974. Nevertheless, even a brief glance at the chart reveals that the production of language arts materials for American Indian languages has been somewhat uneven. The Navajo tribe, with 135,000 members, has been fairly well represented, with 190 publications in the categories laid out on the chart. Other languages with large numbers of speakers and/or potential speakers have fared less well. The Cree, with 70,947 tribal members, have only 16 publications, the Ojibwe

28

with 91,883 have only 8, the Sioux (Lakota, Nakota, Dakota) with 40,000
have only 10. On the other hand, the much smaller language groups of
Alaska are disproportionately well represented. The Kutchin Athabascan,
with a tribal population of 1,138 have 48 materials; the Tanana and Koyukon
with approximately 1,800 speakers have 44, the Siberian Yupik Eskimos of
St. Lawrence Island, who number 750 have 26 native language publications
available to them.

Obviously, many factors are at work here, not the least of which is
the availability of funding for bilingual education. Also to be considered
is the perceived need for bilingual education--most of the Alaskan natives
are monolingual in their native language, while tribes which have had more
prolonged contact with the dominant culture are much more likely to be at
least minimally bilingual in English. Thus it might be argued that the
need for bilingual education and ESL is more immediate in Alaska. Yet
another reason for this discrepancy might be the political awareness,
impact, and unity of the individual tribes.

CHART OF NATIVE NORTH AMERICAN INDIAN
LANGUAGES AND LANGUAGE ARTS MATERIALS

This chart is modeled after the chart presented by William O. Bright
in his article in the New Encyclopedia Brittanica (1974); however, we have
omitted all extinct languages and those spoken by fewer than ten persons.
For Indian languages the figures for number of speakers are also taken
from Bright (op. cit.). Population figures for American Indian tribes
were taken from Murdock and O'Leary (1975) when they were available for
the entire language group as defined by Bright. All figures for Eskimo
and Aleut languages were taken from Krauss (1973).

We do wish to point out that it does not list all the American Indian
languages we know of; however, it does list all the ones we received bilingual
education information about. Also there are some problems with the geographic
location which we did not correct.

29

LANGUAGE	LOCATION	Population	No. of Speakers	Dictionaries	Grammars	Primary Materials	Adult Reading	Primary ESL
NA-DENE								
ATHABASCAN								
Carrier, Chilcotim	British Columbia	3,862	1,500+	-	-	-	-	-
Chipewyan, Slave, Yellowknife	Northwest Terr.	3,113	4,400+	1	1	3	-	-
Chiricahua, Mescalero Apache	S. New Mexico	1,600	1,100+	-	-	-	-	-
Dogrib, Bear Lake, Hare	Northwest Terr.	1,746	1,400	-	-	1	-	4
Haida	British Columbia	1,500	700	1	-	3	-	-
Hupa	NW California	1,100	50	-	-	-	-	-
Jicarilla Apache	N. New Mexico	1,928	1,000	-	-	4	-	2
Kutchin	Alaska, Yukon	1,138	1,200	1	-	45	2	-
Navajo	Ariz., New Mex.	135,000	80,000+	2	5	87	58	38
Sekani, Beaver, Sarsi	Alberta	1,556	450+	-	-	-	-	-
Tahltan, Kaska	Northwest Terr.	1,606	300+	-	-	-	-	-
Tanaina, Ingalik, Nabesna, Ahtena	Alaska	------	1,400+	1	-	1	1	-
Tanana, Koyukon, Han, Tutchone	Alaska	------	1,800+	-	-	39	5	-
Tlingit	SE Alaska	7,800	1,000+	1	-	11	-	-
W. Apache	W. Arizona	7,500	8,000+	1	-	3	-	-

LANGUAGE	LOCATION	Population	No. of Speakers	Dictionaries	Grammars	Primary Materials	Adult Reading	Primary ESL
MACRO-ALGONKIAN								
ALGONKIAN								
Arapaho, Atsina, Nawathenehena	E. Colorado	4,512	1,000+	-	-	-	-	-
Blackfoot	Mont., Alberta	17,231	5,000+	2	-	-	-	-
Cheyenne	E. Wyoming	6,872	3,000+	-	-	-	-	-
Cree, Naskapi, Montagnais	E. Canada	70,947	35,000	2	1	10	2	1
Delaware	C. Atlantic Cst.	3,507	10+	-	-	-	-	-
Fox-Sauk-Kickapoo	S. of Great Lakes	3,431	1,500	-	-	-	-	-
Malecite, Passamaquoddy	New England, Maritime	1,636	900+	1	-	-	-	-
Menominee	Great Lakes	4,307	300+	-	-	-	-	-
Mic Mac	Maritime Prov.	8,465	3,000+	-	-	2	-	-
Ojibwa (Chippewa), Ottawa, Algonkin, Salteaux	S. Ontario	91,883	41,000+	1	1	5	1	-
Penobscot, Abnaki	New England	616	50+	-	-	-	-	-
Potawatomi	Michigan	5,459	100+	-	-	-	-	-
Shawnee	SC United States	2,208	300+	-	-	-	-	-
YUROK	NW California	3,000	10+	-	-	-	1	-
POMO	NC California	2,626	140	-	1	-	-	-

LANGUAGE	LOCATION	Population	No. of Speakers	Dictionaries	Grammars	Primary Materials	Adult Reading	Primary ESL
PALAIHNIHAN								
Achomawi	NE California	980	10+	1	-	-	-	-
WASHO	EC California, Nevada	1,200	100	-	-	-	-	-
KAROK	NW California	1,406	100+	-	-	-	-	-
PENUTIAN								
YOKUTSAN (Yokuts)	SC California	791	10+	1	-	-	1	-
MAIDUAN (Nisenan)	NC California	-------	10+	1	-	-	-	-
WINTUN Patwin Wintu, Nomlaki	 NC California NC California	1,650	 10+ 20+	 - -	 - -	 - -	 - -	 - -
MIWOK-COSTANOAN	SC California	-------	50	2	-	-	-	-
KLAMATH-MODOC	SC California	2,100	100+	-	-	-	-	-
SAHAPTIAN								
Nez Perce	WC Idaho	1,987	500+	-	1	-	-	-
Sahaptin (Klikitat, Umatilla, Walla Walla, Warm Springs, Yakima	NC Oregon	4,995	1,400+	-	1	-	-	-
CHINOOKIAN	NW Oregon SW Washington	800	20	-	-	-	-	-
TSIMSHIAN	WC British Columbia	8,200	3,000	-	-	-	-	-

32

LANGUAGE	LOCATION	Population	No. of Speakers	Dictionaries	Grammars	Primary Materials	Adult Reading	Primary ESL
ZUNI	WC New Mexico	5,155	3,000+	-	1	-	-	-
AZTEC-TANOAN								
KIOWA-TANOAN								
Kiowa	Oklahoma	4,337	2,000	-	-	-	-	-
Tewa	NC New Mexico	4,778	2,000	-	-	1	-	-
Tiwa	NC New Mexico	3,983	2,200+	-	-	-	-	-
Towa	NC New Mexico	1,448	1,200	-	-	-	-	-
MUSKOGEAN								
Alabama, Koasati	Alabama	646	300+	-	-	-	-	-
Choctaw, Chickasaw	N. Mississippi	25,616	12,000+	2	2	1	2	1
Mikasuki, Hitchiti	NW Florida	-------	700	-	-	-	-	-
Muskogee (Creek), Seminole	Georgia, Florida	22,059	10,300+	-	-	13	-	-
MACRO-SIOUAN								
SIOUAN								
Crow	E. Montana	4,208	3,000	-	1	1	-	-
Dakota (Sioux)	N. Plains	40,000	15,000+	4	-	2	1	3
Hidatsa	N. Dakota	1,100	500+	-	-	-	-	-
Omaha, Osage, Ponca, Kansa, Quapaw	Central Plains	9,365	1,200+	-	-	1	-	-

LANGUAGE	LOCATION	Population	No. of Speakers	Dictionaries	Grammars	Primary Materials	Adult Reading	Primary ESL
Winnebago	Wisconsin	2,832	1,000+	-	-	-	-	-
IROQUOIAN								
Cherokee	S. Appalachians, Oklahoma	66,150	10,000	2	-	11	2	1
Mohawk	New York		1,000+	2	2	4	-	-
Oneida	New York		1,000+	-	-	-	-	-
Seneca, Cayuga, Onondaga	New York	41,815	2,600+	1	-	1	1	-
Tuscarora	North Carolina		100+	-	1	-	-	-
CADDOAN								
Arikara	Dakotas	928	200+	-	-	-	-	-
Caddo	Ark., Oklahoma	1,207	300+	-	-	-	-	-
Pawnee	Kansas	1,928	400+	-	-	-	-	-
Wichita	Tex., Oklahoma	485	100+	-	-	-	-	-
YUCHI	S. Appalachians	-------	100+	-	-	-	-	-
HOKAN								
YUMAN								
Delta Yuman (Cocopa)	Colorado River Delta	441	300+	-	-	-	-	-
Diegueno, Kiliwa	S. & Baja Calif.	-------	10+	1	1	-	-	-
Mohave, Yuma	Lower Colo. Riv.	2,290	2,000	-	-	1	-	-

LANGUAGE	LOCATION	Population	No. of Speakers	Dictionaries	Grammars	Primary Materials	Adult Reading	Primary ESL
Walapai, Havasupai, Yavapai	NW Arizona	2,370	900	-	-	-	1	-
UTO-AZTECAN								
Cahuilla	S. California	600	10+	-	-	-	1	-
Comanche	N. Texas	4,250	1,500	-	-	-	-	-
Hopi	N. Arizona	7,236	3,000+	-	-	1	1	2
Kawaiisu, Ute, Chemehuevi, S. Paiute	SE Calif., S. Nev., S. Utah, SW Colorado	4,615	3,000+	1	-	1	-	-
Luiseno	S. California	900	100+	1	-	1	-	-
Mono	EC California	500	100+	-	-	-	-	-
N. Paiute, Bannock, Snake	NE Calif., SE Ore., N. Nev., S. Idaho	3,300	2,000	-	-	-	-	-
Panamint, Gosiute, Shoshone	C. Nev., N. Utah, SW Wyoming	5,300	5,000+	1	-	-	2	-
Pima-Papago	S. Arizona	17,700	13,000+	2	1	2	2	1
UNCLASSIFIED								
KERESAN (Acoma)	NW New Mexico	8,877	7,000	-	-	-	1	-
KUTENAI	Mont., Idaho, BC	1,150	300+	-	-	-	-	-
CHIMAKUAN								
Quileute	NW Washington	200	10+	-	-	-	-	-

LANGUAGE	LOCATION	Population	No. of Speakers	Dictionaries	Grammars	Primary Materials	Adult Reading	Primary ESL
SALISH								
Bella Coola	WC Brit. Columbia	575	200+	-	-	-	-	-
Coeur d'Alene	N. Idaho	440	100	-	-	-	-	-
Halkomelem	SW Brit. Columbia	7,652	1,000+	-	-	-	-	-
Lilloet	C. Brit. Columbia	2,374	1,000+	-	-	-	-	-
Middle Columbia (Salish), Wenatchee	E. Washington	200	200	1	-	-	-	-
Okanagon, Sanpoil, Lake, Colville	S. Brit. Columbia	4,500	1,000+	-	-	-	-	-
Pend d'Oreille, Flathead, Spokan (Salish), Kalispel	N. Idaho	3,952	600+	-	1	-	-	-
Shuswap	E. Brit. Columbia	3,675	1,000+	-	1	-	-	-
S. Puget Sound Salish	W. Washington	2,500	50+	1	1	-	-	-
Squamish	SW Brit Columbia	2,500	100+	-	1	-	-	-
Straits Salish	SW Washington	4,300	500	-	1	-	-	-
Thompson	C. Brit. Columbia	2,647	1,000+	-	-	-	-	-
Upper Chehalis, Cowlitz, Lower Chehalis, Quinault	W. Washington	1,000	10+	-	-	-	-	-
WAKASHAN								
Bella Bella, Heiltsuk	WC Brit. Columbia	1,198	100+	-	-	-	-	-

LANGUAGE	LOCATION	Population	No. of Speakers	Dictionaries	Grammars	Primary Materials	Adult Reading	Primary ESL
Kitamat, Haisla	WC Brit. Columbia	1,966	100+	-	-	-	-	-
Kwakiutl	WC Brit. Columbia		1,000+	-	-	-	-	-
Makah	NW Washington		500	-	-	-	-	-
Nitinat	Vancouver Island	4,600	10+	-	-	-	-	-
Nootka	Vancouver Island		1,000+	-	-	-	-	-
ESKIMO-ALEUT								
ALEUT	Alaska	2,300	600+	-	-	5	-	-
ESKIMO								
Siberian Yupik	St. Lawrence Island	-------	750	-	-	22	4	
Yupik	W. Alaska	-------	17,000	-	1	102	1	8
Innuit	E. Alaska NW Terr.	-------	20,000	2	2	99	17	4

Now let us consider briefly the categories of language arts materials represented in the chart. The first category, "Dictionaries," includes also word lists and vocabularies. Even so, only forty such items were produced in these ten years, representing only 27 languages. While it is true that many dictionaries of native North American languages were written prior to 1965, almost all of these were written by anthropologists and linguists for their professional peers, and not for the use of the native people. Unfortunately, this is also true of many of the dictionaries in the current collection. There is a great scarcity of dictionaries directed to the native language speaking population, or toward children who are learning either the native language, English, or both.

The same qualifications can be made of the "Grammars," the second category on the chart. There are only 27 of these, representing 21 languages, and again they are almost entirely linguistically oriented. Linguistic investigation and reportage is an essential step toward bilingual education, but it still leaves unfilled the need for grammars usable in classroom native language education.

The category "Primary Materials" includes all beginning and intermediate native language materials with the exception of dictionaries and grammars. Included in this column are primers, alphabet books, story books and other materials developed for both school children and adults who are just learning to speak and/or read the native language. We were able to collect 482 primary materials. However, of the 108 languages on the chart, only 30 had even one such piece of writing developed for or by them. In addition, almost all of the materials in this category are designed with native language as their subject matter. There are very few materials which use the native language as the vehicle for education in other areas, such as mathematics.

In the category, "Adult Reading Materials," 108 materials have been collected in 22 languages. Included in this category are any native

language or bilingual materials suitable for adult reading. They include
linguistic transcription of native myths and legends and a large number of
religious tracts, hymnals, and translations of all or part of the Bible.
While the development of adult reading materials logically follows the
development of primary materials, it is also a fact that unless there is
a body of literature in a language, there is little incentive to become
literate in that language. We see here a need for the development of
native language adult reading--whether the works be original texts or
translations of works already available in other languages.

The final category on the chart lists "Primary ESL Materials,"
developed especially for native North American tribes. In this area we
have counted 61 items developed for ten groups of people--the lowest
number of language groups yet represented in any category. One reason
for this may be that the need for native language materials is perceived
as greater, since primers in English exist, as well as ESL primers not
directed toward any particular language or cultural group. However, as
we have already indicated, there is a real need for ESL materials which
are written either about or from the cultural context of the child who is
the target audience. In addition to this problem of the subject matter
of the materials, the problems arising from specific language differences
must be dealt with in designing ESL materials. Since most "general" ESL
materials have been developed for Spanish-speaking Americans, they reflect
the language and culture of this large minority group, and are therefore
not entirely suitable for Native American ESL programs. Nor are ESL
programs developed for one group of Native Americans transferrable without
change or introductory material for use with a second group of Native
Americans. The young Cree facing the dual challenge of learning to read
and learning English will be only slightly less confused by an ESL reader
written about the Chicano culture than he would be by a reader about Dick
and Jane. While he may recognize the children in a Navajo ESL text as
Indians, he will be little more at home with the Navajo environment--cultural
and ecological, than he would be with the way of life and physical
surroundings of suburban white middle-class Americans.

39

This is not to say that the materials developed as ESL texts for any one group, Indian or non-Indian, have no use with any other group. It is merely to say that they must not be used without reference to the differences between the new and old target groups. With these differences in mind, materials may be amended in language and/or cultural content, or prefatory material may be supplied to acquaint the new reader with the unfamiliar concepts and words which he will encounter in the unamended text.

Having looked down the chart at the entries for each column, let us look again across the columns to see how well represented the various peoples listed here are. Of the one hundred and eight groups listed here, only five cultures have entries in each of the five columns on the chart. These five are the Navajo, the Cree, the Choctaw-Chickasaw, and Pima-Papago, and the Innuit. Of these five only the Navajo have a well balanced representation in all five columns. The Cree, Choctaw-Chickasaw and Pima-Papago have very few materials represented here, and the Cree materials are particularly heavily centered in the primary native language materials column. The Innuit have a large number of materials, but again they are disproportionately weighted toward primary native language materials--99 out of 124 items fall into this column.

If we look to see how many groups are well represented in primary native language materials (having 10 or more items in this column), we find only ten such groups--the Navajo, Cree, and Innuit whom we have already mentioned, plus two Northern Athabaskan groups--the Kutchin and the Tanana-Koyukon, the Tlingit, Cherokee, Seminole, Siberian Yupik, and the Yupik.

The only languages for which ten or more adult native language materials have been collected are the Navajo and the Innuit. The only language for which more than ten ESL materials have been developed is the Navajo. If we then lower our sights and ask how many peoples not yet

40

mentioned have had more than five items represented in at least three columns, we find three--the Ojibwa-Salteaux, the Sioux, and the Mohawk, and a fourth if we combine the two Apache groups, the Western Apache and the Jicarilla Apache.

This gives us a total of only fourteen native languages of America north of Mexico for which more than five language arts materials have been collected here. That is to say there are only fourteen native languages out of the extant one hundred and eight, for which we have been able to locate any significant "publications" in the area of bilingual, native language, and ESL education.

As we have seen, then, despite the excellent work done in bilingual education in these ten years, the field is still in its developmental stage with large gaps remaining to be filled. The major need is, of course, for wider coverage--bilingual education has yet to touch many groups of native peoples. Within this development of wider linguistic coverage, we need a broader range of materials. Specifically lacking are the following: (1) native language dictionaries and grammars suitable for the use of elementary and secondary teachers and/or their students; such works would facilitate the development of many other language arts materials as well as being useful in the classroom in and of themselves. (2) Instructional materials at all levels and in all subjects in the native language. A curriculum which incorporates a class in the native language is no more bilingual than the average American high school which has a French teacher. Only if both languages are used as the medium of instruction is the curriculum truly bilingual. (3) Materials, both ESL and native language, which are aimed at newly literate adults and at children. Such works should include translations of useful works available in other languages and new "creative" works by native people written either in their language or in English. They should reflect the present status of the audience to which they are addressed as well as their traditional lifestyle. They should provide entertainment as well as enlightenment.

41

It may seem idealistic to ask for this type of expansion of materials development. However, we maintain that without it true bilingual education cannot succeed. The powers of governmental and private funding establishments and the people who depend upon them for support in this endeavor must decide whether they regard bilingual education as (a) an experiment to which they are not fully committed; (b) a means of easing non-English-speaking people into becoming fluent and literate in English, in order eventually to wean them entirely from the native language; or (c) a vital program aimed at literacy and fluency in both the native language and English. If the answer is (a) or (b), the materials collected here are merely interesting curios, of temporary value only. If the answer is (c), these materials can only be the beginning of a flood of varied materials which must and will be produced in the coming years.

REFERENCES

ADAMS, EVELYN C.
    1946   American Indian Education, New York, Arno Press.

BAUER, EVELYN
    1971   A history of bilingual education in BIA schools. in Robert
                Rebert, et al. Bilingual Education for American Indians.
                Bureau of Indian Affairs, Curriculum Bulletin 3. Washington,
                D.C., Government Printing Office.

BERRY, BREWTON
    1968   The education of the American Indians; a survey of the
                literature. U.S. Department of Health, Education, Welfare,
                Office of Education, Bureau of Research. Washington, D.C.,
                Government Printing Office.

    1972   The histories of American Indian education. in Jeanette
                Henry, ed., The American Indian reader: education. San
                Francisco, Indian Heritage Press, p. 29-37.

BRIGHT, WILLIAM O.
    1974   North American Indian languages. New Encyclopedia Brittanica.
                Chicago, Encyclopedia Brittanica, Inc., vol. 13, p. 208-213.

COHEN, FELIX S.
    1942   Handbook of federal Indian law. Washington, D.C., Government
                Printing Office.

COLLIER, JOHN
    1934   Our Indian policy has definite aims. Letter to the editor,
                Editorial section, New York Times, June 10, 1934, p. 5.

    1963   From every zenith. Denver, Sage Books.

CONVERSE, FRANCIS
    1836   Life of John Eliot, the apostle to the Indians. Library
                of American Biography, Series 1, vol. 5. Boston: Hilliard,
                Gray and Co.

43

COOK, MARY JANE and MARGERT AMY SHARP
　　1966　　Problems of Navajo speakers in learning English. Language
　　　　　　　Learning, vol. 16, no. 1 & 2, p. 21-30.

DAWES, HENRY L.
　　1899　　Have we failed the Indians? Atlantic Monthly, August,
　　　　　　　Vol. 84, p. 280-285.

DOZIER, EDWARD P.
　　1972　　The teacher and the Indian student. in Jeanette Henry, ed.
　　　　　　　The American Indian reader: education. San Francisco,
　　　　　　　Indian Heritage Press, p. 21-26.

EVVARD, EVELYN and GEORGE C. MITCHELL
　　1972　　Sally, Dick and Jane at Lukachukai. Journal of American
　　　　　　　Indian Education, Vol. 5, no. 3, p. 2-6.

GRAHAM, PATRIC E. and JUDSON H. TAYLOR
　　1969　　Reservations and Tribal customs, history and languages; a
　　　　　　　survey of students' opinions. Journal of American Indian
　　　　　　　Education, Vol. 8, no. 3, p. 19-26.

HAGAN, WILLIAM T.
　　1971　　American Indians. Chicago, University of Chicago Press.

HAVIGHURST, ROBERT J.
　　1970　　The education of Indian children and youth: summary report
　　　　　　　and recommendations, U.S. Office of Education. Washington,
　　　　　　　D.C., Government Printing Office.

KLUCKHOHN, CLYDE
　　1963　　Mirror for man. New York, Fawcett.

KRAUSS, MICHAEL
　　1973　　Eskimo-Aleut. Current Trends in Linguistics, Vol. 10,
　　　　　　　p. 796-902.

LANDAR, HERBERT
　　1973　　The tribes and languages of North America: a checklist.
　　　　　　　Current Trends in Linguistics, Vol. 10, p. 1253-1441.

LEIBOWITZ, ARNOLD H.
    1971   A history of language policy in American Indian schools. in
                 Robert Rebert et al., Bilingual Education for American
                 Indians. Washington, D.C., Bureau of Indian Affairs,
                 Curriculum Bulletin 3, p. 1-6.

LYDEKKER, JOHN WOLFE
    1938   The faithful Mohawks. Cambridge, Cambridge University Press.

MACLEAN, HOPE
    1973   A review of Indian education in North America. rev. ed.
                 Toronto: Ontario Teachers' Federation.

MORISON, SAMUEL ELIOT
    1936   Three centuries of Harvard 1636-1936. Cambridge, Mass.,
                 Harvard University Press.

MURDOCK, GEORGE PETER and TIMOTHY J. O'LEARY
    1975   Ethnographic Bibliography of North America. New Haven,
                 Human Relations Area Files Press. 5 vols.

OHANESSIAN, SIRARPI, et al.
    1969   Conference on Navajo orthography. Arlington, Va., Center
                 for Applied Linguistics.

RICHARDSON, LEON B.
    1932   History of Dartmouth College. Hanover: Dartmouth College
                 Press.

SALISBURY, LEE H.
    1967   Teaching English to Alaska natives. Journal of American
                 Indian Education. Vol. 6, No. 2, p. 1-13.

SCHMECKEBIER, LAURENCE F.
    1927   The office of Indian Affairs; its history, activities, and
                 organization. Baltimore, John Hopkins Press.

U.S. CONGRESS. HOUSE.
    1934   Congressional Record, 73rd Congress, Second Session, Vol. 78,
                 Part 2.

U.S. CONGRESS. HOUSE. COMMITTEE ON INDIAN AFFAIRS.
    1934   Hearings on House Resolution 7902, 73rd Congress, 2nd Session.

U.S. CONGRESS. SENATE
    1969   Indian education: a national tragedy - a national challenge.
                 Report of the Special Subcommittee on Indian Education.

U.S. DEPARTMENT OF THE INTERIOR
    1886   Annual report of the Indian Commissioner to the Secretary of
                 the Interior, 1885.

U.S. GOVERNMENT
    1823   Journals of the American Congress: 1774-1788. Washington,
                 Way and Gideon.

1905-1906   Journals of the Continental Congress: 1774-1789.

WALKER, WILLARD
    1969   Notes on native writing systems and the design of native
                 literacy programs. Anthropological Linguistics, Vol. 11,
                 no. 5, p. 148-166.

WASHBURN, WILCOMB E.
    1971   Red man's land/white man's law. New York: Scribner's Sons.

    1973   The American Indian and the United States. New York, Random
                 House.

WEAVER, YVONNE J.
    1967   A Closer Look at TESL on the Reservation. Journal of American
                 Indian Education. Vol. 6, no. 2, p. 26-30.

WILLIAM AND MARY COLLEGE
    1970   The history of the College of William and Mary. Baltimore.
                 John Murphy and Co.

ZINTZ, MILES V.
    1971   What classroom teachers should know about bilingual education.
                 in Robert Reder et al., Bilingual Education for American
                 Indians. Washington, D.C., Bureau of Indian Affairs,
                 Curriculum Bulletin 3, p. 39-58.

V.   HOW TO USE THE BIBLIOGRAPHY

Limitations of the material included.

This bibliography includes all works available to us which have been
or might be used in native language education, bilingual education, or
English as a Second Language education for native North Americans. It
includes linguistic publications only when their subject matter is broad
enough to be of interest to the non-linguist, i.e., grammars and dictionaries, and when the texts were comprehensible to the reader without formal
education in linguistics. English as a Second Language materials which
were not specifically developed for native North Americans have not been
included, because many lists of such materials are available, and it was
felt that our limited resources might be better spent if we limited our
search to native North American materials. A further limitation of the
material is that only English language materials whose main purpose was
language instruction were included--other subject areas, such as math,
social studies, and science were excluded when these subjects were presented
in English, even though the materials were developed for native North
Americans.

All available materials written wholly or partially in Indian or
Eskimo languages were included, whether they were developed as educational
materials or not. The broader scope here is justified by the fact that
there are so few such materials and that they have seldom been gathered
together. These materials include religious publications, linguistic
transcriptions of traditional texts and reprints of early reports of native
languages.

All materials included were produced or reproduced in the ten year
period between 1965 and 1974. This period was chosen because it includes
the major increase in production of these materials which followed (in the
United States) the passage of the Bilingual Education Act.

47

In addition to materials developed for or useful in language learning, instructions for producing such materials and bibliographies of such materials were included in the body of the bibliography. Critiques, evaluations, and descriptions of these materials were not sought. However, when particularly interesting examples of such publications were discovered, they were included in the first Appendix.

The second Appendix presents the language arts curriculum of one English as a Second Language program--that of CITE, Inc., formerly head-quartered in Los Angeles. While there have been several such programs in this country and Canada, the CITE materials were chosen for full representation here because (a) although they are not culture-specific (the few culture-specific CITE products have been included under NAVAJO in the main body of the bibliography), they were developed for the Navajo people, with the particular English language problems and the cultural context of that group in mind, and (b) the CITE materials were readily available to us.

Only "printed word" materials were included in the bibliography. This includes "fugitive materials"--manuscripts, mimeographed materials, etc., but does not include films, cassettes, or records. When such non-book materials are available in conjunction with an item in our list we have mentioned this in the annotation of that item.

Organization of the entries

In the first and largest section of the bibliography the entries are presented under the native language group for which they were developed. These languages are presented alphabetically. Within each native language there is a further subdivision into (a) bilingual materials--not necessarily equally divided between the native language and English, but materials which contain some amount of both languages. This includes materials mainly in English with only a few words or sections in the native language, as well as materials mainly in the native language with instructions and notes in

English sufficient to allow the non-native language speaker to use them;
(b) materials monolingual in the native language; (c) materials monolingual
in English; and (d) materials of which the language composition is not
known, because neither the materials nor an adequate description of them
was available. The sequence of subdivisions within a language is shown
below:

        CHEROKEE
            CHEROKEE - BILINGUAL
            CHEROKEE - MONOLINGUAL, CHEROKEE
            CHEROKEE - MONOLINGUAL, ENGLISH
            CHEROKEE - NOT KNOWN

Within each of these subdivisions, entries are arranged alphabetically by
author (where known), responsible corporate body, or title.

    Where there was some disagreement in the materials over the name or
spelling of a native language, we have used Herbert Landar's "The Tribes
and Languages of North America: a Checklist," (1973) as the final authority.
It might be noted here that SIBERIAN YUPIK as used in this bibliography does
not refer to YUPIK speakers who reside in Soviet Siberia, but to a small
group of Yupik speakers who migrated from Siberia to St. Lawrence Island,
Alaska, and who speak a type of Yupik significantly different from the
speech of the Yupik of mainland Alaska.

    Interfiled with the specific language entries are sections covering
materials developed for an area which includes more than one language group.
These sections are ESKIMOS, INDIANS OF CALIFORNIA, INDIANS OF THE SUBARCTIC,
and INDIANS OF THE SOUTHWEST. Following the specific language section of
the bibliography are three sections containing materials not addressed to
specific native language groups or areas. These sections are GENERAL
BILINGUAL, GENERAL ENGLISH AS A SECOND LANGUAGE, and GENERAL LANGUAGE.
Following these three sections are the two appendices mentioned previously.
Again, within each of these sections, the entries are arranged alphabetically by author.

Individual entries and annotation.

The notation for each entry includes as much bibliographic information
as was available from the work itself and from research. In many cases this
information is less complete than we could wish, due either to the nature
of the work or it unavailability to us. When works were unavailable, either
because they were no longer in print, or because we did not have the funds
with which to purchase them, the notation "Not Available" follows the
citation. When a secondary source provided information for annotation of
an unavailable work, that source is cited within the parentheses, following
"Not Available," e.g., ("Not Available" - Idaho BAI, p. 231). For the sake
of brevity, these secondary sources have been presented in abbreviated
form. The full citation for these abbreviations follows:

1. CAIL Newsletter = Fidelholtz, ed. Conference of American
   Indian Languages Clearinghouse Newsletter. Center for
   Applied Linguistics, Arlington, Virginia.

2. Correll NBSI #1 = Correll, et al. Navaho Bibliography with
   Subject Index, Supplement No. 1. Navajo Tribe, Window Rock,
   Arizona, 1973.

3. Idaho BAI = Idaho State Department of Education. Books about
   Indians, Boise, Idaho, 1971.

4. Kari NLB = Kari, James. Navajo Language Bibliography,
   University of New Mexico, Albuquerque, New Mexico, 1973.

5. Krauss CTL = Krauss, Michael. "Eskimo-Aleut," in Current
   Trends in Linguistics, Vol. 10, 1973, Mouton, The Hague,
   p. 1285-1366.

6. Martin Survey = Martin, Jeannette. A survey of the current
   study and teaching of North American Indian languages in the
   United States and Canada. Center for Applied Linguistics,
   Arlington, Virginia, 1975.

7. Nafziger = Nafziger, Alyce J. American Indian Education, A
    Select bibliography, Supplement No. 1. New Mexico State
    University, University Park, New Mexico, 1970.

8. Spolsky ABNRM = Spolsky, et al. Analytical bibliography of
    Navajo reading materials, University of New Mexico,
    Albuquerque, 1970.

9. Whiteside = Whiteside, Don. Aboriginal People, National
    Indian Brotherhood, Ottawa, Ontario, 1973.

There are two additional notes which sometimes appear at the end of a
citation. The first cites Dissertation Abstracts, and gives the number
assigned to the work in that publication. This citation was used only
when the work being abstracted was not available to this project. The
second cites ERIC (Education Resources Information Center) and was used
only when the work in question was available to us only through the ERIC
files; many other cited works are undoubtedly available through ERIC, but
time did not permit a cross check to ascertain what ERIC numbers had been
assigned to them. If there is no cited secondary source, but a work listed
as "Not Available" is annotated, the information for this annotation was
obtained from the person or organization cited as responsible for the work.

Effort was made to include in the citations the full address of the
projects or organizations which produced the materials. It is hoped that
this will be helpful to the reader who wishes to obtain the material cited
or contact the issuing agency.

The annotation is divided into two parts--the prose description of
the work, directly below the notation, and the abbreviated marking code
in the "Content" and "Level" columns in the right margin. It is hoped
that this dual approach will satisfy the needs of both those who wish to
skim rapidly through the bibliography for works of particular interest to
them, and those who wish to have some information about particular works.

Abbreviations used in the "Content" column are:

    voc - vocabulary, where a conscious effort to teach words and meanings is made

    phon - phonology, where sound systems are discussed

    pron - pronunciation, where emphasis is placed on oral use of language

    gram - where there is a conscious teaching of language structure

    desc - description and/or history of a language

    lit - literature, including legends, traditional stories, and stories written for pedagogical purposes (literature is not used here as an achievement term)

    script - where an alphabet or syllabary other than the Roman is used and explained

    bibl - bibliography

    test - tests of language learning

    theor - theory of language learning or teaching

    meth - methodology of language teaching

Abbreviations used in the "Level" column are:

    prim - primary level instruction, whether for children or adults

    int - intermediate level of difficulty in reading

    adv - advanced level in difficulty in reading

    col - materials for users beyond secondary level of education

    self - self-teaching materials

SOURCES OF THE MATERIAL

In addition to searching the holdings of the University Research Library at UCLA, and those of the American Indian Studies Center Library on the same campus, we made extensive efforts to contact workers in the field of native language and bilingual education in the United States and Canada. Letters of inquiry were sent to all of the following individuals and groups.

The following people contributed materials and information to the current bibliography, and we wish to express our gratitude.

Alaska State Operated School System
Stanley Friese - Superintendent
650 International Airport Road
Anchorage, Alaska 99502

Amiotte, Lowell R., Director
Center of Indian Studies
Black Hills State College
Spearfish, South Dakota 57783

Barnes, Barbara, Project Director
Title IV Program
Salmon River Central School
Fort Covington, New York

Baumgartner, David C., Director
Barrow Day School
Box 169
Barrow, Alaska 99723

Bogart, Linda M.
Migrant Heritage Studies Project
Geneseo Migrant Center
State University College
Geneseo, New York

Cassell, Virginia C.
Program Officer, Office of
   Bilingual Education
Department of Health, Education
   & Welfare
Office of Education
Washington, D.C. 20202

Center for In-Service Education
Post Office Box 754
Loveland, Colorado 80537

Cherokee Bilingual Education Center
Post Office Box 769
Tahlequah, Oklahoma 74464

Cornelius, Neil
Oneida Band Office
R.R. 2
Southwold, Ontario

Dorris, Michael
Department of Anthropology
Dartmouth College
Hanover, New Hampshire 13755

Elgin, Dr. Suzette
California State University
5402 College Avenue
San Diego, California 92115

Emarthle, Mary, Project Secretary
Seminole Bilingual Project
Hokkoten Punayetv
East Central University
Ada, Oklahoma 74820

Fadden, Ray
Onchiota, New York 12968

Fidelholtz, James L., Editor
CAIL Clearinghouse Newsletter
Center for Applied Linguistics
1161 N. Kent Street
Arlington, Virginia 22209

Hill, Faith
Wycliffe
5909 Burbach/
Holzhausen, Germany

Holisky, D.A.
University of Chicago
Department of Linguistics
5828 S. University Avenue
Chicago, Illinois

54

Holzmueller, Diana
Assistant Education Program Director
University of Alaska
College, Alaska 99702

Jacobsen, William H., Jr.
Department of English
University of Nevada
Reno, Nevada

Kendall, Bonnie
Vassar College
Poughkeepsie, New York

Kindred, Jim
Bilingual Specialist
Blanding Indian Education Center
Post Office Box 425
Blanding, Utah 84511

Kowalczyk, Emil
Bureau of Indian Affairs
Post Office Box 3-8000
Juneau, Alska 99801

Laughlin, Dr. Robert M.
Center for the Study of Man
Department of Ethnology
Smithsonian Institution
Washington, D.C.

Leap, Dr. William
Director, American Indian Projects
1611 North Kent Street
Arlington, Virginia 22209

Leavitt, Robert M.
Maine Indian Education
Motakmiqeui Skalhawossol
Indian Township, Maine 04668

Levi, Peter Jr., Coordinator
Big Cove Band Council
Big Cove Reserve
R.R. 1
Rexton, New Brunswick

MacCarty, Colin
Assistant Director Special Services
Bilingual Education
Alaska Unorganized Borough School
   District

McGary, Jane
Alaska Native Language Center
University of Alaska
Fairbanks, Alaska 99701

Mailer, William
Cultural Heritage Program
Bethel Regional High School
Bethel, Alaska 99559

Manitou Community College
R.C. Gagne
Post Office Box 30
Ecowi, Labelle, Quebec JOT 1CO

Maring, Joel
Department of Anthropology
Southern Illinois University
Carbondale, Illinois 62901

Martin, Jeanette
2521 W. Third Avenue
Durango, Colorado 81301

Martin, Larry
State of Minnesota
Department of Education
Capitol Square Building
550 Cedar Street
St. Paul, Minnesota 55101

Miller, Wick R.
Linguistics Department
University of Utah
Salt Lake City, Utah 84112

Mitchell, Mary L.
Native Language Office
Lakehead District Office DIAND
200 S. Syndicate Avenue
Thunder Bay, Ontario

Morrison, James D., Consultant
Choctaw Bilingual Education Program
Southeastern State College
Durant, Oklahoma   74701

Mueller, Richard
Box 329
Fort Yukon, Alaska   99740

Munro, Pamela
Department of Linguistics
University of California
La Jolla, California   92037

Navajo Christian Reading
Route 1, Box 2F
Cortez, Colorado   81321

Newell, Wayne A., Project Director
Wabnaki Bilingual Education Project
River Road, Box 291
Calais, Maine   04619

Nome Agency
Box 1108
Nome, Alaska   99762

Northern Indian California Education
   Project
526 A. Street
Eureka, California   95501

Old Coyote, Elnora
Box 415
Crow Agency, Montana   59034

Perrin, Kathleen, Director
Alaska Bilingual Education Center
4510 Airport Road
Anchorage, Alaska   99502

Powell, J.V.
Department of Anthropology
University of British Columbia
Vancouver, British Columbia

Printup, Marjorie
5086 Walmore Road
Sanborn, New York   14132

Pulu, Tupou
Alaska State Operated School System
650 International Airport Road
Anchorage, Alaska   99502

Rankin, Robert L.
Department of Linguistics
University of Kansas
Lawrence, Kansas   66045

Spolsky, Bernard
Department of Linguistics
1805 Roma, N.E.
Albuquerque, New Mexico   87131

Streiff, Paul
3304 Roma, N.E.
Albuquerque, New Mexico   87106

Warren, David
U.S. Department of the Interior
Bureau of Indian Affairs
Institute of American Indian Arts
Cerillos Road
Santa Fe, New Mexico   87501

Wells, Dr. Robert N.
St. Lawrence University
Canton, New York   13617

Werner, Dr. Oswald
Northwestern University
Department of Anthropology
Evanston, Illinois

Williams, Marianne Mithun
Department of Linguistics
SUNY Albany
1400 Washington Avenue
Albany, New York   12222

The following were either unable to respond or were not in a position to offer material relevant to our search.

Abeel, David
St. Lawrence University
Canton, New York   13617

Abeyta, Joe
Education Specialist
Box 580
Santa Fe, New Mexico   87532

Abrams, George, H.J.
Western Washington State College
College of Ethnic Studies
Bellingham, Washington   98225

Afcan, Paschal L.
Eskimo Language Specialist
University of Alaska
Box 95207 CNER

Afcan, Pat, Director
Yupik Language Center
St. Mary's Mission High School
St. Mary's, Alaska

Ahrvey, Gina P.
Department of English
University of Arizona
Box 3062
Flagstaff, Arizona   86001

Alford, Dan K.
Assistant Director/Linguist
Box 175
Ashland, Montana   59003

Anallo, Tim, Director
Native American Language Insittute
Cerilos Road
Santa Fe, New Mexico   87501

Antell, Dr. Will
Capitol Square Building
550 Cedar
St. Paul, Minnesota   55101

Apache Culture Center
c/o Edgar Perry
Post Office Box 507
Fort Apache, Arizona   85926

Archibeque, Sophie
Elementary Teacher
San Felipe Day School
Algodones, New Mexico   87001

Askan, Marie
Santa Clara
Espanola, New Mexico   87532

Atanasoff, Dave
Lake Valley School, Principal
Post Office Box 238
Crownpoint, New Mexico   87313

Auleta, Elizabeth
State University College at Oswego
Oswego, New York   13126

Bacon, Herbert, Program Consultant
411 E. 13th Street
Claremore, Oklahoma   74017
(918) 341-5625

Baker, Lynn D.
Rocky Boy Reservation
Box Elder, Montana   59521

Barss, Arliss J.
Cooperative College Center
State University at Buffalo
465 Washington Street
Buffalo, New York   14203

Baskin, Wade, ESL Consultant
Southeastern State College
Durant, Oklahoma   74701

Bekis, Mac, Bilingual Staff
Post Office Box 1420
Cortez, Colorado 81321

Benedict, Ernest
R.D. 3
Cornwall Island
Ontario, Canada

Benton, S. William
Education Administrator
Box 347
Bethel, Alaska 99559
(907) 543-2745

Bilingual Education Program
University of South Dakota
School of Education
Vermillion, South Dakota 57069

Bitsie, Oscar, Project Director
Best of Both Cultures for Navajo/Zuni
    Children
Gallup McKinley County Schools
Post Office Box 1318
Gallup, New Mexico 87301

Blackthunder, Elijah
Northern State College
Sisseton, South Dakota

Blackman, Charlie
Blue Quills Native Education Council
Box 279
St. Paul, Alberta, Canada
(403) 645-4455

Bradley, Helen
Advisory School Board Member
Post Office Box 67
San Fidel, New Mexico 87049
(505) 287-3292

Brigham Young University
Department of Linguistics
Provo, Utah

Bryde, Father John F.
Holy Rosary Mission
Pine Ridge, South Dakota

Bunney, Curtis & Estelle
SIL-Literacy
Post Office Box 51
San Carlos, Arizona 85550

Burnaby, Barbara
Cree Language Consultant
9219-96 Street
Edmonton, Alberta, Canada

Chavez, Everett F.
Language Developer
Box 1295
Santo Domingo, New Mexico 87052

Field Coordinator
Cheyenne River Sioux Tribe
Eagle Butte, South Dakota 57625
(605) 964-8686

Chico, Theresa V.
Post Office Box 67
San Fidel, New Mexico 87049

Chino, Gyrus
Community Coordinator
Box 97
San Fidel, New Mexico 87049

Cochiti Elementary School
Pena Blanca, New Mexico 87041
(505) 465-2260

Cohen, Stanley
State Agricultural College
Canton, New York 13617

Coit, Shirley C., Librarian
University of Texas, Box 13
El Paso, Texas 79968
(915) 747-5337

Coleman, Caroline
Post Office Box 843
San Juan Pueblo, New Mexico
(515) 455-2366

Coley, Raymond
State University College
Brockport, New York 14420

Cook, John
Hogansburg, New York 13655

Coolidge, Joseph
Kuskokwim Community College
Box 581
Bethel, Alaska
(907) 543-2047

Cowen, Agnes, Project Director
Cherokee Bilingual Education Program
Post Office Box 769
Tahlequah, Oklahoma 74464
(918) 456-6177

Crawler, Shirley
Curriculum Development
Morly, Alberta, Canada
881-3986

Creighton, Mary
66B Fremont Street
Somerville, Massachusetts 02145

Crow Bilingual Education Project
Crow Agency Public School
Crow Agency, Montana 59022
(505) 638-2209

Davis, Wallace, Project Director
Sanostee Boarding School
Shiprock, New Mexico 87420
(505) 723-2401

Donne, John
Department of Anthrpology
Oregon State University
Corvallis, Oregon

Duran, Elizabeth C.
Niagara University
Niagara, New York 14109

Education Division
Indian Affairs Branch
Indian Affairs & Northern Development
1849 Yonge Street
Toronto 7, Ontario, Canada

Efrat, Barbara
Provincial Museum
Victoria, British Columbia

Einhorn, Arthur
Box 286
Lowville, New York 13367

Ekstrom, Jonathan & Margaret
512 Cottonwood
Winslow, Arizona 86047
(602) 289-4964

Head, Curriculum Services
Elementary and Secondary E. Division
Education Branch
400 N. Laurier Avenue, W.
Ottawa, Ontario, Canada L1A 044

Ellis, C. Douglas, Chairman
Department of Linguistics
McGill University
Post Office Box 6070
Montreal 101, Quebec, Canada

Internship in Ethnic Studies Library
Office of the Director
Fisk University Library
Nashville, Tennessee 37203

Bosdick, Donald J.
BIA Education Code 520
1951 Constitution Avenue, N.W.
Washington, D.C. 20242

Fox, Sandra J.
Education Specialist
Aberdeen Area Office, BIA
Aberdeen, South Dakota 57401

Francis, Gordon
Big Cove, Kent County
New Brunswick

Frasier, Dr. Vance C.
College of Education
University of Arizona
Tucson, Arizona 85721

Frenier, Pasqualita
VISTA Language Program
Santa Clara, New Mexico

Fuchs, Dr. Estelle
College of Education
Hunter College
695 Park Avenue
New York, New York 10021

Garrett, James B.
Cornell University
Ithaca, New York 14850

Gentry, Robert
Education Department
University of Oklahoma
Norman, Oklahoma

Gillie, Bernard, Director
Intercultural Curriculum Development
    Project
University of Victoria
Post Office Box 1700
Victoria, British Columbia V8W 2Y2

Goldbas, Mervyn
State University College
Fredonia, New York 14063

Golnick, Bill
Oneida Language Project
Sacred Heart Seminary
Oneida, Wisconsin

Graves, Byron L.
Bemidji State College
Bemidji, Minnesota 56601

Gullo Anthony S.
Niagara County Community College
Niagara Falls, New York 14303

Guyer, Dan, Superintendent
Rice Public School No. 20
San Carlos, Arizona 85550

Hagan, Dr. William T.
State University College
Fredonia, New York 14603

Hammond, Patricia
Foreign Languages
310 Will Rogers Building
Oklahoma City, Oklahoma 73105

Hamp, Eric P.
University of Chicago
5828 So. University
Chicago, Illinois 60637

Havill, Thomas L.
Keene State College
Keene, New Hampshire 03431

Headley, Ida D.
University State College
Cortland, New York 13045

Herrick, Earl M., Professor
English Department
Texas A & I University
Kingsville, Texas 78363

Hertzberg, Dr. Hazel W.
Columbia University
Teachers College
New York, New York 10027

Hertzman, Michele
Cazenovia College
Cazenovia, New York 13035

Hesbon, Jan
Migrant Center
State University College
Geneseo, New York 14454

Hess, Thom
Department of Indian Studies
University of Washington
Seattle, Washington

Hill, Jerry M.
College of Education
University of Arizona
Tucson, Arizona 85721

Hinton, Leanne
Social Science Department
University of Dallas
Livingston, Texas

Holthaus, Gary H.
Executive Director
3111 C. Street
Anchorage, Alaska

Hull, Walt
Department of Linguistics
University of Kansas
Lawrence, Kansas   66045

Hunter, Emily
Cree Language Teacher
Goodfish Lake
Alberta, Canada

Institute for Cultural Pluralism
College of Education, Room 117
University of New Mexico
Albuquerque, New Mexico   87106

Instructional Service Center
Professional Library
Post Office Box 66
Brigham City, Utah   84302

Jacob, Randy, Assistant Director
742 Vet Village
Durant, Oklahoma   74701

Jacobs, Roderick, Dr.
Department of Linguistics
University of Hawaii
Honolulu, Hawaii

Jacobsen, Wm. H., Jr.
Department of English
University of Nevada
Reno, Nevada   89507

Jahner, Elaine
American Language Coordinator
Apple Creek Road
Bismarck, North Dakota   58501

Jemison, Allan
Gowanda, New York   14070

Johnson, Mary Ann
Route 9, Box 6
Albuquerque, New Mexico   87105

Kaneshiro, Vera
Language Specialist
4182-26th Street
Fort Wainwright, Alaska   99703

Kari, James
Alaska Native Language Center
University of Alaska
Fairbanks, Alaska   99701

Kenney, John
St. Lawrence University
Canton, New York   13617

King, Dr. Paul
State Agricultural & Technical
   College
Alfred, New York   14805

King, Richard
Studies of Intercultural Education
University of Victoria
Post Office Box 1700
Victoria, British Columbia   V8W 2Y2

Kito, John R.
Director, Bilingual Education
650 International Airport Road
Anchorage, Alaska   99701

Kuipers, Art H.
University of Leiden
Netherlands

Krzemien, Gerald D.
Erie Community College
Main & Youngs Road
Buffalo, New York

Lanquist, Norman
Institute ESL & Indian American
    Culture
Eastern Arizona University
Thatcher, Arizona 85552

Larouche, Mrs. K., Librarian
Clayton Brown Public School
Box 7000
Hearst, Ontario, Canada

Lazore, Chief Lawrence
Box 368
Hogansburg, New York 13655

Lee, George P.
Executive Vice President & Director
The College of Ganado
Ganado, Arizona 86505

Leighton, Dr. E. Roby
Director, Bilingual-Bicultural
    Project
Rough Rock Demonstration School
Chinle, Arizona 86503

Lewis, Mr. Mekko
Department of Linguistics
University of Kansas
Lawrence, Kansas 66045

Lewis, Robert E.
Governor of Zuni
Post Office Box 338
Zuni, New Mexico 87327

Little, Camillie M.
Project Director
Box 407
Lame Deer, Montana 59043

Loneman Day School
Oglala, South Dakota 57764

Lowe, Bertha
Coordinator, Inupiat Bilingual
650 International Airport Road
Anchorage, Alaska 99502

Lujan, Lena M.
Staff/Native American Studies
1812 Las Lomas, N.E.
Albuquerque, New Mexico 87106

MacKenzie School District
Yellowknife, Northwest Territory
Canada

MacLean, Edna
Language Specialist
Post Office Box 90612
Fairbanks, Alaska 99701

MacLean, Joanne L.
Salmon River Central School District
Fort Covington, New York 12937

MacLeod, Ida
1625 Bader Crescent
Saskatoon, Saskatchewan
Canada

Makois, Alice
Social Counselor
Saddle Lake Reservation
Box 1515
St. Paul, Alberta, Canada

Mansfield, F.R.
School Principal
Isleta, New Mexico 87104

Manuelito, Kathryn
Language Arts Coordinator
Box 186
Ramah, New Mexico 87321

Martin, Pierce, Project Director
Choctaw Bilingual Education Program
Broken Box Public Schools
Box 207
Broken Bow, Oklahoma 74728

Martinez, Esther
Box 715
San Juan, New Mexico 87566

Massey, Gill D.
Assistant Director
Post Office Box 139
420 No. 4th Street
Bismarck, North Dakota   58501

Maus, Cyrin T.
Title VII Project Director
Post Office Box 44021 Tamiami Station
Miami, Florida   33144

Mendez, Arturo
Project Director
Grants Bilingual-Bicultural Education
    Program
Post Office Box 8
Grants, New Mexico

Micmac Association of Cultural
    Studies
Box 961
Sydney, Nova Scotia

Miller, Wick
Department of Anthropology
University of Utah
Salt Lake City, Utah

Milliea, Mrs. Mildred
Site 5, Box 2
Big Cove, Kent County
New Brunswick

Mills, Faynell
Tri-Director
Post Office Box 769
Tahlequah, Oklahoma   74464

Mississippi Band of Choctaw Indians
Bilingual Education Project
RFD 7, Box 21
Philadelphia, Mississippi   39350

Mitchell, Mike
Cornwall Island, Ontario, Canada

Mofsie, Louis
2335 Hudson Terrace
Fort Lee, New Jersey   07024

Montroy, George E.
Mater Dei College
Ogdensburg, New York   13669

Murie, Robert P.
Project Director
Chippewa-Cree Bilingual Education
    Project
School District #87
Rocky Boy Reservation
Box Elder, Montana   59521

Nicklas, Thurston Dale
Linguistics Consultant
916 Hilltop Drive
Lawrence, Kansas   66044

Nichols, John
Department of Linguistics
University of Wisconsin
Milwaukee, Wisconsin

North American Indian Club
Baptist Church
Grace and Dudley Street
Syracuse, New York   13200

Oberholser, Christian
Project Director
Acomita Day School
Post Office Box 96
San Fidel, New Mexico   87049

O'Donnell, Dr. Thomas F.
State University College
Brockport, New York   14420

Oklahoma City Council of Choctaws
Post Office Box 94924
Oklahoma City, Oklahoma   73109

Chief Oren Lyons
Onondaga Nation
Nedrow, New York   13120

Ortiz, Ramona
Box 96
Acomita Day School
San Fidel, New Mexico   87049

Pacini, Claudia
Acoma Bilingual Project
Acoma, New Mexico 87049
(505) 287-2860

Paisano, Gabriel
Associate Judge
Post Office Box 194
Laguna, New Mexico 87026

Patrick, Ike
Post Office Box 781
Pendleton, Oregon 97801

Perry, Edgar, Director
Box 507
Fort Apache, Arizona 85926

Phillips, Dale
Community Liaison
3100 Avenue
Yuma, Arizona

Phone, Wima
Cultural Education Program
Post Office Box 57
Dulce, New Mexico 87528

Pierce, Lyman
4515 Edinberg Drive
Woodbridge, Virginia 22191

Poage, Lonn
US BIA
Nome Agency Bilingual Resource Center
Nome, Alaska

Poitras, Charles
Harvard University
13 Appian Way
Cambridge, Massachusetts 02138

Pulu, Tupore L., Acting Director
Native Language Programs
State of Alaska
Alaska State Operated School System
650 International Airport Road
Anchorage, Alaska 99502

Quaempts, Peter S.
Director of Indian Studies
Post Office Box 100
Pendleton, Oregon 97801

Queal, Beverly K.
Education Specialist
4206 West Virginia Avenue, Apt. 5
Phoenix, Arizona 85009

Quinault Tribal Council
Taholah, Washington

Ramons, Elaine E.
Vice President
Post Office Box 479
Sitka, Alaska 99835

Reed, Irene
Material Development
Box 95207 CNER
Fairbanks, Alaska 99701

Richburg, Dr. James R.
Division of Social Sciences and
   Special Education
Florida Junior College
Southside Campus
Jacksonville, Florida 82207

Rigsby, Bruce
Department of Anthropology
University of New Mexico
Albuquerque, New Mexico 87106

Risingsun, Ted
Project Director
Northern Cheyenne Bilingual
   Education Program
Box 6
Lame Deer, Montana 59043

Rock Point School
Chinle, Arizona 86505

Rodriguez, Ray
Box 96
San Fidel, New Mexico 87049

Rourke, Anna
Librarian
Akwesásne Cultural Center Library
Rural Route
Hogansburg, New York

SEDL
800 Brazos
Austin, Texas   87801

St. Labre Indian School
Ashland, Montana   59003

Saluskin, Alex
Yakima Tribe
Toppenish, Washington

Salvador, Wilbert
Acomita Day School
Acomita, New Mexico

Sanchez, Josephine
Bilingual Aide
Box 96
Acomita Day School
San Fidel, New Mexico

Sanderson, Milford M.
Director of Federal Projects
Ganado Public Schools
Ganado, Arizona   86505

Sarracino, Lawrence J., Treasurer
Post Office Box 194
Laguna, New Mexico   87026

Sarracino, Millie
Bilingual Aide
Box 96
Acomita Day School
San Fidel, New Mexico   87049

Scannell, James J., Jr.
Boston College
Chestnut Hill, Massachusetts   02167

Scott, Freddie J.
Post Office Box 194
Laguna, New Mexico   87026

Schultz, Hal, Principal
Acomita Day School
Acomita, New Mexico

Searles, Fr. Thaddeus
Post Office Box 37
Philadelphia, Mississippi   39350

Segerstrom, Harold
State Education Department
Albany, New York   12200

Serna, Leonila
501 Indiana, S.E., Apt. C
Albuquerque, New Mexico   87108

Sioux City American Indian Center
313 Omaha Street
Sioux City, Iowa   51103

Skye, Jim
Woodland Indian Institute
Post Office Box 1506
Brantford, Ontario   N3T 5V6

Smith, Ronald V.
Post Office Box 191
Laguna, New Mexico   87026

South Dakota University
Department of Education
Vermillion, South Dakota

Sullivan, Daniel
State University at Potsdam
Potsdam, New York   13676

Title I Project
Southern Pueblos Agency
1000 Indian School Road, N.W.
Albuquerque, New Mexico   87107

Southwestern Cooperative Educational
    Laboratory, Inc.
117 Richmond Drive
Albuquerque, New Mexico

Speirs, Randall H. and Anna F.
SIL Linguist & Teacher
Route 2, Box 60
Espanola, New Mexico 87432

Stilwel, Lucille
Research Assistant
1404 San Mateo, S.E.
Albuquerque, New Mexico 87108

Stotss, Mary
Barrow School Board President
University of Alaska, Box 147
Barrow, Alaska 99723

Stringfield, James
Superintendent
Route 3
Seminole, Oklahoma 74868

Sundown, Corbett
299 Lone Road
Basom, New York 14013

Swentzell, Rina
Culture Diversity Specialist
New State Department of Education
Communicative Arts Unit
Santa Fe, New Mexico 87501

Symes, Dr. Martha
Western Washington State College
College of Ethnic Studies
Bellingham, Washington 98225

Taliman, Anacita
Santa Clara Box 99
Espanola, New Mexico 87432

Tarrant, Josephine
350 Joralemon Street
Belleville, New Jersey 07109

Taylor, Allan R.
Director
University of Colorado Lakhota
    Project
Department of LInguistics
University of Colorado
Boulder, Colorado 80302

Tennant, Edward A.
Language Specialist
4900 Overland, N.E.
Albuquerque, New Mexico 87109

Thunder Bay Office
DIAND
200 S. Syndicate Avenue
Thunder Bay, F
Ontario, Canada

Tidzump, Malinda L.
Post Office Box 119
Fort Ashakie, Wyoming 82514

Tonemah, Stuart A.
Hinman Box 498
Dartmouth College
Hanover, New Hampshire 03755

Townsend, W. Cameron
Founder and Director
Summer Institute of LInguistics
Box 248
Waxhaw, North Carolina 28173

Toya, Patrick E.
JOM Liaison
Post Office Box 226
Jemez, New Mexico 87024

Twoyoungmen, John R.
Curriculum Development
Morely, Alt, Canada

Tyson, Jean
Education Specialist
Post Office Box 356
Sells, Arizona 85634

Vallo, Lois
Post Office Box 8
Grants, New Mexico 87020

Van Naerseen, Margaret
Bilingual Eduation Specialist
400 Maryland Avenue, S.W.
Washington, D.C. 20202

Vicenti, Arnold
Box 552
Dulce, New Mexico 87528

Vineyard, William
Southwest Indian Polytechnic Institute
Albuqerque, New Mexico 87114

Waddell, Jack
Department of Anthropology
Purdue University
Lafayette, Indiana 47907

Wall, Gertrude
Box 447
Zuni, New Mexico

West, David
Post Office Box 44021
Tamiami Station
Miami, Florida 33144

Whetter, Mrs. K.
DIAND
55 St. Clair Avenue, E.
Toronto, Ontario, Canada

White, Lincoln C.
St. Lawrence University
Canton, New York 13617

White, Minerva
Hogansburg, New York 13655

Wilson, Allan
Department of Linguistics
University of New Mexico
Gallup Branch
Gallup, New Mexico

Wohlgemuth, Emil
ESL Coordinator
Bent-Mescalero School
Mescalero, New Mexico 88340

Yokayo School
Attn: Diane Abella, Guadalupe
    Lopez, Karen Mitchell, Pamela
    Mitchell
355 W. Clay Street
Ukiah, California 95482
(707) 462-7207

Yup'ik Eskimo Language Workshop
Koskokwim Community College
Bethel, Alaska

Zia Day School
San Ysidro, New Mexico 87053

Zuni, Mary Martha
Post Office Box 62
Isleta, New Mexico 87022

Zuni Elementary School
Zuni, New Mexico 87327

BIBLIOGRAPHY

ACOMA - BILINGUAL

1. Maring, Joel. Acoma language and culture; a bilingual/
   bicultural manual. Partial manuscript received
   from author. ca. 1969.

   Intended for use by the Acomita Day School Bilin-   desc   self
   gual/Bicultural program and for people of Acoma   gram
   tribal community. Includes some cultural material,   phon
   grammar, phonology, and morphology.

2. Miller, Wick R. Acoma grammar and texts. University of
   California Publications in Linguistics, #45,
   Berkeley, California. 1965, 259 pp.

   Various aspects of grammar of Acoma, including pho-   phon   col
   nology, morphophonemics, verb themes, noun themes,   gram   self
   derivation, and syntax. Also Acoma and English
   translations of texts of myths - Acoma version
   precedes English version of each myth.

ACHUMAWI - BILINGUAL

3. Olmsted, D.L. Achumawi dictionary. University of
   California, Berkeley, California. 1966, 158 p.

   Achumawi-English, English-Achumawi dictionary,   voc   col
   based on the research of Jaime de Angulo with this   bibl   self
   California tribe. Dictionary is designed for
   comparative linguistics.

ALEUT - BILINGUAL

   Kraus, Michael. Eskimo-Aleut. in Current Trends in
       Linguistics, 1973, Vol. 10, p. 1285-1366.

   See under ESKIMO

   Pilling, James C. Bibliography of the Eskimo language.
       AMS Press, New York, 1973, 116 p.

   See Pilling under GENERAL LANGUAGE

ALEUT - MONOLINGUAL, ALEUT

4. Alaska State-Operated Schools System. Alqux̂ tutat?
   (What can you hear?) (Western dialect). Alaska
   State-Operated School System, 650 International
   Airport Road, Anchorage, Alaska. 1974, 34 pp.

Series of answers to the title question, using   voc   prim
sounds from the Alaskan environment, e.g., snow-
mobile, goose. Workbook section in back of book.
Illustrated.

5. Atka Village. Angaginaagamagis tunumkaasaqangis (Told
    by older people). Atka Village, Alaska. 1973,
    64 p.

    Several tales about life on Atka in the past.   lit   adv.

6. _____. Tunumkaazam itxalax̂tangis (Miscellaneous
    stories). Atka Village, Alaska. 1973, 23 p.

    Series of short stories, fictional and true,   lit   int
    including a fable from Aesop. Illustrated.

7. Bergsland, Knut. Niiĝuĝim aaznukaa/Atkan Aleut Primer.
    Atka Village, Alaska. 1973, 70 p.

    Primer concentrates on various letters, presenting   voc   prim
    groups of words which use that letter. Progresses
    to simple sentences. Illustrated.

8. _____. Niiĝĝim tunugan ilakuchangis (Elements of
    Atkan Aleut). Atka Village, Alaska. 1973, 31 p.

    Short vocabulary and basic grammar of Atkan Aleut,   voc   int
    for speakers of Aleut.   gram

9. Dirks, Larry Sr. Nam-hadan itx̂ayginaax̂s (Reindeer hunt
    on the South Side). Atka Village, Alaska. 1973,
    16 p.

    True story about a reindeer hunt. Illustrated.   lit   int

10. Dirks, Moses. Atx̂am kugan mataliin anĝaĝiilazas (Life
    on Atka). Atka Village, Alaska. 1973, 42 p.

    Discussion of life and activities on Atka - chil-   lit   int
    dren's games, school, church, fishing, the arrival
    of big ships with supplies, etc. Illustrated.

11. _____. Atx̂am qangis (Atkan fishes). Atka Village,
    Alaska. 1973, 38 p.

    Factual discussion of the various fish in the waters lit   int
    around Atka. Illustrated.

12. Dirks, Moses. Samusis achixaasingis (Arithmetics).
    Atka Village, Alaska. 1973, 11 p.

    Numerals, short word problems and time telling.   lit   prim
    Illustrated.

13. Dirks, Moses and Sally Snigaroff. Hilaakax̂t ii? (Can
     you read?). Atka Village, Alaska. 1973, 30 p.

     Discussion of objects, animals and activities of   lit   int
     life on Atka. Illustrated.

14. _____. Hilal alug̑il (Read and write). Atka
     Village, Alaska. 1973, 20 p.

     Workbook with space for students to write about   voc   int
     various everyday objects pictured and described.
     Illustrated.

15. Dirks, William Sr. Latug̑ing (My grandfather). Atka
     Village, Alaska. 1973, 13 p.

     Story about author's grandfather. Illustrated.   lit   int

16. Golley, Nadesta. Atx̂am hitnisangis (Atkan plants).
     Atka Village, Alaska. 1973, 46 p.

     Factual discussion of various plants native to   lit   int
     the area around Atka Village. Illustrated.

17. _____. Hilaqulim adungizulax (Short readings).
     Atka Village, Alaska. 1973, 15 p.

     Six short texts, fictional and true, realistic   lit   int
     and imaginary. Illustrated.

18. _____. Hilada (Read). Atka Village, Alaska.
     1973, 15 p.

     Primer. One word is concentrated on per page,   lit   prim
     then used in a few short sentences. Illustrated.   voc

19. _____. Taangulam kiig̑uusii (The mountain of thirst).
     Atka Village, Alaska. 1973, 11 p.

     Story about a young boy who finds a pond.   lit   int
     Illustrated.

20. _____. Unangam hlakuchaa ivaanax̂ (The little
     Aleut boy John). Atka Village, Alaska. 1973,
     15 p.

     Story about the daily life and chores of a young   lit   int
     Aleut boy. Illustrated.

21. Marsh, Bruce D. Translated by Moses Dirk. Atx̂ax̂ matal
     txin agunaa (The building of Atka Island). Atka
     Village, Alaska. 1973, 10 p.

     Geological discussion of the formation of the   lit   adv.
     Aleutian Islands, Atka in particular. Illustrated.

70

22. Snigaroff, S. Hamaa hlax̂ aasal isugix̂ (The boy and the
        seal) (Atkan dialect). University of Alaska, Alaska
        Native Language Center, Fairbanks, Alaska. 1973,
        15 p. (ERIC ED111193).

     Elementary reader. Illustrated.   lit   int

ALEUT - NOT KNOWN

23. Tabios, Derenty (Translator). Arirqanek nuyalek pinga'un
        tan'erlit-hlu (Sugcestun dialect). Alaska Native
        Language Center. University of Alaska, Fairbanks,
        Alaska. 1972, 48 p. (Not Available).

24. _____. Nupahlkiaq kep'arkat ililihlrat (Sugcestun
        Dialect). Alaska Native Language Center, University
        of Alaska, Fairbanks. 1973, 20 p. (Not Available)

25. _____. Tan'erlinguasaaq pehlahleq. Alaska Native
        Language Center. University of Alaska, Fairbanks.
        1973, 25 p. (Not Available).

26. Tabios, Derenty and Jeffry Leer. Igapet (Sugcestun dia-
        lect). Alaska Native Language Center, University
        of Alaska, Fairbanks. 1972, 24 p. (Not Available).

27. Tabios, Derenty and Seraphim Meganack. Sugcestun Unigkuat
        (Sugcestun dialect). Alaska Native Language Center,
        University of Alaska, Fairbanks. 1972, 38 p. (Not
        Available).

ALGONKIAN - BILINGUAL

     Pilling, James C. Bibliography of the Algonkian languages.
        AMS Press, New York. 1973, 614 p.

     See Pilling under GENERAL LANGUAGE

ALGONKIAN - MONOLINGUAL, ENGLISH

28. Minnerly, Carol. An adaptation to Louise Lancaster's
        Introducing English for Algonquian speaking Children.
        New York State Migrant Center, Geneseo, New York.
        1973, 19 p. (Not Available).

     Deals with the problems of teaching and learning   meth   col
     English as a second language. Discusses lexocen-   theor
     trism of American education system. Addressed to
     particular problems of speakers of Algonkian
     languages.

29. Pentland, David H., C. Douglas Ellis, Carol A. Simpson,
       and H. Christoph Wolfart. A Bibliography of
       Algonquian Linguistics. University of Manitoba,
       Anthropology Papers, No. 11. Winnepeg, Manitoba.
       1974, 85 p.   (Not Available - CAILC Newsletter,
       Vol. III, #2 1975).

       Covers all Algonquian languages, as well as Yurok,   bibl   self
       Wiyot and Beothok to 1974. Approximately 1200
       entries.

ALGONKIAN - see also CREE, CHIPPEWA, OJIBWA. PASSAMAQUODDY, MALECITE-
       PASSAMAQUODDY, MIC-MAC, SAULTEAUX, BLACKFOOT

APACHE - BILINGUAL

30. American Bible Society. The New Testament. American
       Bible Society, New York. 1966, 1041 p.

       New Testament in Apache with half-page English   lit   self
       translations on same pages as Apache equivalent.
       Some illustrations in black and white.

31. Jicarilla Apache Cultural Awareness Program. Jicarilla
       Apache legends. Jicarilla Apache Cultural Aware-
       ness Program, Dulce, New Mexico. 1974. (Not
       Available).

32. _____ . Trees on the reservation. Jicarilla Apache
       Cultural Awareness Program, Dulce, New Mexico.
       1974. (Not Available).

33. _____ . Coyote and the rabbit. Jicarilla Apache
       Cultural Awareness Program, Dulce, New Mexico.
       1974. (Not Available).

34. Vicenti, Arnold and Wilma Phone. English translation
       by Filomena Pono. Nake'yah ji ali'ma'i: Animals
       of the reservation. Jicarilla Apache Cultural
       Awareness Program, Dulce, New Mexico. 1974, 28 p.
       (Not Available).

       Description of animals found on Apache reservation.   lit   prim
       Illustrated

35. White Mountain Apache Culture Center. Keys to reading
       Apache. White Mountain Apache Culture Center,
       P.O. Box 507, Fort Apache, Arizona. 1972, 52 p.

       Workbook for reading and writing Apache. Includes   phon   int
       review of sound system, short stories in Apache,   voc
       with English translation. Illustrated. Instruc-   lit
       tion in English.

36. White Mountain Apache Culture Center. Western Apache
     dictionary. White Mountain Apache Tribe, Fort
     Apache, Arizona. ca. 1973, 135 p.

     Dictionary designed to help translate Oral History   voc   self
     Program created by the White Mountain Apache Tribe   gram
     of Whiteriver, Arizona. Bulk of book is English-   pron
     Apache dictionary. Appendices contain grammar and
     pronunciation helps, maps of Athapaskan language
     family, lists of plant names and kinship terms,
     and Apache calendar.

37. White Mountain Apache Culture Center Staff. Writing
     Apache. White Mountain Apache Culture Center,
     P.O. Box 507, Fort Apache, Arizona. 1972, 20 p.

     Workbook for practicing writing Apache. Words   script prim
     are half spelled-out with blanks for students to
     fill in. Illustrated. Instruction in English.

38. Whiteriver Public Schools. Curriculum program for the
     Apache language. Whiteriver Public Schools,
     Arizona. 1969, 110 p.   (ERIC ED025757).

     Contains English-Apache word list, list of encli-   voc   prim
     tics with meanings and illustrations of usage,   phon
     chart of Apache vowels and consonants, pronouns,
     numbers and conversation patterns. Also contains
     an Apache reader presenting full phonemic range in
     simple words and short sentences, and a story about
     an Indian boy presented in English and Apache.

APACHE - MONOLINGUAL, ENGLISH

39. Chino, Galbert. My best friend. Jicarilla Apache
     Cultural Awareness Program, Dulce, New Mexico.
     1974, 9 p.   (Not Available).

     Story about a pet horse, for grades 3-5. Written   lit   int
     and illustrated by a fifth grade student.

40. Jicarilla Apache Cultural Awareness Program. I used to
     be afraid. Jicarilla Apache Cultural Awareness
     Program, Dulce, New Mexico. 1974. (Not Available).

     Reader to teach "used to be - but now I'm not"
     construction. Grades 1-3. Written and illustrated   gram   prim
     by elementary students at Dulce.

ATHABASKAN

     See CHIPEWYAN, KOYUKAN, KUTCHIN, UPPER KUSKOKWIM, TANANA,
     DOGRIB, TANAINA, APACHE, NAVAJO, INDIANS OF SUBARTIC,
     and Pilling under GENERAL LANGUAGE

ELACKFOOT - BILINGUAL

41. Frantz, Donald G. Toward a generative grammar of Black-
     foot. Summer Institute of Linguistics of University
     Of Oklahoma, Norman, Oklahoma. 1971, 142 p.

     Work intended for linguists and has a heavy bias   gram col
     toward theoretical linguistics. Nonlinguists with   theor
     some knowledge of Blackfoot may find it of some use.

42. Redhorn, Peter. A guide to the spoken Blackfeet Indian
     language into English. Late 1960's.

     List of words that are of practical use to visitors   voc   prim
     to the Browning, Montana area or the Blackfoot   pron   self
     reservation. Basic pronunciation key is given.
     Words not listed alphabetically. Numbers and days
     of week listed. Small map of reservation and brief
     description of terrain. Amateur effort.

43. Taylor, Allan R. A grammar of Blackfoot. Ph.D. Disser-
     tation, University of California, Berkeley. 1969,
     340 p.   (Not Available - Dissertation Abstract
     #70- 13,183).

     Description of phonology and morphology of Black-   phon col
     foot as spoken in Montana and Alberta. Linguisti-   gram self
     cally oriented, and thereby difficult for nonlin-   bibl
     guist to use. However, contains annotated biblio-
     graphy of published materials on Blackfoot language
     from 1710-1969.

BODEGA MIWOK

     See MIWOK

CAHUILLA - BILINGUAL

44. Seiler, Hansjakob. Cahuilla texts with an introduction.
     Indiana University, Bloomington, Indiana. 1970,
     204 p.

     Collection of myths in Cahuilla; Cahuilla version   lit   col
     precedes English translation on verso. Sentences   gram self
     are numbered to facilitate translation. Introduc-
     tion contains some points of grammar.

CHEROKEE - BILINGUAL

45. Alexander, J.T. (Compiler). A dictionary of the
     Cherokee Indian language. Distributed by Raven
     Hail, P.O. Box 35733, Dallas, Texas. 1971, 359 p.

English-Cherokee, Cherokee-English dictionary.   voc   col
In former section Cherokee words are given both   script self
in Cherokee syllabary and in English translitera-
tion. In latter section, only the Cherokee
syllabary form of the word is given. Very little
explanation of given definitions; no illustrations
of usage. Preface has some information about the
Cherokee syllabary. Small list of sample phrases.

46. American Baptist Publication Society. Cherokee hymn
        book. American Baptist Publication Society,
        Philadelphia. Distributed by Raven Hail, P.O.
        Box 35733, Dallas, Texas. ca. 1970, 96 p.

     Hymns in the Cherokee language. Titles given   voc   self
     only in English. Index by title, but only   script
     Cherokee titles used here. No musical notation.   lit
     Transcription equivalents from Cherokee sylla-   pron
     bary to English alphabet. Also a page of expla-
     nation of sounds.

47. Cherokee Bilingual Education Program. Cherokee folk-
        tales, Book I. Cherokee Bilingual Education
        Program, P.O. Box 769, Tahlequah, Oklahoma.
        1974, 201 p.

     Collection of six stories, some of them folk-   lit   adv
     tales, other recollections of earlier periods in
     Cherokee history. Cherokee language version
     presented in small print at beginning of each
     story, English language version in small print
     follows.

48. _____. Cherokee folktales, Book III. Cherokee
        Bilingual Education Program, P.O. Box 769,
        Tahlequah, Oklahoma. 1974, 61 p.

     Six Cherokee folktales, presented first in large   lit   adv
     print English, then in small type, single space
     Cherokee. Illustrated.

49. _____. Cherokee Writing booklets I-IV. Cherokee
        Bilingual Education Program, P.O. Box 769,
        Tahlequah, Oklahoma. 1974, 82 p.

     Workbooks for practicing writing in Cherokee   script prim
     syllabary. Instructions are in English. Each
     page is a work sheet with space for practicing
     individual symbols and words made up of those
     symbols. Progression in difficulty from two
     syllable/symbol words to multisyllable words, to
     sentences and paragraphs.

50.   Cherokee Bilingual Education. Primer V, teacher's edition.
         Cherokee Bilingual Education Program, P.O. Box 769,
         Tahlequah, Oklahomah. 1974, 37 p.

         Lesson plans to accompany Primer V (see under   meth prim
         CHEROKEE - MONOLINGUAL, CHEROKEE). Instructions
         for teacher given in English. Includes planned
         dialogue for teacher and students in Cherokee.

51.   Chiltoskey, Mary Ulmer. Cherokee words with pictures.
         The Stephens Press, Asheville, North Carolina.
         1972, 56 p.

         Word list alphabetically in English followed by   voc   elem
         Cherokee syllabary equivalent, with subscript   script
         pronunciation of syllabic elements. Small line
         drawings illustrate many entries. Also included
         are a short phrase list, numbers, months, people's
         names, and words to two hymns (to be sung to
         tunes of 'Amazing Grace' and 'What a Friend We
         Have in Jesus'). Work is apparently aimed at
         non-Cherokee children interested in the language.
         Could be useful for beginning literacy for
         Cherokee speakers.

52.   Cowen, Agnes and Martin Cochran. Life of famous
         Cherokee Men. Cherokee Bilingual Education
         Program, P.O. Box 769, Tahlequah, Oklahoma.
         1974, 123 p.

         Five biographies of Cherokee men, including Will   lit   int
         Rogers and Sequoyah, who achieved fame. Each
         biography preceded by study guide in English and
         Cherokee language version of story. Stories are
         then given in English, using large type. Illus-
         trated with line drawings.

53.   Kilpatrick, Anna G. An Introduction to Cherokee.
         Cherokee Bilingual Education Program, Tahlequah,
         Oklahoma. Revised edition 1972, 67 p.

         Bilingual and language instruction. Including   pron prim
         pronunciation drill, basic sentences for memori-   voc   self
         zation, drills on variations of sentences.   lit
         Emphasis on oral Cherokee. Contains 18 lessons
         and three Cherokee stories in English transla-
         tion. Stories illustrated.

54.   Pulte, William and Durbin Feeling. Conversational
         Cherokee Lessons 1-30 with accompanying tapes.
         Cherokee Bilingual Education Program, P.O. Box
         769, Tahlequah, Oklahoma. ca. 1970, 129 p.

A series of lessons in spoken Cherokee to be used   voc   int
with or without Cherokee-speaking instructor.   gram
Each lesson includes dialogue and vocabulary
drill in Cherokee, with English translation; and
discussion of vocabulary and grammar employed in
drill.

55. Pulte, William and Agnes Cowen. Cherokee oral language
     program, Vol. I-VI. Cherokee Bilingual Program,
     Tahlequah, Oklahoma. 1971-1972 (Experimental
     Edition).

     One hundred and fifty (150) lessons of progres-   voc   prim
     sive difficulty in spoken Cherokee. Unpaginated,   pron   self
     no table of contents or index.

56. Pulte, William and Adalene Smith. A Cherokee syllabary
     primer, Vol. I-IV. Cherokee Bilingual Program,
     Tahlequah, Oklahoma. 1972 (Experimental Edition).

     Eighty-two (82) lessons progressing from   voc   prim
     single words to paragraphs in the Cherokee sylla-   script self
     bary. Illustrated, but no pagination, table of   pron
     contents or index.

57. Smith, Adalene and Agnes Cowen. Cherokee songs.
     Cherokee Bilingual Program, Tahlequah, Oklahoma.
     1972, 34 p.

     Cherokee songs in Cherokee syllabary, English   lit   self
     transliteration and English translation. The
     titles are in English and often in Cherokee as
     well. No musical notation, table of contents or
     index.

58. Spade, Watt and Willard Walker. Indian names and
     Whiteman numbers. In William Slager (Editor).
     English for American Indians, Bureau of Indian
     Affairs, Washington, D.C. 1971, pp. 74-75.

     Amusing story about Cherokees confronted with   lit   adv
     white American bureaucracy. Presented in Cherokee
     syllabary on verso and English translation on
     recto.

59. Walker, Willard. Cherokee primer. Carnegie Corpora-
     tion Cross-Cultural Education Project of the
     University of Chicago, Tahlequah, Oklahoma.
     ca. 1965, 68 p.

     Primer for beginning readers. Pages of words   voc   prim
     and accompanying illustrations. Words are
     presented in English, in Cherokee syllabary and
     in English transliteration.

CHEROKEE - MONOLINGUAL, CHEROKEE

60. Cherokee Bilingual Education Program. Primer V.
     Cherokee Bilingual Education Program, P.O. Box
     769, Tahlequah, Oklahoma. 1974, 22 p.

     Children's book for practice in reading Cherokee.   voc   prim
     Written in Cherokee syllabary. Illustrated.   script
     Fifteen lessons.

61. _____. Workbook, Primer 1-4. Cherokee Bilingual
     Education Program, P.O. Box 769, Tahlequah,
     Oklahoma. 1974, 81 p.

     Practice in reading Cherokee syllabary. Progresses   voc   prim
     from two-syllable words through single sentences   script int
     to short stories. Each lesson focuses on parti-
     cular word(s) or syllable(s). Illustrated.

62. Cowen, Agnes. Cherokee Roman script primer, Vol. I-X.
     Cherokee Bilingual Education Program, P.O. Box
     769, Tahlequah, Oklahoma. 1974, 159 p.

     Series of children's readers in Cherokee, written   voc   prim
     in Roman alphabet rather than Cherokee syllabary.   script
     Each page has large picture illustrating an
     object or action which is described in short
     sentences below.

63. Crittenden, Carl (Compiler). Cherokee Roman script
     readers I-IV. Cherokee Bilingual Education
     Program, P.O. Box 769, Tahlequah, Oklahoma.
     1974, 93 p.

     Each volume is prefaced by a chart showing   script prim
     Cherokee syllabary symbol for Roman script syllable   voc
     and Cherokee words using that syllable (in Roman
     script transliteration). Each page then deals
     with one syllable, three or more words containing
     syllable and an illustration of one of the words.

CHEROKEE - MONOLINGUAL, ENGLISH

64. Cherokee Bilingual Education Program. Cherokee folk-
     tales, book II. Cherokee Bilingual Education
     Program, P.O. Box 769, Tahlequah, Oklahoma. 1973,
     165 p.

     Seven tales of Cherokee folklore and life.   lit   adv
     Several stories accompanied by study guide and/or
     glossary of difficult English words. Illustrated.

78

65. Hoyt, Anne K. Bibliography of the Cherokees. South
     Central Regional Education Lab Corporation.
     Little Rock, Arkansas. 1968, 61 p,   (ERIC
     ED023533).

     Extensive bibliography of books, government publi-   bibl self
     cations, periodical articles, and theses published
     between 1832 and 1968 on all phases of Cherokee
     life. Shorter listings on Cherokee education and
     language.

CHICKASAW - BILINGUAL

66. Humes, Jesse and Vinnie May Humes. A Chickasaw dictio-
     nary. The Chickasaw Nation, Oklahoma. 1973, 258 p.

     Actually a word list with pronunciations. Arrange-   voc   self
     ment is English to Chickasaw with a respelling of   pron
     latter to indicate pronunciation. Simple guides
     to pronunciation precede word list.

CHINOOKAN

     See WISHRAM

CHIPEWYAN - BILINGUAL

67. Garr, Ben. Guide to understanding Chipewyan I. Indian
     and Northern Education, University of Saskatchewan,
     Saskatoon, Canada. 1972.

     Introduction to the comprehension of written and   phon self
     some spoken Chipewyan. Also explanation of sound   voc
     system. Dialect used is Patuanak. Vocabulary list   test
     of English words and their Chipewyan equivalents.

68. Paul, Simon. Introductory Chipewyan; basic vocabulary.
     Indian and Northern Education, University of
     Saskatchewan, Saskatoon, Saskatchewan. ca. 1967,
     60 p.

     Work introduces the 38 sounds of Chipewyan.   voc   prim
     Part I introduces a word in English and in   phon self
     Chipewyan and some short   sentences using new
     Chipewyan word. Part II is vocabulary and phrase
     list. Rest is a workbook with several English
     phrases and places for student to write Chipewyan
     equivalent. No preface or table of contents.
     Pagination sporadic.

69.   Reynolds, Margaret. Chipewyan workbook. Indian and
          Northern Curriculum Resources Center, University
          of Saskatchewan, Saskatoon, Saskatchewan. ca.
          1972 (Not Available).

      Workbook for children aged 4 to 7. Series of   voc   prim
      lessons including exercises such as filling
      in missing vowel and matching the English to
      Chipewyan word. Illustrated.

70.   _____. Guide to understanding Chipewyan II.
          Indian and Northern Education, University of
          Saskatchewan, Saskatoon, Saskatchewan. ca. 1972.

      Series of lessons that deal with grammar, vocabu-   voc   int
      lary. Preface indicates most of material was   gram
      taken from Goddard's Analysis of Cold Lake Dialect,   phon
      Linguistic Structures of Native America, and
      International Journal of American Linguistics.
      Brief summation of sound system. See entry above -
      Garr, Benn. Guide to understanding Chipewyan I.

71.   Richardson, Marry W. Chipewyan grammar. Northern
          Canada Evangelical Mission, Cold Lake, Alberta.
          1968. (Not Available - Martin, Survey, p. 40).

CHIPPEWA - BILINGUAL

72.   Verwyst, Chrysostom. Chippewa exercises. Ross and
          Haines, Incorporated, Minneapolis, Minnesota,
          1971, 500 p.   (Reprint of Holy Childhood School
          Print, Harbor Springs, Michigan. 1901).

      Despite early date of original publication, this   voc   self
      is a thorough and useful book of Chippewa vocabu-   gram
      lary and grammar. It is presented in ninety (90)   pron
      lessons, including verb and noun paradigms,
      conversational phrases, etc. Aimed at non-Chippewa
      speaking, non-linguists who wish to work among
      Chippewa. Introduction to modern reprint by
      John D. Nichols, provides linguistic setting of
      Chippewa and additional information on pronuncia-
      tion.

CHIPPEWA - MONOLINGUAL, ENGLISH

73.   Minnesota Historical Society. Chippewa and Dakota
          Indians; a subject catalog of books, pamphlets,
          periodicals and manuscripts in the Minnesota
          Historical Society. St. Paul, Minnesota, 1969,
          127 p.

Catalog providing access to Chippewa and Dakota   bibl col
texts. Two main divisions are "Books, Pamphlets,   self
Periodicals" and "Manuscripts."

CHIPPEWA

See also OJIBWA

CHOCTAW - BILINGUAL

74. Badger, Herbert A. A Descriptive grammar of Mississippi
     Choctaw. Doctoral Dissertation, University of
     Southern Mississippi. 1971, 84 p.   (Not Availa-
     ble - Dissertation Abstract #71- 28,823).

     Transformational grammar of Choctaw as spoken by   gram col
     descendants of scattered remnants of that tribe
     which remained in Mississippi when main body of
     tribe was removed to Oklahoma. Linguistically
     oriented.

75. Choctaw hymn book. John Knox Press, Richmond, Virginia.
          1966, 252 p.   (Reprint of 1858 edition.)

     Hymns are classified by subject: Awakening and   lit   self
     Inviting, Sin, etc. Some titles and hymns in
     English and Choctaw, others only in Choctaw.
     "Articles of Faith" and "Solemnization of
     Marriage" in both Choctaw and English.

76. Downing, Todd. Chahta nompa: An Introduction to the
     Choctaw language. Choctaw Bilingual Education
     Program, Southeastern State College, Durant,
     Oklahoma. 1971, 23 p.

     Nine chapters providing a well organized, intelli-   voc   self
     gently written introduction to Choctaw for the   gram prim
     layman. Includes some historical and ethnographic
     background on the Choctaw.

77. Littlejohn, Joseph E. A Handbook for teachers and
     aides of the Choctaw bilingual education program.
     Southeastern State College, Durant, Oklahoma.
     1971, 26 p.   (ERIC ED054902).

     Discussion of needs of Choctaw children, references   meth self
     to materials available for in-service training and   voc
     classroom use. Also includes a list of Choctaw
     terms with definitions.

78. Nicklas, Thurston D. Choctaw morphology. Southeastern
         Oklahoma State College, Durant, Oklahoma. 1970,
         27 p.   (ERIC ED048582).

         Discusses Choctaw word structure, definitions of   voc   self
         frequently used terms, articles, conjunctions and   gram
         personal pronouns.

79. _____. Choctaw morphology. Southeastern Oklahoma
         State College, Durant, Oklahoma. 1971, 59 p.
         (ERIC ED058789).

         Discussion of articles, conjunctions, pronouns,   voc   self
         adjectives, verb parts. Morphophonemic changes   morph col
         considered throughout discussion.   gram

80. _____. A Choctaw orthography. Southeastern
         Oklahoma College, Durant, Oklahoma. 1970, 12 p.
         (ERIC ED048583).

         Description of an essentially phonemic ortho-   script self
         graphy. Sample text given in Choctaw, with
         English translation.

     Pilling, James Constantine. Bibliography of the
         Muskogean languages. AMS Press, New York. 1973,
         114 p.

         See Pilling under GENERAL LANGUAGES

81. Watkins, Ben. Choctaw definer. Southeastern Indian
         Antiquities Survey, Incorporated, Box 12392,
         Nashville, Tennessee. 1972, 84 p. (Reprint of
         publication by J.W. Baldwin, Van Buren, Arkansas, 1892)

         English-Choctaw dictionary with six-page appendix   voc   self
         showing conjugation of verbs "buy" and "sell."   gram
         Some mistakes in typesetting and spelling. Note
         original date of publication.

CHOCTAW - MONOLINGUAL, ENGLISH

     Ohannessian, Sirarpi. Teaching English to speakers of
         Choctaw, Navajo, and Papago; a contrastive approach.
         Prepared at the Center for Applied Linguistics for
         the Bureau of Indian Affairs. Center for Applied
         Linguistics, Washington, D.C. 1969, 138 p.

         See under GENERAL ESL

82. Southeastern State College. Choctaw bilingual educa-
         tion program. Southeastern State College, Durant,
         Oklahoma. 1973, 62 p.   (ERIC ED085363).

Description of program emphasizing use of Choctaw   meth self
language as vehicle of instruction, improvement of   col
self image of Choctaw children, and employment of
bilingual teachers and aids. Also contains teacher
handbook.

CLALLUM

See SALISH

CREE - BILINGUAL

83. Anderson, Anne (Narnoya Ayiman). Let's learn Cree.
     Edmonton. 1970, 106 p. (Not Available -
     Whiteside).

84. Cree Alphabet Book. Key to the Cree syllabic characters.
     In William Slager (Editor). Language in American
     Indian Education. Bureau of Indian Affairs,
     Albuquerque, New Mexico. Spring 1972, pp. 110-112.

     Chart of Cree syllabary with transliteration, fol-   voc   prim
     lowed by two pages of illustrations with English   script
     label, Cree syllabary label, and English trans-
     literation of Cree word.

85. Ellis, C. Douglas. Spoken Cree: west coast of James
     Bay, part 1. Revised edition. Department of
     Missions, Anglican Church of Canada, Toronto.
     1971 (Not Available - Martin, Survey, p. 40).

86. Kingfisher Indian Day School Students. Our Cree dic-
     tionary. Kingfisher Indian Day School, Kingfisher
     Lake, via Central Patricia, Ontario, Canada. 1970.
     (Not Available - CAILC Newsletter, Vol. 1, No. 2,
     p. 13).

87. McLeod, Barbara. The Cree language. Indian and
     Northern Curriculum Resources Center, University
     of Saskatchewan, Saskatoon, Saskatchewan. ca.
     1967, 71 p.

     Primer in written Cree. Picture of vocabulary   voc   prim
     item is followed by word in English, word in Cree,
     and a simple declarative sentence in English and
     in Cree using that word.

88. The Native people. The Alberta Native Communications
       Society, Room B1, 100 Avenue Building, 100 Avenue
       and 104 Street, Edmonton, Alberta. Monthly issues
       from May 1970 - December 1974 (collection incom-
       plete).

       Monthly review of national, local, and tribal   lit   self
       news. Each issue contains numerous articles in
       the Cree language using Cree syllabary.

89. The Saskatchewan Indian. The Saskatchewan Indian, 1114
       Central Avenue, Prince Albert, Saskatchewan.
       Monthly issues from July/August 1971 - October
       1973 (collection incomplete).

       Official voice of the Federation of Saskatchewan   lit   self
       Indians. Intended to serve as an effective
       vehicle for Indian opinion. Each issue contains
       an article in the Cree language.

90. Soveran, Marilylle. From Cree to English, part one:
       The sound system. Saskatchewan University, Saska-
       toon, Saskatchewan. Indian and Northern Curricu-
       lum Resources Center. 1968, 80 p.   (ERIC
       ED025755).

       Provides specific teaching instructions with   pron   self
       facial diagrams to illustrate oral production of
       English sounds difficult for Cree speakers, and
       discussion of differences between two languages
       which provide difficulties. Detailed pronuncia-
       tion drill included. Knowledge of linguistics is
       not required of reader.

91. Tait, Joyce and George Sesequaysis. Introduction to
       Cree language. Indian and Northern Education,
       University of Saskatchewan, Saskatoon, Saskatche-
       wan. ca. 1967, 105 p.

       Four lessons in three volumes. Four tapes corre-   voc   self
       spond to lessons. Course intended for native   phon   sec
       speakers of English at high school or adult level.   gram
                                                                 pron

92. Wolfart, Hans C. An outline of Plains Cree morphology.
       Ph.D. Dissertation, Yale University. 1969,
       299 p. (Not Available - Dissertation Abstract
       #70- 17,442).

       Sets out the grammatical categories of Plains Cree,   gram   col
       as spoken in Alberta and Saskatchewan, then gives
       detailed analysis of paradigms of nouns, pronouns
       and verbs. Also outlines word formation.

93.   Wolfart, Hans C. Plains Cree: a grammatical study. Trans-
      actions of the American Philosophical Society, New
      Series, Vol. 63, Part 5, Philadelphia. 1973,
      90 p. (Not Available - CAILC Newsletter, Vol. 2,
      No. 2, 1974).

      Linguistic work of general scope. Attempt to   gram col
      describe structure of words in Plains Cree.
      Intended as a tool for further, more detailed
      studies. Includes a sample text.

94.   Wolfart, H. Christoph and Janet F. Caroll. Meet Cree.
      A Practical guide to the Cree language. University
      of Alberta Press, Edmonton. 1973, 63 p.   (Not
      Available - CAILC Newsletter, Vol. 2, No. 2, 1974).

      Not an attempt to teach Cree, but an explanation   phon self
      of major differences between Cree and English.   gram
      Includes sounds of Cree, and grammar.

CREE - MONOLINGUAL, CREE

95.   Bearskin, Daisy. Mančata (transliteration of Cree
      syllabary by KLA) (Eastern dialect). Ontario
      Region, Department of Indian and Northern Affairs,
      Toronto, Ontario. 1974, 10 p.   (Not Available).

      Booklet about building a wigwam. Illustrated.

96.   Fort George Federal School Staff and Students. Nistam
      hiyiyomasiniikan (transliteration from Cree sylla-
      bary by KLA) (Eastern Cree dialect). Ontario
      Region, Department of Indian and Northern Affairs,
      Toronto, Ontario. 1971, 34 p   (Not Available).

      A first reading book.

97.   Pash, Nellie. Apamitanoč natohosčič (transliteration of
      Cree syllabary by KLA) (Eastern dialect). Ontario
      Region, Department of Indian and Northern Affairs,
      Toronto, Ontario. 1974, 12 p.   (Not Available).

      Booklet about animals encountered while following
      a trapline. Illustrated.

98.   Tekakwitha, Sister Catherine. Ayamitata ininimohin
      (transliteration of Cree syllabary by KLA) (Fort
      Albany dialect). Ontario Region, Department of
      Indian and Northern Affairs, Toronto, Ontario.
      1974, 16 p.   (Not Available).

      Story of a boy home from school for summer vaca-
      tion.

CREE - MONOLINGUAL, ENGLISH

99. Bear, Robert. Cree legends. Indian and Northern Educa-
        tion, University of Saskatchewan, Saskatoon, Sas-
        katchewan. ca. 1965, 62 p.

      Legends collected in taped interviews with Cree-   lit   int
      speaking people, telling stories in native language.   self
      Attempt is to make English translation conform to
      Cree usage as closely as possible. Stories untitled.

CROW - BILINGUAL

100. Kaschube, Dorothea. Structural elements of the language
        of the Crow Indians of Montana. University of
        Colorado Studies, Series in Anthropology, No. 14,
        University of Colorado, Boulder, Colorado. 1967,
        109 p.

      Includes discussion of stems, morphophonemic   gram   col
      changes, and analysis of translation of Crow   voc
      tape. Also includes dictionary of stems and
      inventory of consonants and vowels.

101. Toineeta, Joy, Euna Rose He Does It, Dora Rides Horse,
        Dale Old Horn. The Crazy one. In William Slager
        (Editor), Language in American Indian Education,
        Bureau of Indian Affairs, Albuquerque, New Mexico.
        Fall 1971, pp. 84-85.

      Story about a mischevious Crow boy and some trouble   lit   self
      he causes. Presented first in Crow, then in
      English translation.

CUPEÑO - BILINGUAL

102. Hill, Jane H. and Rosinda Nolasquez. Mulu'wetam: the
        first people; Cupeño oral history and language,
        including a dictionary and grammatical sketch of
        Cupeño. Malki Museum Press, Morongo Indian Reser-
        vation, Banning, California. 1973, 198 p.

      Collection of oral histories, myths, accounts of   lit   self
      old religious ceremonies, reminiscences, stories   voc
      for children, and songs of Cupeño people of   gram
      southern California presented in English and
      Cupeño. Cupeño-English and English-Cupeño dic-
      tionary and a grammatical sketch also included.

DAKOTA

      See SIOUX

DIEGUEÑO - BILINGUAL

103. Couro, Ted and Christina Hutcheson. Dictionary of Mesa
      Grande Diegueño. Malki Museum Press, Morongo
      Indian Reservation, Banning, California. 1973,
      118 p,

      Diegueño-English, English-Diegueño dictionary.   voc   col
      More detailed in former part, although latter sec-   gram self
      tion is longer. Some points of grammar in last
      ten pages. Introduction by Margaret Langdon,
      Associate Professor for Linguistics at University
      of California, San Diego. For linguistic scholars
      and Indian people.

104. Langdon, Margaret. A grammar of Diegueño: The Mesa
      Grande dialect. University of California Publica-
      tions in Linguistics No. 66, Berkeley. 1970,
      200 p.

      Contains chapters of (1) Phonemes; (2) Principles   voc   col
      of word formation; (3) Morphophonemics; (4) The   phon
      noun; (5) Inflection; (6) Syntactic affixes; and   bibl
      (7) Syntax. Has a bibliography.   gram

DOGRIB - BILINGUAL

105. MacDiarmid, J.A. Tendi goes beaver snaring. Curriculum
      Division, Department of Education, Northwest
      Territories, Canada. 1972, 13 p,

      Young Indian boy goes trapping beaver in winter.   lit   int
      Book 7 in Stories about Tendi series. Tendi
      speaks some Dogrib, in story. Illustrations in
      color by B. Abraham.

DOGRIB - MONOLINGUAL, ENGLISH

106. Football, Virginia. Tesqua and the chief's son.
      Curriculum Division. Department of Education,
      Northwest Territories, Canada. 1972, 32 p.

      Book 6 of Dogrib Legends series. Plot of   lit   int
      Cinderella genre. Chief's son finds Tesqua's lost
      moccasin and searches for her. They meet, marry
      and live happily ever after. Illustrated by B.
      Abraham.

87

107. MacDiarmid, J.A. Johnny goes hunting. Curriculum Division,
      Department of Education, Yellowknife, Northwest Territories,
      Canada. 1972, 29 p.

      Story of Johnny's hunting trip with his father.   lit   int
      Their prey are caribou and moose.

108. _____. Johnny goes to Yellowknife. Curriculum Divi-
      sion, Department of Education, Yellowknife, Northwest
      Territories, Canada. 1972, 21 p.

      Johnny, a young Indian boy, visits the city.   lit   int
      Illustrations in color by Wallace T. Murphy.

109. _____. Tendi's mossbag. Curriculum Division, Depart-
      ment of Education, Yellowknife, Northwest Territories,
      Canada. 1872, 15 p.

      First book in Stories About Tendi series. Tells of   lit   prim
      Tendi as a baby and his father and mother. Illustra-
      tions by B. Abraham.

ESKIMO - BILINGUAL

      Canada, Department of Information. Elementary Education in
      the Northwest Territories, a handbook for curriculum
      development. Curriculum Division, Department of Educa-
      tion, Northwest Territories, Canada. ca. 1970, 313 p.

      See under GENERAL ESL

110. Hofmann, T.R. Writing in the Eskimo classroom. Cahiers
      Linguistiques D'Ottawa, Ottawa University, Ontario.
      1973. Vol. 7. No. 3. 5 p. (ERIC ED102870).

      New syllabic writing system for transcribing Eskimo   script self
      languages is suggested as being more viable than one
      currently in use.

      Pilling, James C. Bibliography of the Eskimo Language.
      AMS Press, New York. 1973, 116 p.

      See Pilling under GENERAL LANGUAGES

111. Pitseolak. Pictures out of my life. From recorded inter-
      views with Dorothy Eber, University of Washington,
      Seattle. 1972, 91 p.

      Biographical stories of Eskimo life written both in   lit   self
      English and in Eskimo, including forward and picture   col
      captions. Illustrated from stone cuts and engravings
      by the author, one of many artists of the Cape Dorset
      region.

112. Ray, Lieutenant P.H. and John Murdock. A vocabulary of
      the Eskimos of Point Barrow and Cape Smythe. Shorey
      Book Store, Seattle. 1965, 11 p. (Reprint of edition
      by Government Printing Office, Washington, D.C. 1885).

      Vocabulary lists in English and Eskimo. Words are   voc   self
      grouped in subject classes, i.e., persons, parts of
      the body, kinship terms. Verbs are partially conjugated.
      Note original date of publication. No information on
      pronunciation or grammar provided.

ESKIMO - MONOLINGUAL, ENGLISH

113. Alaska State-Operated School System. What can you hear?
     Alaska State-Operated School System, 650 International
     Airport Road, Anchorage. 1974, 34 p.

      Series of answers to the title question, using sounds   voc   prim
      from the environment of the far north, e.g., snowmobile,
      goose. Workbook section in back of book. Illustrated.

114. _____. What can you see? Alaska State-Operated School
      System, 650 International Airport Road, Anchorage,
      1974, 34 p.

      Series of answers to the title question, using familiar   voc   prim
      Alaskan sights, e.g., raven, river. Illustrated.

115. _____. What can you see? Alaska State-Operated School
      System, 650 International Airport Road, Anchorage.
      1974, 96 p.

      Sixteen short stories about things and people an Eskimo   lit   int
      boy and girl see in their village. Illustrated.

116. _____. What can you smell? Alaska State-Operated
      School System, 650 International Airport Road,
      Anchorage. 1974, 20 p.

      Series of answers to the title question. Aromas are   voc   prim
      taken from the surroundings of the target population,
      e.g., wet fur, coffee. At the back of the book the
      child can choose words to fill the blank in the sen-
      tence "I can smell _____" and can match the pic-
      ture of an item to the word for that item.
      Illustrated.

117. Alaska State-Operated School System. What do you like to
       Eat? Alaska State-Operated School System, 650 Inter-
       national Airport Road, Anchorage. 1974, 33 p.

       Series of answers to the title question, using food   voc   prim
       items familiar to Eskimos, e.g., caribou, blue-
       berries. Workbook section in back of book.
       Illustrated.

118. Benton, S. William. A set of picture cards for use in
       teaching English verbs to Eskimo and Indian children
       in Alaska. Bureau of Indian Affairs Schools, Bureau
       of Indian Affairs, Bethel, Alaska. 1969, 67 p.
       (ERIC ED080249).

       Set of 23 cards to aid in teaching English verbs,   voc   prim
       using contractions and informal speech. Illustra-
       tions show situations familiar to the students.

119. Hofman, T.R. Teaching the Eskimo syllabics. In the
       Northian, University of Saskatchewan, College of
       Education, Saskatoon, Saskatchewan. 1970, Vol. 7,
       No. 4, 12 p.

       Argument in favor of syllabic writing as opposed   script   self
       to alphabets. New methods of teaching syllabics   meth
       for Eskimos are suggested to support this argu-
       ment. Examples of Eskimo syllables used.

       Holzmueller, Diana Lynn. Multi-media resource list;
       Indian and Eskimo culture in the North. Center for
       Northern Educational Research, University of Alaska,
       College, Alaska, in collaboration with the Insti-
       tute of Social, Economic and Government Research.
       1973, 59 p.

       See under GENERAL BILINGUAL EDUCATION

       Hopkins, Thomas R. Language testing of North
       American Indians. Paper delivered at Conference
       on Problems in Foreign Language Testing, English
       Language Institute, University of Michigan,
       Ann Arbor. September 28-30, 1967.

       See under INDIANS OF SUBARCTIC

       Kraus, Michael. Alaska Native Language Center Report
       1973. Alaska Native Language Center, University
       of Alaska, Fairbanks. 1973, 24 p.

       See under INDIANS OF SUBARCTIC

ESKIMO - MONOLINGUAL, ENGLISH cont'd

120. Kraus, Michael. Eskimo-Aleut. in Current Trends in
        Linguistics, Mouton, The Hague. 1973, Vol. 10,
        p. 1285-1366.

        Descriptive article about the various Eskimo   desc   self
        and Aleut languages and dialects. Includes a   bibl   col
        review of work in this field and an extensive
        bibliography.

ESKIMO

      See also INNUIT, SIBERIAN YUPIK, YU'PIK

GITKSAN - BILINGUAL

121. Hindle, Lonnie and Bruce Rigsby. A short practical
        dictionary of the Gitksan language. reprinted
        from Northwest Anthropological Research Notes,
        Moscow, Idaho. 1973, 60 p.

        Dictionary based on dialects of Gitksan spoken   voc   self
        in Hazelton and Kispiax, northern British Columbia.
        Intended as an initial reference work for guidance
        and use of Gitksan people.

GWICH'IN

      See KUTCHIN

HAIDA - MONOLINGUAL, ENGLISH

      Dall, W.H. et al. Languages of the tribes of the
        extreme Northwest -- the Aleutians and adjacent
        territories. Shorey Book Store, Seattle, Washington,
        1970, 47 p. (Reprinted from Contributions to
        American Ethnology, Vol. 1, Washington, D.C.
        1877).

      See under INDIANS OF SUBARCTIC

122. Kess, Joseph. A bibliography of the Haida language.
        Canadian Journal of Linguistics, Fall, 1968.
        Vol. 14, p. 63-5.

        Brief bibliography of monographs and articles   bibl   self
        in French and English dealing with the Haida
        language.

HAIDA - NOT KNOWN

123. Lawrence, Erma (Editor). Haida noun dictionary. Alaska
        State Language Center, University of Alaska, Fair-
        banks, Alaska. 1972, 68 p. (Not Available).

124. _____. Haida language workshop reader. Alaska
        State Language Center, University of Alaska,
        Fairbanks, Alaska. 1972, 34 p. (Not Available).

125. _____. Haida word lists, Volume 1. Alaska State
        Language Center, University of Alaska, Fairbanks,
        Alaska. 1972, 26 p. (Not Available).

126. Natkong, Jessie, Christine Edenso and Bob Cogo. Xáadas
        kil asgyáan gin-gáay. Alaska State Language
        Center, University of Alaska, Fairbanks, Alaska.
        1973, 27 p. (Not Available).

HOPI - BILINGUAL

127. American Bible Society. The epistle of Paul the
        apostle to the Romans. Paul Jesus ayaatnihqat
        peniata Rome ep tuptsiivni'yunquamuy amumii.
        American Bible Society, New York. Distributed
        by Raven Hail, P.O. Box 35733, Dallas, Texas.
        1966, 59 p.

        New Testament Book of Romans presented in both   lit   self
        English and in Hopi.

HOPI - MONOLINGUAL, HOPI

128. Albert, Roy and Charlie Talawepi. Coyote tales.
        Northern Arizona Supplementary Education
        Center, Northern Arizona University, Flagstaff,
        Arizona. 1970, 300 p.

        Twenty Hopi stories, several about coyote.   lit   int
        Ranging in difficulty from first through third
        grade reading level. Each story paginated
        separately. Illustrated.

HOPI - MONOLINGUAL, HOPI cont'd

129. Black, Robert. Hopi grievance chants: a mechanism
         of social control. in Dell Hymes and William Bittle
         (Editors). Studies in Southwestern Ethnolin-
         guistics. Mouton, The Hague, 1967, p. 54-67.

      While mainly a study of the cultural function   lit   col
      of these chants, this article does give the   phon   self
      texts of some representative chants in Hopi
      with literal English translation. A brief
      phonetic key to Hopi is included.

HOPI - MONOLINGUAL, ENGLISH

130. Talaswaima, Terrance. The Eagle hunt. Hopi Action
         Program, Oraibi, Arizona. 1974, 12 p.

      Story about two young Hopi boys who capture   lit   int
      baby hawks to participate in the ritual of the
      Eagle hunt and the subsequent sacrifice of the
      birds. Illustrated in full color.

131. _____. Hopi bride at the home dance. Hopi
         Action Program, Oraibi, Arizona. 1974, 21 p.

      Description of traditional final wedding   lit   int
      ceremony of the Hopi and the preparations for
      it. Hopi words are used for ceremonial
      objects, foods, etc. Illustrated with full
      color paintings.

INDIANS OF CALIFORNIA

      Heizer, Robert F. Languages, territories, and names
         of California tribes. University of California,
         Berkeley. 1966, 62 p.

      See under GENERAL LANGUAGE

132. Parrish, Sidney. How sickness came to the people.
         Ya-ka-ma Indian Education and Development,
         Incorporated, P.O. Box 11339, Santa Rosa,
         California. 1974, 16 p.

      Traditional coyote tale, in simple English.   lit   int
      Illustrated.

133. _____. The owl story. Ya-ka-ma Indian Educa-
         tion and Development, Incorporated, P.O. Box
         11339, Santa Rosa, California. 1974, 8 p.

      Story about how Owls attacked an Indian couple   lit   int
      and put fear in the people. Illustrated.

INDIANS OF CALIFORNIA cont'd

134.   Parrish, Sidney. The slug woman. Ya-ka-ma Indian Educa-
          tion and Development, Incorporated, P.O. Box
          11339, Santa Rosa, California. 1974, 12 p.

          Story about the supernatural Slug Woman and her   lit   **adv**
          vengeance on an Indian youth who breaks the
          laws of his people. Illustrated.

INDIANS OF SOUTHWEST

       Hymes, Dell H. and William E. Bittle (Editors).
          Studies in southwestern ethnolinguistics.
          Meaning and history in the language of the
          American Southwest. Mouton, Paris, The Hague.
          1967, 467 p.

          See under GENERAL LANGUAGE

INDIANS OF SUBARCTIC - BILINGUAL

135.   Dall, W.H., J. Furuhelm and George Gibbs. Languages
          of the tribes of the extreme Northwest - The
          Aleutians and adjacent territories. Shorey
          Book Store, Seattle, Washington. 1970, 47 p.
          (Reprinted from Contributions to American
          Ethnology, Vol. 1, Washington, D.C. 1877).

          Vocabulary lists for various dialects of   voc   self
          Tlingit, Haida, Innuit, Kwakiutl, and other
          languages of the Arctic and Subarctic. Note,
          however, original date of publication.

136.   The River Times. Fairbanks Native Association, 102
          Lacey Street, Fairbanks, Alaska. July 31,
          1973, Vol. II, No. 8, p. 3.

          This issue of the newspaper has an untitled   voc   self
          article with a list of northern Athabaskan
          words with English translations.

137.   _____. Fairbanks Native Association, 102
          Lacey Street, Fairbanks, Alaska. Monthly,
          September 7, 1973 - December 1973.

          Monthly newspaper containing a review of   voc   self
          national, local and tribal news from the
          Athabaskan, Aleut and Eskimo viewpoint. Each
          issue includes an article on the Athabascan
          language.

INDIANS OF SUBARCTIC - MONOLINGUAL, ENGLISH

Alaska State-Operated School System. What can you
hear? Alaska State-Operated School System,
650 International Airport Road, Anchorage,
Alaska. 1974, 34 p.

See under ESKIMO

138. Alaska State-Operated School System. What do you
hear? Alaska State Operated School System,
650 International Airport Road, Anchorage,
Alaska. 1974, 72 p.

Twelve short stories about sounds two Athabaskan   lit   int
boys hear. Illustrated.

139. Beaulieu, Antoine. Getting lime. Canarctic
Publishing, Limited, Yellowknife, Northwest
Territories, Canada for Curriculum Division,
Department of Education, Northwest Territories,
Canada. 1973, 15 p.

How the Indians extracted lime from rocks for   lit   int
sale to Hudson's Bay Company. Some uses of   hist
lime mentioned.

Benton, S. William. A Set of picture cards for use
in teaching English verbs to Eskimo and Indian
children in Alaska. Bureau of Indian Affairs
Schools, Bureau of Indian Affairs, Bethel,
Alaska. 1969, 67 p.

See under ESKIMO

Canada, Department of Information. Elementary
education in the Northwest Territories; a
handbook for curriculum development. Curriculum
Division, Department of Education, Northwest
Territories, Canada. ca. 1970, 313 p.

See under GENERAL ESL

Holzmueller, Diana Lynn. Multi-media resource list;
Indian and Eskimo culture in the North. Center
for Northern Educational Research, University
of Alaska, College, Alaska, in collaboration
with the Institute of Social, Economic and
Government Research. 1973, 59 p.

See under GENERAL BILINGUAL EDUCATION

INDIANS OF SUBARCTIC - MONOLINGUAL, ENGLISH cont'd

Indian Affairs Branch. Linguistic and cultural
affiliations of Canadian Indians. Indian
Affairs Branch, Government of Canada, Queen's
Printer, Ottawa. 1967, 26 p.

See under GENERAL LANGUAGE

140. Krauss, Michael. Alaska Native Language Center
Report 1973. Alaska Native Language Center,
University of Alaska, Fairbanks, Alaska. 1973,
24 p.

Includes a description of the Center's activities   desc   self
to date of publication, and description of the
languages of Alaska.

141. Mullen, Dana. LEREC: learning English as a second
language through recreation. Saskatchewan
Newstart, Incorporated, Prince Albert, Saskatchewan. 1972, 263 p. (ERIC ED064993).

A program for use in summer recreation projects   meth   col
in northern Canada. Combines recreational   voc
activities for children of all ages with   gram
practice in English vocabulary and sentence
structure. Includes list of phrases and words
to use. Outlines training necessary for
recreation leaders.

National Library of Canada. Indian-Innuit authors:
an annotated bibliography. National Library of
Canada, Ottawa, Ontario, Canada. 1974, 108 p.

See under INNUIT

142. Sikkuark, Nic. Book of things you will never see.
Keewatin Region Education Office, Department
of Education, Curriculum Division, Government
of Northwest Territories, Yellowknife, Canada.
1973, 25 p.

Story of imaginary and impossible animals and   lit   int
events.

96

INDIANS OF SUBARCTIC - MONOLINGUAL, ENGLISH cont'd

143. Sikkuark, Nic. What animals think. Keewatin Region
          Education Office, Department of Education,
          Curriculum Division, Government of Northwest
          Territories, Yellowknife, Canada. 1973, 39 p.

      Different animals pictured on each page, with   lit   int
      what the animal "thinks" in English opposite   voc
      the picutre. Included are polar bear, fish,
      sea lions, wolves, caribou, and birds.

144. Unka, Helene. Working for wages. Curriculum
          Division, Department of Education, Northwest
          Territories, Canada. 1973, 19 p.

      Story of a woman's recollections of her child-   lit   adv
      hood at the turn of the century, when white   hist
      man's economy made employment available for
      Indians. Illustrated in color.

INDIANS OF SUBARCTIC

      See also DOBRIB, KOYUKON, KUTCHIN, TANACROSS, TANAINA,
      UPPER KUSKOKWIM, UPPER TANANA, NIKOLAI

INNUIT - BILINGUAL

145. Afcan, P. and Naqeak, J. Analgaam qimmini (Pat's
          dogs) (Barrow dialect). Alaska Native Language
          Center, University of Alaska, Fairbanks, Alaska.
          1973, 25 p. (Not Available).   prim

146. Alaska State-Operated Schools. My family (Report).
          Alaska State-Operated Schools, Anchorage, Alaska.
          1974, 35 p. (ERIC ED098797).

      Elementary reader in Inupiat (Innuit) with   lit   prim
      English translation following. Illustrated.

147. _____. Noorvik reader. Alaska State-Operated
          Schools, Anchorage, Alaska. 1974, 108 p.

      Series of one or two paragraph stories about   lit   int
      the history of Noorvik and life there today.
      Story is presented first in Noorvik dialect,
      then in English. Illustrated.

INNUIT - BILINGUAL cont'd

148. Alaska State-Operated Schools. Teller Reader. Alaska
      State-Operated Schools, Anchorage. 1974, 108 p.

      Series of one or two paragraph long stories   lit   int
      about life in Teller, past and present. Story
      is presented first in Teller dialect, then in
      English. Illustrated.

149. _____. Upper Kobuk reader. Alaska State-
      Operated Schools, Anchorage, Alaska. 1974, 88 p.

      Series of one or two paragraph long stories   lit   int
      about life in the villages of Ambler, Kobuk, and
      Shungnak; at present and in the past. Each
      story is presented first in Kobuk dialect, then
      in English. Illustrated.

150. Barrow School. Aġviq (The Whale). Barrow School,
      North Slope Borough School District, Box 307,
      Barrow, Alaska. 1974, 31 p. (Not Available).   prim

151. Barrow School. Akḷunaaliuġniq natchium amianiñ
      (Making rope from sealskin). Barrow School,
      North Slope Borough School District, Box 307,
      Barrow, Alaska. 1974, 15 p. (Not Available).   adv

152. _____. Annuġarriuġniq niġrutit amiŋiññiñ
      (Making clothing from animal skins). Barrow
      School, North Slope Borough School District,
      Box 307, Barrow, Alaska. ca. 1974, 24 p.
      (Not Available).   adv

153. _____. Apuyyaq (Snowhouse). Barrow School,
      North Slope Borough School District, Box 307,
      Barrow, Alaska. 1974, 12 p. (Not Available).   adv

154. _____. Iḷisaurrim maqpiġaaŋi (Teacher's book-
      guide to workbook I and II). Barrow School,
      North Slope Borough School District, Box 307,
      Barrow, Alaska. 1974, 43 p. (Not Available).   col

155. _____. Kutiq (Kutiq). Barrow School, North
      Slope Borough School District, Box 307, Barrow,
      Alaska. 1974, 7 p. (Not Available).   prim

156. _____. Natchiqsiuŋniq kuvraqtuqḷugich (Catching
      seal with a seal net). Barrow School, North
      Slope Borough School District, Box 307, Barrow,
      Alaska. 1974, 10 p. (Not Available).   adv

INNUIT - BILINGUAL cont'd

157. Barrow School. Piraksrat (Things to do). Barrow School,
        North Slope Borough School District, Box 307,
        Barrow, Alaska. 1972, 22 p. (Not Available).   prim

158. _____. Utuqqaich aŋuniunnat tiŋmiaġruŋnullu
        qaugannulla (Old hunting equipment for hunting
        birds and ducks). Barrow School, North Slope
        Borough School District, Box 307, Barrow,
        Alaska. 1974, 11 p. (Not Available).   adv

159. Canada, Curriculum Section, Education Division.
        Igloolik (Reader). Northern Affairs Branch, Depart-
        ment of Indian Affairs and Northern Development,
        Ottawa. 1965 (Not Available - Kraus CTL, p. 1341).

     In English, syllabics and roman orthography.

160. Canadian Arctic Producers. Arctic women's workshop.
        Department of Indian Affairs and Northern Develop-
        ment and Canadian Arctic Producers, Box 4130 Station
        "E", Ottawa, Ontario. 1974, 92 p.

     Report on Canadian national meeting of Arctic women.   lit   adv
     Focuses on Arctic crafts and ways of improving
     income through them. Includes a list of delegates,
     observers, translators. Presented in both English
     and Innuit. Illustrated with photographs of work-
     shop.

161. Charput, Therese and Rachel Erkloo. The story of
        Papik, an Eskimo Boy. Department of Indian
        Affairs and Northern Development, Ottawa.
        1965, 50 p. (Not Available - Kraus CTL,
        p. 1335).

     In English, syllabics and roman orthography.

162. Inuit Tapirisat of Canada. INUIT and the law. Inuit
        Tapirisat of Canada, 222 Somerset Street West,
        Ottawa, Ontario. 1974, 138 p.

     A basic introduction to Canadian law and govern-   lit   adv
     ment, particularly in regard to its relationship   self
     to the Native Peoples of Canada. Divided into
     four sections - Making of Law, Administration
     of Justice, Basic Concepts of Law, and Govern-
     ment Services. Includes charts of electoral
     districts, governmental organization. Book is
     presented in both English and Inuit. Illustrated.

INNUIT - BILINGUAL cont'd

163. Inuttituut. Minister of Indian and Northern Affairs,
      Ottawa. Quarterly issues from Summer 1972-
      Winter 1974.

      Quarterly magazine in three languages: Inutt   lit   self
      (Innuit), French and English. Review of
      national and tribal news of the Innuit people.

164. Jamassee, Nicotye. Nicotye and her family. Curricu-
      lum Section, Education Division, Northern Affairs
      Branch, Department of Indian Affairs and Northern
      Development, Ottawa. 1965, 27 p. (Not Available -
      Kraus CTL, p. 1341).

      In English, syllabics and roman orthography.

165. Kaveolook, Harold. Allagich iglunich Iñupiat (Diffe-
      rent kinds of Eskimo houses). Barrow School
      Inupiat Program, Barrow, Alaska. 1974-75, 21 p.

      Description in Iñupiat (Innuit) of building and   lit   int
      furnishing of traditional Iñupiat homes. Illus-
      trated with line drawings and floor plans.
      English translation at back of book.

166. Kayak, Lily. Have you ever seen a walrus? (Pond
      Inlet dialect). Curriculum Division, Depart-
      ment of Education, Government of the Northwest
      Territories, Canada. 1973, 54 p.

      English alphabet book. Each letter is intro-   script   prim
      duced, accompanied by an English word that   voc
      begins with that letter, the Innuit equivalent
      of that word (both in Innuit syllabary and in
      English transliteration) and a question employing
      that word. Question is in English, syllabics,
      and transliteration. A photograph illustrates
      the question.

167. Webster, Donald H. Inupiat Eskimo dictionary. Alaska
      University, College, Alaska. 1970, 211 p.
      (ERIC ED062896).

      Consists of vocabulary from North and Northwest   voc   self
      Alaska villages. Words classified by subject: script
      terms relating to people, heavens, earth and
      atmosphere, place, time and descriptives; and
      other words. North Alaska dialect words noted
      with (N). Index in English. Also guide to
      Eskimo writing.

INNUIT - BILINGUAL cont'd

168. Webster, Donald H. and Roy Ahmaogak. Iñupiat/New
          Testament. American Bible Society, New York,
          1966, 1503 p. (Not Available - Kraus CTL,
          p. 1364).

INNUIT - MONOLINGUAL, INNUIT

169. Ahvakana, F. Auaqqanam quliaqtannik.(Barrow dialect).
          University of Alaska, Alaska Native Language
          Center, Fairbanks, Alaska. 1975, 17 p. (Not
          Available).

      Advanced legends.   adv

170. Alaska State-Operated School System. Annutit iqaluk
          tinmiat (Birds, fish and animals) (Deering,
          Buckland dialect). Alaska State-Operated School
          System, 650 International Airport Road, Anchorage,
          Alaska. 1974, 25 p.

      Names of various Alaska fauna. Each name is   voc   prim
      illustrated by a drawing of the animal.

171. _____. Aŋŋutit qaluich tiŋmiuratlu (Birds,
          fish and animals) (Noorvik dialect). Alaska
          State-Operated School System, 650 International
          Airport Road, Anchorage, Alaska. 1974, 25 p.

      Names of various Alaskan fauna. Each name is   voc   prim
      illustrated by a drawing of the animal.

172. _____. Qanusimik naivik? (What can you smell?)
          (Shishmaref dialect). Alaska State-Operated
          School System, 650 International Airport Road,
          Anchorage, Alaska. 1974, 48 p.

      Series of short essays about the various things   lit   int
      two Eskimo children smell. Illustrated.

173. _____. Qanusimik qinilguiñ? (What can you see?)
          (Shishmaref dialect). Alaska State-Operated
          School System, 650 International Airport Road,
          Anchorage, Alaska. 1974, 34 p.

      Series of answers to the title question, using   voc   prim
      familiar Alaskan sights, e.g., raven, river.
      Illustrated.

INNUIT - MONOLINGUAL, INNUIT cont'd

174.   Alaska State-Operated School System. Qanusiq nagua-
       ǵuiyn niǵikhavgu? (What do you eat?) (Shish-
       maref dialect). Alaska State-Operated School
       System, 650 International Airport Road,
       Anchorage, Alaska. 1974, 33 p.

       Series of answers to the title question, using   voc   prim
       food items familiar to Eskimos, e.g., caribou,
       blueberries. Workbook section in back of book.
       Illustrated.

175.   _____. Sumik naivik? (What can you smell?)
       (Ambler, Kobuk, Shungnak, Selawik dialects).
       Alaska State-Operated School Sytem, 650 Inter-
       national Airport Road, Anchorage, Alaska. 1974,
       20 p.

       Series of answers to title question. Aromas   voc   prim
       taken from surroundings of Inupiat speakers.
       Workbook section at back of book. Illustrated.

176.   _____. Sumik naivik? (What can you smell?)
       (Ambler, Kobuk, Shungnak, Selawik dialects).
       Alaska State-Operated School System, 650 Inter-
       national Airport Road, Anchorage, Alaska. 1974,
       48 p.

       Series of short essays about the various things   lit   int
       a pair of Eskimo children smell. Illustrated.

177.   _____. Sumik nigisuguuvich? (What do you eat?)
       (Kivalina dialect). Alaska State-Operated School
       System, 650 International Airport Road,
       Anchorage, Alaska. 1974, 33 p.

       Series of answers to the title question, using   voc   prim
       food items familiar to Eskimos, e.g., caribou,
       blueberries. Workbook section in back of book.
       Illustrated.

178.   _____. Sumik niǵisuuguuvit? (What do you eat?)
       (Koyuk dialect). Alaska State-Operated School
       System, 650 International Airport Road, Anchorage,
       Alaska. 1974, 33 p.

       Series of answers to the title question, using   voc   prim
       food items familiar to Eskimos, e.g., caribou,
       blueberries. Workbook section in back of book.
       Illustrated.

INNUIT - MONOLINGUAL, INNUIT cont'd

179.   Alaska State-Operated School System. Sumik niĝisuuvich?
          (What do you eat?) (Noorvik dialect). Alaska
          State-Operated School System, 650 International
          Airport Road, Anchorage, Alaska. 1974, 33 p.

       Series of answers to title question, using food   voc   prim
       items familiar to Eskimos, e.g., caribou, blue-
       berries. Workbook section in back of book.
       Illustrated.

180.   _____. Sumik niĝisuuvich? (What do you eat?)
          (Ambler, Shungnak, Kobuk dialects). Alaska
          State-Operated School System, 650 International
          Airport Road, Anchorage, Alaska. 1974, 33 p.

       Series of answers to the title question, using   voc   prim
       food items familiar to Eskimos, e.g., caribou,
       blueberries. Workbook section in back of book.
       Illustrated.

181.   _____. Sumik tusraavich? (What can you hear?)
          (Noorvik dialect). Alaska State-Operated School
          System, 650 International Airport Road, Anchorage,
          Alaska. 1974, 34 p.

       Series of answers to the title question, using   voc   prim
       sounds from the environment of the Far North,
       e.g., snowmobile, goose. Workbook section in
       back of book. Illustrated.

182.   _____. Tiŋmiat, aqaluit suli niĝrutit (Birds,
          fish and animals) (Kivalina dialect). Alaska
          State-Operated School System, 650 International
          Airport Road, Anchorage, Alaska. 1974, 25 p.

       Names of various Alaskan fauna. Each name is   voc   prim
       illustrated by a drawing of the animal.

183.   _____. Tiŋmiaruich, aqaluichlu suli aŋnutitlu
          (Birds, fish and animals) (Noatak dialect).
          Alaska State-Operated School System, 650
          International Airport Road, Anchorage, Alaska.
          1974, 25 p.

       The names of various fauna of Alaska. Each name   voc   prim
       is illustrated by a drawing of the animal.

INNUIT - MONOLINGUAL, INNUIT cont'd

184. Alaska State-Operated School System. Tiŋmiirat,
     qaluich, aŋŋutillu (Birds, fish and animals)
     (Ambler, Kobuk, Shungnak, Selawik dialects).
     Alaska State-Operated School System, 650
     International Airport Road, Anchorage, Alaska.
     1974, 25 p.

     Names of various Alaskan fauna. Each name is   voc   prim
     illustrated by a drawing of the animal.

185. Barrow School. Aakagivigiñ (Are you my mother?)
     Barrow School, North Slope School District, Box
     307, Barrow, Alaska. ca. 1972, 57 p. (Not
     Available).   prim

186. _____. Aimatkut (Aimaq's family). Barrow
     School, North Slope School District, Box 307,
     Barrow, Alaska. ca. 1972, 22 p. (Not Available).   prim

187. _____. Akⱡaq minuaqtuǵiaǵman (Brown Bear goes
     to school). Barrow School, North Slope School
     District, Box 307, Barrow, Alaska. ca. 1974,
     16 p.   prim

188. _____. Annuǵaavut paŋmapak (Clothing we wear
     now). Barrow School, North Slope School
     District, Box 307, Barrow, Alaska. 1974, 22 p.
     (Not Available).   prim

189. _____. Aŋun aŋuniaqtuaq taǵiumi (A man goes
     hunting on the Ocean). Barrow School, North
     Slope School District, Box 307, Barrow, Alaska.
     1974, 10 p. (Not Available).   prim

190. _____. Apayauq paannaliuqtuq (Apayauq made a
     friend). Barrow School, North Slope School
     District, Box 307, Barrow, Alaska. 1974, 7 p.
     (Not Available).   inter

191. _____. Atchagat (Alphabet). Barrow School,
     North Slope School District, Box 307, Barrow,
     Alaska. ca. 1972, 49 p. (Not Available).   prim

192. _____. Grammar rules. Barrow School, North
     Slope School District, Box 307, Barrow, Alaska.
     ca. 1974, 9 p. (Not Available).   inter

193. _____. Ilalugich ilaŋŋaǵlugiḷlu savaaksrat
     (Adding and subtracting workbook). Barrow School,
     North Slope School District, Box 307, Barrow,
     Alaska. 1974, 7 p. (Not Available).   prim

INNUIT - MONOLINGUAL, INNUIT cont'd

194. Barrow School. Iqiasuannayuglu qupquġiaġlu (The
      Ten-Legged polar bear). Barrow School, North
      Slope School District, Box 307, Barrow, Alaska.
      ca. 1974, 16 p. (Not Available).   prim

195. _____. Kisitchisa qulinuaglaan (Let's count to
      ten). Barrow School, North Slope School District,
      Box 307, Barrow, Alaska. ca. 1974, 28 p. (Not
      Available).   prim

196. _____. Natchiq (The Seal). Barrow School, North
      Slope School District, Box 307, Barrow, Alaska.
      ca. 1974, 23 p. (Not Available).   inter

197. _____. Niġrutiŋich nunapta - tuttu (Animals of
      our land - caribou). Barrow School, North Slope
      School District, Box 307, Barrow, Alaska.
      ca. 1974, 10 p. (Not Available).   prim

198. _____. Niġrutitigun maqpiġaat - qaugak (Animal
      book - duck). Barrow School, North Slope School
      District, Box 307, Barrow, Alaska. ca. 1974,
      14 p. (Not Available).   prim

199. _____. Nuvuk aŋuniaqti (Nuvuk the hunter).
      Barrow School, North Slope School District, Box
      307, Barrow, Alaska. ca. 1974, 24 p. (Not
      Available).   inter

200. _____. Savaaksrat Iñupiatun maqpiġaat I (Inupiat
      workbook I). Barrow School, North Slope School
      District, Box 307, Barrow, Alaska. 1974, 13 p.
      (Not Available).   prim

201. _____. Savaaksrat Iñupiatun maqpiġaat II
      (Inupiat workbook II). Barrow School, North
      Slope School District, Box 307, Barrow, Alaska.
      1974, 21 p. (Not Available).   prim

202. _____. Taiñġurat (Vowels). Barrow School, North
      Slope School District, Box 307, Barrow, Alaska.
      ca. 1974, 25 p. (Not Available).   inter

203. _____. Tiŋmiaŋillu niġrutiŋillu nunapta (Birds
      and animals of our land). Barrow School, North
      Slope School District, Box 307, Barrow, Alaska.
      ca. 1974, 12 p. (Not Available).   prim

204. _____. Uqaluich iglugiiksitaaksrat (Words to be
      matched). Barrow School, North Slope School
      District, Box 307, Barrow, Alaska. 1974, 6 p.
      (Not Available).   prim

INNUIT - MONOLINGUAL, INNUIT cont'd

205. Blanchett/Teeluk/Brow/Ahsoak/Sovalik. Savaktugut suli
       piurraqtugut (We work and we play) (Barrow dialect).
       University of Alaska, Alaska Native Language Center,
       Fairbanks, Alaska. 1973, 20 p. (Not Available).   prim

206. Inuttituut. Minister of Indian and Northern Affairs,
       Ottawa. Quarterly issues from Winter 1969 to
       Winter and Spring 1972.

       Quarterly magazine written entirely in Inutt   lit   self
       (Innuit).

207. Jackson, E. Tulugaġlu agṅauraġlu (The raven and the
       little girl) (Barrow dialect). University of
       Alaska, Alaska Native Language Center, Fairbanks,
       Alaska. 1974, 22 p. (Not Available).   int

208. MacLean, E. Avilaitgatigiik (The two friends) (Barrow
       dialect). University of Alaska, Alaska Native
       Language Center, Fairbanks, Alaska. 1974, 48 p.
       (Not Available).

       With worksheets.   adv

209. _____. Lessons and games for Iñupiaq as a second
       language (Barrow dialect). University of Alaska,
       Alaska Native Language Center, Fairbanks, Alaska.
       1974, 36 p. (Not Available).   prim

210. _____. Malguk quliaqtuak: aahaalliglu, aniq-
       paktuaq aviŋŋaq (Two stories: The old squaw and
       its ducklings, The large lemming) (Barrow
       dialect). University of Alaska, Alaska Native
       Language Center, Fairbanks, Alaska. 1974, 14 p.
       (Not Available).   int

211. _____. Savaaksrat I (Workbook I). (Barrow dialect).
       University of Alaska, Alaska Native Language Center,
       Fairbanks, Alaska. 1974, 25 p. (Not Available).   prim

212. _____. Suva una? (What is it doing?) (Barrow
       dialect). University of Alaska, Alaska Native
       Language Center, Fairbanks, Alaska. 1973, 29 p.
       (Not Available).   prim

213. _____. Suva una? Worksheets (Barrow Dialect).
       University of Alaska, Alaska Native Language Center,
       Fairbanks, Alaska. 1974, 10 p. (Not Available).   prim

INNUIT - MONOLINGUAL, INNUIT cont'd

214. MacLean, E. Uqaluich (Barrow dialect). University
        of Alaska, Alaska Native Language Center,
        Fairbanks, Alaska. 1973, 30 p. (Not Available).   prim

215. _____. Uqaluich sivulligñiisaaŋich (Beginning
        letters of words). Alaska Native Language
        Program, Center for Northern Educational Research,
        University of Alaska, Fairbanks, Alaska. 1973,
        23 p.

        Inupiq alphabet book. Each page features one   voc   prim
        letter in upper and lower case with illustrations
        and captions of four items that begin with that
        letter.

216. Mather, E. and Aiken, M. Iqiasuaq aviŋŋaq (The lazy
        mouse) (Barrow dialect). University of Alaska,
        Alaska Native Language Center, Fairbanks, Alaska.
        1973, 18 p. (Not Available).   prim

217. Nageak, V. and Demientieff/MacLean. Ataataluqiik
        (Barrow dialect). University of Alaska. Alaska
        Native Language Center, Fairbanks, Alaska. 1974,
        104 p. (Not Available).

        A legend.   adv

218. Nashaknik, H. and Nageak, J. Anułhuyuk (Barrow
        dialect). University of Alaska, Alaska Native
        Language Center, Fairbanks, Alaska. 1973, 54 p.
        (Not Available).   adv

219. Norton, L. and H. Schnare. Aahahaaŋaaq. (Kobuk dialect).
        University of Alaska, Alaska Native Language
        Center, Fairbanks, Alaska. 1974, 24 p. (Not
        Available).   int

220. Rudolph, G. Iñupiaq worksheets (Barrow dialect).
        University of Alaska, Alaska Native Language
        Center, Fairbanks, Alaska. 1974, 78 p. (Not
        Available).   prim

221. Teeluk, M. and Hopson, A. Aqargig tuluqaq ugrugnau-
        raglu (Ptarmigan, raven, and shrew) (Barrow
        dialect). University of Alaska, Alaska Native
        Language Center, Fairbanks, Alaska. 1973, 14 p.
        (Not Available).   int

222. Teeluk, M. and N. Sheldon. Qanuq kayuqtuq kavaiqsiruaq
        (How the fox turned red) (Kobuk dialect).
        University of Alaska, Alaska Native Language
        Center, Fairbanks, Alaska. 1973, 24 p. (Not
        Available).   int

INNUIT - MONOLINGUAL, ENGLISH

Dahl, W.H. et al. Languages of the tribes of the
extreme Northwest - The Aleutians and adjacent
territories. Shorey Book Store, Seattle,
Washington, 1970, 47 p. (Reprinted from
Contributions to American Ethnology, Vol. 1,
Washington, D.C. 1877).

See under INDIANS OF THE SUBARCTIC

223. National Library of Canada. Indian-Inuit authors: an
annotated bibliography. National Library of
Canada, Ottawa, Ontario, Canada. 1974, 108 p.
(Not Available - Review Northian Vol. II, No. 1,
p. 32).

List of works by Canadian Indian and Inuit   bibl   self
authors published to 1972. Work divided in two
sections - works by Indian and Metis authors and
works by Inuit authors. Within each section,
publications are listed by type. Fifteen works
by native children are included.

INNUIT - NOT KNOWN

224. Ahmaogak, R.R. and D.H. Webster. Iñupiam ukaluŋi
(Iñupiat reader 1) (Barrow dialect). Summer
Institute of Linguistics, P.O. Box 1028,
Fairbanks, Alaska. 1969. (Not Available).

225. _____. Iñupiam ukaluŋi 2 (Iñupiat reader 2)
(Barrow dialect). Summer Institute of Linguis-
tics, P.O. Box 1028, Fairbanks, Alaska. 1971.
(Not Available).

226. Ahvakana, R. Translated by E. MacLean. Tikiġaġmiġguuq...
(In Point Hope, Alaska...) (Barrow dialect).
Alaska Native Language Center, Center for
Northern Educational Research, University of
Alaska, Fairbanks, Alaska. 1973. (Not Available).

227. Aiken, Martha (Translator). Iqiasuak aviññaq. Alaska
State Language Center, University of Alaska,
Fairbanks, Alaska. 1973, 20 p. (Not Available).

228. Ayaryaq, John. Autobiography. Welfare Division,
Northern Administration Branch, Department of
Indian Affairs and Northern Development, Ottawa.
1968, 123 p. (Not Available - Kraus CTL, p. 1332).

INNUIT - NOT KNOWN cont'd

229. Blanchett/Teeluk. Translated by M. Leavitt. Aimaq
     iḷaniḷu (Aimaq and his family) (Barrow dialect).
     Alaska Native Language Center, Center for
     Northern Educational Research, University of
     Alaska, Fairbanks, Alaska. 1973. (Not
     Available).

230. _____. Translated by A. Hopson. Taiguallaruṇa
     (I can read) (Barrow dialect). Alaska Native
     Language Center, Center for Northern Educational
     Research, University of Alaska, Fairbanks,
     Alaska. 1973. (Not Available).

231. Brown, Harvey, Marie Ahsoak and Ernie Sovalik (Trans-
     lators). Savaktugot suli piuraaqtugut. Alaska
     State Language Center, University of Alaska,
     Fairbanks, Alaska. 1973, 22 p. (Not Available).

232. Chambers, Rev. John R. and Rev. Samuel Simmons. The
     Iñupiat Eskimo hymnbook. Fellowship Book Store,
     Barrow, Alaska. 1965, 232 p. (Not Available -
     Kraus CTL, p. 1335).

233. Foster (Translator and Editor). Psalms, Genesis,
     Isaiah (Baffin Island Dialect). Canadian Bible
     Society, Toronto. 1966 (Not Available - Kraus
     CTL, p. 1337).

234. Gagné, Raymond. Eskimo language course. Department
     of Indian Affairs and Northern Development,
     Ottawa. 1966, 364 p. (Not Available - Kraus
     CTL, p. 1338).

235. Gagné, Raymond and Paul Koolerk. Uqalimartaa (Pond
     Inlet Dialect). Education Branch, Department of
     Indian Affairs and Northern Development, Ottawa.
     1968, 79 p. (Not Available - Kraus CTL, p. 1338).

236. Gray, Arthur, Minnie Gray and Wilfried Zibell, trans-
     lators. Jesus-ŋum iñuuḷhanik (Gospel stories in
     Kobuk River Eskimo). Wycliffe Bible Translators,
     Berghausen, Germany. 1966, 37 p. (Not Availa-
     ble - Kraus CTL, p. 1339).

237. Hopson, Alice (Translator). Aqargiq tulugaq
     ugrugnauraglu. Alaska State Language Center,
     University of Alaska, Fairbanks, Alaska. 1973,
     17 p. (Not Available).

238. _____. Taiguallaruna. Alaska State Language
     Center, University of Alaska, Fairbanks, Alaska.
     1973, 61 p. (Not Available).

INNUIT - NOT KNOWN cont'd

239. Kanavurak, B. Uvva Saiḷaq (Here's Sailaq) (Barrow
        dialect). Alaska Native Language Center, Center
        for Northern Educational Research, University of
        Alaska, Fairbanks, Alaska. 1973, 32 p. (Not
        Available).

240. Kaveolook, Harold. Malğuk quliaqtuak: aahaalliglu
        piayaaŋillu; aŋiqpaktuaq aviŋŋaq (Two stories:
        the old squaw and it's ducklings; the large
        lemming) (Barrow dialect). Alaska Native
        Language Center, Center for Northern Educational
        Research, University of Alaska, Fairbanks,
        Alaska. 1974. (Not Available).

241. Leavitt, Marie. Aimaq ilanilu. Alaska State
        Language Center, University of Alaska,
        Fairbanks, Alaska. 1973, 23 p. (Not Available).

242. MacLean, Edna. Avilaitqatigiik, worksheets (The two
        friends, worksheets) (Barrow dialect). Alaska
        Native Language Center, Center for Northern
        Educational Research, University of Alaska.
        Fairbanks, Alaska. 1974. (Not Available).

243. Nageak, James (Translator). Aŋalgaam qimmini.
        Alaska State Language Center, University of
        Alaska, Fairbanks, Alaska. 1973, 29 p. (Not
        Available).

244. Oyagak, Roxy, Jr. Ilatka. Alaska State Language
        Center, University of Alaska, Fairbanks, Alaska.
        1973, 27 p. (Not Available).

245. Pageau, Christiane and Paulusi Uqittuq. Allagit
        allaniarit. Direction generale du Nouveau
        Quebec, Ministere des Richesses Naturelles,
        Canada. 1966, 295 p. (Not Available - Kraus
        CTL, p. 1359).

246. Sheldon, Nita (Translator). Qanuq kayuqtuq
        kaviqsiruaq. Alaska State Language Center,
        University of Alaska, Fairbanks, Alaska. 1973,
        27 p. (Not Available).

247. Spalding, Alec E. Salliq: an Eskimo grammar.
        Education Branch, Department of Indian Affairs
        and Northern Development, Ottawa. 1969, 128 p.
        (Not Available).

INNUIT - NOT KNOWN cont'd

248. Teeluk, Martha. Translated by R. Oyagak. Iḷatka
    (My family) (Barrow dialect). Alaska Native
    Language Center, Center for Northern Educational
    Research, University of Alaska, Fairbanks,
    Alaska. 1973. (Not Available).

249. Webster, D.H. Can you read English? Then you can
    also read Eskimo. Summer Institute of Linguis-
    tics, P.O. Box 1028, Fairbanks, Alaska. 1968.
    (Not Available).

250. Webster, Donald H. Ikaayutit (New Testament helps).
    Wycliffe Bible Translators, Fairbanks, ca. 1968,
    8 p. (Not Available - Kraus CTL, p. 1364).

251. _____. Inupiam uḳaluṇi/Eskimo reading course
    I-II. Summer Institute of Linguistics, Fairbanks,
    1969, 76 p. (Not Available - Kraus CTL, p. 1365).

252. _____. Ḳuliaḳtuaḳ inuusiagun Jesus. (Life of
    Jesus). Summer Institute of Linguistics,
    Fairbanks. Ca. 1967, 16 p. (Not Available -
    Kraus CTL, 1364).

253. _____. Let's Learn Eskimo. Summer Institute
    of Linguistics, Fairbanks. 1968, 66 p. (Not
    Available - Kraus CTL, p. 1364).

254. _____. Unipkaat (Coloring book) (Barrow
    dialect). Summer Institute of Linguistics,
    P.O. Box 1028, Fairbanks. 1971. (Not Available)

255. Webster, Don and Roy Ahmaogak. Iñupiat suuvat?
    (What about the Eskimo?) (Barrow dialect).
    Summer Institute of Lingusitics, P.O. Box 1028,
    Fairbanks, Alaska. 1971. (Not Available).

256. Webster, Donald H. and Wilfried Zibell. Inupiat
    dictionary. University of Alaska and Summer
    Institute of Linguistics, Fairbanks, Alaska.
    1970, 218 p. (Not Available - Kraus CTL,
    p. 1365).

257. Zibell, Wilfried. Aglaich Eskimo alphabet book
    (Coloring book) (Kobuk dialect). Summer
    Institute of Linguistics, P.O. Box 1028,
    Fairbanks, Alaska. 1971. (Not Available).

258. _____. Atuutit mumiksat (Hymnal). Summer Insti-
    tute of Linguistics, P.O. Box 1028, Fairbanks,
    Alaska. 1967, 22 p. (Not Available - Kraus
    CTL, p. 1365).

INNUIT - NOT KNOWN cont'd

259. Zibell, Wilfried. Inupiam Uqaλhi (Kobuk dialect).
     Summer Institute of Linguistics, P.O. Box 1028,
     Fairbanks, Alaska. 1973. (Not Available).

260. _____. Jesus-num inuuλha (Life of Jesus).
     Summer Institute of Linguistics, P.O. Box 1028,
     Fairbanks, Alaska. 1966, 16 p. (Not Available -
     Kraus CTL, p. 1365).

261. _____.Unipchaat I (Animal stories of the Kobuk
     River Eskimos). (Kobuk dialect). Summer Insti-
     tute of Linguistics, P.O. Box 1028, Fairbanks,
     Alaska. 1971. (Not Available).

262. _____. Unipchaat 2 (Animal stories of the Kobuk
     River Eskimos) (Kobuk dialect). Summer Institute
     of Linguistics, P.O. Box 1028, Fairbanks, Alaska.
     1969. (Not Available).

263. _____. Unipchaat 3 (Animal stories of the Kobuk
     River Eskimos). (Kobuk dialect). Summer Insti-
     tute of Linguistics, P.O. Box 1028, Fairbanks,
     Alaska. 1970. (Not Available).

264. Zibell, Wilfried and Pauline Harvey, translators.
     Thessalonians I-II. Summer Institute of
     Linguistics, P.O. Box 1028, Fairbanks, Alaska.
     1968, 28 p. (Not Available - Kraus CTL, p. 1366).

265. _____. Timothy. Summer Institute of
     Linguistics, P.O. Box 1028, Fairbanks, Alaska.
     1968, 22 p. (Not Available - Kraus CTL, p. 1366).

266. _____. Timothy I - II, Thessalonians I-II, Titus.
     Evangelizationsverlag, Berghausen, Germany. 1971.
     (Not Available - Kraus CTL, p. 1366).

267. Zuk, William M. Inuit pinnguarusingit (Eskimo
     games). Department of Indian Affairs and
     Northern Development, Ottawa. 1967, 26 p.
     (Not Available - Kraus CTL, p. 1366).

INUPIAT

     See INNUIT

IROQUOIAN - BILINGUAL

268. Hale, Horatio Emmons (Editor). Iroquois book of
         rites. University of Toronto Press, Toronto,
         Second edition. 1965, 222 p. (Reprint of 1883
         edition).

         Chapter II of Book III of this work deals with   script   self
         Iroquois language. Parts of speech and alphabet   gram
         (16 characters) are described. Sample words   desc
         listed and declined or conjugated. Lord's   voc
         prayer is given in Seneca dialect. Some examples
         of dialectical variation among the six languages
         (Seneca, Cayuga, Oneida, Onondaga, Mohawk,
         Tuscarora) that comprise Iroquoian family are
         given.

      Pilling, James Constantine. Bibliography of the
         Iroquoian languages. AMS Press. 1973, 208 p.

      See Pilling under GENERAL LANGUAGES

IROQUOIAN

      See also MOHAWK, SENECA, TUSCARORA, CHEROKEE, ONONDAGA

KERESAN - BILINGUAL

269. Boas, Franz. Keresan texts, two volumes. AMS Press, New
         York. 1974, 644 p. (Reprinted from Publications of
         the American Ethnological Society, Volume VII,
         Parts 1 and 2, New York. 1928).

         Various myths, legends, folktales and reminis-   lit   self
         cences, presented in English in Part 1 and in   col
         Keresan in Part 2. Lines are numbered in Keresan
         text with these numbers interpolated in English
         text to facilitate comparison.

KERESAN

      See also ACOMA

KOYUKON - BILINGUAL

270.   Alaska State-Operated Schools. Koyuk reader, Alaska
         State-Operated Schools, Anchorage, Alaska. 1974,
         99 p. (ERIC ED095715).

         Elementary reader with alternating pages in   lit   prim
         Koyuk and English. Story of daily family life
         in Koyuk, Alaska. Illustrated.

271.   The River Times. Fairbanks Native Association,
         Fairbanks Native Center, Fairbanks, Alaska.
         January 1974, Vol. III, No. 1, p. 10.

         This issue of the newspaper contains an article   voc   self
         on Koyukon language work at Athabaskan Language
         Workshop.

272.   _____. Fairbanks Native Association, Fairbanks
         Native Center, Fairbanks, Alaska. March 1974,
         Vol. III, No. 3, p. 4

         This issue of River Times contains an article   lit   self
         about the bald eagle, presented in Koyukon and
         in English.

273.   _____. Fairbanks Native Association, Fairbanks
         Native Center, Fairbanks, Alaska. December 1974,
         Vol. III, No. 12, p. 4.

         This issue of the newspaper contains an article   voc   self
         which includes sentences and words in Koyukon.   lit

KOYUKON - NOT KNOWN

274.   Henry, David. Explanation of the sounds used in
         Koyukon. Summer Institute of Linguistics,
         P.O. Box 1028, Fairbanks, Alaska. 1969. (Not
         Available).

275.   _____. Sam (lower Koyukon dialect). Summer
         Institute of Linguistics, P.O. Box 1028,
         Fairbanks, Alaska. 1973. (Not Available).

276.   _____. Vowel and consonant charts (Central
         and Lower Koyukon dialects , Summer Institute
         of Linguistics, P.O. Box 1028, Fairbanks, Alaska.
         1973. (Not Available).

277.   Henry, David and Kay Henry. Dinaak'a (Our Language).
         Summer Institute of Linguistics, P.O. Box 1028,
         Fairbanks, Alaska. 1969. (Not Available).

114

KOYUKON - NOT KNOWN cont'd

278. Henry, David and Kay Henry. Dinaak'aa reading book
     one. Summer Institute of Linguistics, P.O. Box
     1028, Fairbanks, Alaska. 1966. (Not Available).

279. _____. Hadohzil-eeyah (We are reading). Summer
     Institute of Linguistics, P.O. Box 1028,
     Fairbanks, Alaska. 1969. (Not Available).

280. Henry, David C., Kay Henry and Sally Hudson. Sam
     (Central Koyukon dialect). Summer Institute
     of Linguistics, P.O. Box 1028, Fairbanks, Alaska.
     1972. (Not Available).

281. Henry, David, Kay Henry, Marie D. Hunter, Eliza Jones
     and others. Dinaak'a (Our langauge). Summer
     Institute of Linguistics, P.O. Box 1028,
     Fairbanks, Alaska. 1973. (Not Available).

282. Henry, David C. and Members of the Koyukon Cultural
     Enrichment Program. Consonants (Central
     Koyukon dialect). Summer Institute of Linguis-
     tics, P.O. Box 1028, Fairbanks, Alaska. 1973.
     (Not Available).

283. _____. Consonants (Lower Koyukon dialect).
     Summer Institute of Linguistics, P.O. Box 1028,
     Fairbanks, Alaska. 1973. (Not Available).

284. Henry, David C. and Koyukon Cultural Enrichment
     Program. Dibaa asdlaan? (Who am I?) (Central
     Koyukon dialect). Summer Institute of Linguis-
     tics, P.O. Box 1028, Fairbanks, Alaska. 1973.
     (Not Available).

285. _____. Dinaa aslaan? (Who am I?) (Lower
     Koyukon). Summer Institute of Linguistics,
     P.O. Box 1028, Fairbanks, Alaska. 1973. (Not
     Available).

286. _____. Dot'aan? (What is he doing?) (Lower
     Koyukon). Summer Institute of Linguistics,
     P.O. Box 1028, Fairbanks, Alaska. 1973. (Not
     Available).

287. _____. Dot'aan? (What is he doing) (Central
     Koyukon dialect). Summer Institute of Linguis-
     tics, P.O. Box 1028, Fairbanks, Alaska. 1973.
     (Not Available).

288. _____. Dotson' nonot'oh (Translation and adapta-
     tion of Raven got fooled) (Central Koyukon).
     Summer Institute of Linguistics, P.O. Box 1028,
     Fairbanks, Alaska. 1973. (Not Available).

KOYUKON - NOT KNOWN cont'd

289.	Henry, David C. and Koyukon Cultural Enrichment
	Program. Dotson' nonot'oh (Translation and
	adaptation of Raven got fooled) (Central
	Koyukon). Summer Institute of Linguistics,
	P.O. Box 1028, Fairbanks, Alaska. 1973. (Not
	Available).

290.	_____. Hadohudigi-eeyah (I am learning)
	(Central Koyukon). Summer Institute of Linguis-
	tics, P.O. Box 1028, Fairbanks, Alaska. 1973.
	(Not Available).

291.	_____. Hadohudigi-eeyah (I am learning) (Lower
	Koyukon). Summer Institute of Linguistics,
	P.O. Box 1028, Fairbanks, Alaska. 1973. (Not
	Available).

292.	_____. My alphabet (Central Koyukon dialect).
	Summer Institute of Linguistics, P.O. Box 1028,
	Fairbanks, Alaska. 1973. (Not Available).

293.	_____. My alphabet (Lower Koyukon). Summer
	Institute of Linguistics, P.O. Box 1028,
	Fairbanks, Alaska. 1973. (Not Available).

294.	Hudson, Sally. Paul dineega oko antaalkaan (Transla-
	tion and adaptation of Normie's moose hunt).
	Summer Institute of Linguistics, P.O. Box 1028,
	Fairbanks, Alaska. 1973. (Not Available).

295.	Hunter, Marie D. Daałtł'idzee tok'eekaa (Translation
	and adaptation of the three bears) (Central
	Koyukon dialect). Summer Institute of Linguis-
	tics, P.O. Box 1028, Fairbanks, Alaska. 1973.
	(Not Available).

296.	Jones, Eliza. Tobaan atsah (Crying on the beach)
	(Central Koyukon dialect). Summer Institute
	of Linguistics, P.O. Box 1028, Fairbanks, Alaska.
	1973. (Not Available).

297.	Lolnitz, Doria. K'adoants'idnee (three folk tales).
	Summer Institute of Linguistics, P.O. Box 1028,
	Fairbanks, Alaska. 1973. (Not Available).

298.	Semaken, Ottie G. Doatsoan' yokoay k'idogheełtaan
	(The raven flies for light). Summer Institute
	of Linguistics, P.O. Box 1028, Fairbanks, Alaska.
	1973. (Not Available).

KOYUKON - NOT KNOWN cont'd

299. Simon, Velma. Deeltsa aa dil-aa k'idoghee/taan (The
          mouse saves his uncle) (Central Koyukon dialect).
          Summer Institute of Linguistics, P.O. Box 1028,
          Fairbanks, Alaska. 1973. (Not Available).

KUTCHIN - BILINGUAL

300. The River Times. Fairbanks Native Association,
          Fairbanks Native Center, Fairbanks, Alaska.
          March 12, 1974, Vol. III, No. 1, p. 4.

      This issue of the newspaper has a story in   lit   self
      English with a Kutchin translation.

KUTCHIN - MONOLINGUAL, KUTCHIN

301. Alaska State-Operated School System. Jidii dintth'ak?
          (What can you hear?). Alaska State-Operated
          School System, 650 International Airport Road,
          Anchorage, Alaska. 1974, 34 p.

      Series of answers to the title question, using   voc   prim
      sounds from the environment of the Far North,
      e.g., snowmobiles, geese. Workbook section in
      back of book. Illustrated.

302. _____. Jidii dintth'ak? (What can you hear?).
      Alaska State-Operated School System, 650
      International Airport Road, Anchorage, Alaska.
      1974, 72 p.

      Twelve short stories about sounds two Athabascan   lit   int
      boys hear. Illustrated.

303. Chalkyitsik Bilingual Teachers. Jidii t'inchy'sa?
          (What is this?). Alaska State-Operated School
          system, Alaska Unorganized Borough School District,
          650 International Airport Road, Anchorage, Alaska.
          1972, 11 p. (Not Available).

304. Druck, Leah. Johnny (Translation and adaptation of
          Johnny). Alaska State-Operated School System,
          Alaska Unorganized Borough School District, 650
          International Airport Road, Anchorage, Alaska.
          1972, 16 p. (Not Available).

KUTCHIN - MONOLINGUAL, KUTCHIN cont'd

305. Druck, Leah. Jok drin Johnny dee'ya' (Translation and adaptation of A day with Johnny). Alaska State-Operated School System, Alaska Unorganized Borough School District, 650 International Airport Road, Anchorage, Alaska. 1972, 16 p. (Not Available).

306. _____. Moses (Translation and adaptation of "Tendi") Alaska State-Operated School System, Alaska Unorganized Borough School District, 650 International Airport Road, Anchorage, Alaska. 1972, 11 p. (Not Available).

307. _____. Moses khya t'ah'in ts'a' Juk kee'in nilji (Translation and adaptation of Tendi goes trapping and fishing). Alaska State-Operated School System, Alaska Unorganized Borough School District, 650 International Airport Road, Anchorage, Alaska. 1973, 20 p. (Not Available).

308. _____. Moses nahaazhrii (Translation and adaptation of Tendi goes hunting). Alaska State-Operated School System, Alaska Unorganized Borough School District, 650 International Airport Road, Anchorage, Alaska. 1973, 32 p. (Not Available).

309. _____. Moses tsal nya' ohtsuu (Translation and adaptation of Little Tendi's moss bag). Alaska State-Operated School System, Alaska Unorganized Borough School District, 650 International Airport Road, Anchorage, Alaska. 1972, 13 p. (Not Available).

310. _____. Moses tsee keechee'yaa (Translation and adaptation of Tendi goes beaver hunting). Alaska State-Operated School System, Alaska Unorganized Borough School District, 650 International Airport Road, Anchorage, Alaska. 1972, 13 p. (Not Available).

311. _____. Moses vats'at (Translation and adaptation of Tendi's blanket). Alaska State-Operated School System, Alaska Unorganized Borough School District, 650 International Airport Road, Anchorage, Alaska. 1972, 8 p. (Not Available).

312. Druck, Leah, Moses Gabriel and Minnie Salmon. Nich'it tsal (Little girl). Alaska State-Operated School System, Alaska Unorganized Borough School District, 650 International Airport Road, Anchorage, Alaska. 1972, 10 p. (Not Available).

118

KUTCHIN - MONOLINGUAL, KUTCHIN cont'd

313. Druck, Leah, Moses Gabriel and Minnie Salmon. Tsyaa
tsal (Little boy). Alaska State-Operated School
System, Alaska Unorganized Borough School
District, 650 International Airport Road,
Anchorage, Alaska. 1972, 12 p. (Not Available).

314. Fields, Mary and Mae Peter. Ch'anky'aa gwandak
(Ghost story). Alaska State-Operated School
System, Alaska Unorganized Borough School
District, 650 International Airport Road,
Anchorage, Alaska. 1972, 14 p. (Not Available).

315. _____. Johnny N.C. Co Noozhii (Translation and
adaptation of Johnny at the "Bay"). Alaska
State-Operated School System, Alaska Unorganized
Borough School District, 650 International
Airport Road, Anchorage, Alaska. 1972, 13 p.
(Not Available).

316. Fields, Mary. Tony dinjik enjit naazhrii (Translation and adaptation of Normie's moose hunt).
Alaska State-Operated School System, Alaska
Unorganized Borough School District, 650 International Airport Road, Anchorage, Alaska. 1972,
24 p. (Not Available).

317. Fiitt, Nena. Songs in Gwich'in. Alaska State-
Operated School System, Alaska Unorganized
Borough School District, 650 International
Airport Road, Anchorage, Alaska. 1972, 5 p.
(Not Available).

318. Gabriel, Moses. Nin kweei dehtʎy'aa (Animal book).
Alaska State-Operated School System, Alaska
Unorganized Borough School District, 650 International Airport Road, Anchorage, Alaska. 1973,
26 p. (Not Available).

319. Kutchin Bilingual Teachers. Tr'iinin drin dee'in
(Translation and adaptation of What a child does
in a day). Alaska State-Operated School System,
Alaska Unorganized Borough School District, 650
International Airport Road, Anchorage, Alaska.
1972, 22 p. (Not Available).

320. Mueller, Richard. Dinjii zhraai tsal (Little black
man). Alaska State-Operated School System,
Alaska Unorganized Borough School District, 650
International Airport Road, Anchorage, Alaska.
1972, 27 p. (Not Available).

KUTCHIN - MONOLINGUAL, KUTCHIN cont'd

321. Mueller, Richard. Gwich'in ginjik dęhtły'aa (A
     beginning reader). Summer Institute of Linguis-
     tics/Wycliffe Bible Translators, Box 329, Fort
     Yukon, Alaska. 1969, 12 p. (Not Available).

322. _____. Jesus nankak gwaadaai vagnanaak gwedhaa
     dai' (Illustrated life of Jesus). David C. Cook
     and Wycliffe Bible Translators, Box 329, Fort
     Yukon, Alaska. 1967, 16 p. (Not Available).

323. _____. Let's speak Kutchin. Summer Institute
     of Linguistics, P.O. Box 1028, Fairbanks, Alaska.
     1970 (Not Available - Martin, Survey, p. 39).

324. _____. Sho zhrąąi tik, nich'it tsal haa googwandak
     (The three bears and a little girl). Alaska State-
     Operated School System, Alaska Unorganized
     Borough School District, 650 International
     Airport Road, Anchorage, Alaska. 1972, 40 p.
     (Not Available).

325. Peter, K. Ch'arah'ee dęhtły'aa. University of Alaska,
     Alaska Native Language Center, Fairbanks, Alaska.
     1973, 12 p. (Not Available).

326. _____. Dinjii zhuu gwandak (Gwich'in stories).
     Alaska State-Operated School System, Alaska
     Unorganized Borough School District, 650 Inter-
     national Airport Road, Anchorage, Alaska. 1974,
     76 p. (Not Available).

327. _____. Gineerinlyaa (Gwich'in poems). University
     of Alaska, Alaska Native Language Center,
     Fairbanks, Alaska. 1974, 15 p. (Not Available).   lit   int

328. _____. Gwich'in "ABC" dęhtły'aa (Kutchin "ABC"
     workbook). University of Alaska, Alaska Native
     Language Center, Fairbanks, Alaska. 1974, 48 p.
     (Not Available).   prim

329. _____. Gwich'in workbook. University of Alaska,
     Alaska Native Language Center, Fairbanks, Alaska.
     1974, 29 p. (Not Available).

330. _____. Shih dǫǫ daazhyaa (The four food groups).
     University of Alaska, Alaska Native Language
     Center, Fairbanks, Alaska. 1974, 11 p. (Not
     Available).

331. _____. Vak'aandaii (Touch it). University of
     Alaska, Alaska Native Language Center, Fairbanks,
     Alaska. 1974, 19 p. (Not Available).   prim

KUTCHIN - MONOLINGUAL, KUTCHIN cont'd

332. Peter, K. and T. Pulu. Geh t̸oh ih'aa yindhan? (Do
       you want to eat boiled rabbit?). Alaska State-
       Operated School System, Alaska Unorganized
       Borough School District, 650 International
       Airport Road, Anchorage, Alaska. 1974, 33 p.
       (Not Available).

333. Peter, K., T. Pulu and M. Pope. Jidii a̸tsan? (What
       can you smell?). Alaska State-Operated School
       System, Alaksa Unorganized Borough School
       District, 650 International Airport Road,
       Anchorage, Alaska. 1974, 48 p. (Not Available).

334. _____. Jidii dinitth'ak? (What do you hear?).
       Alaska State-Operated School System, Alaska
       Unorganized Borough School District, 650 Inter-
       national Airport Road, Anchorage, Alaska. 1974,
       72 p. (Not Available).

335. _____. Jidii dintth'ak? (What do you hear? -
       Colorbook). Alaska State-Operated School System,
       Alaska Unorganized Borough School District, 650
       International Airport Road, Anchorage, Alaska.
       1974, 34 p. (Not Available).

336. Peter, Mae. Jii nąąi t'ee shalak (This is my family).
       Alaska State-Operated School System, Alaska
       Unorganized Borough School District, 650 Inter-
       national Airport Road, Anchorage, Alaska. 1972,
       26 p. (Not Available).

337. Salmon, Minnie. Johnny vagood̸it drin (Translation
       and adaptation of Johnny's present). Alaska
       State-Operated School System, Alaska Unorganized
       Borough School District, 650 International
       Airport Road, Anchorage, Alaska. 1972, 10 p.
       (Not Available).

338. Sapir/Fredson, K. Peter. Sapir John Haa, googwandak
       1 (Sapir-Fredson Stories, 1). University of
       Alaska, Alaska Native Language Center, Fairbanks,
       Alaska. 1974, 12 p. (Not Available).   adv

339. _____. Sapir John Haa, googwandak 2 (Sapir-
       Fredson Stories, 2). University of Alaska,
       Alaska Native Language Center, Fairbanks, Alaska.
       1974, 19 p. (Not Available).   adv

340. _____. Sapir John Haa, googwandak 3 (Sapir-
       Fredson Stories, 3). University of Alaska,
       Alaska Native Language Center, Fairbanks, Alaska.
       1974, 20 p. (Not Available).   adv

KUTCHIN - MONOLINGUAL, KUTCHIN cont'd

341.   Tritt, Lincoln. Moses vitr'ii' (Translation and
          adaptation of Tendi's canoe). Alaska State-
          Operated School System, Alaska Unorganized
          Borough School District, 650 International
          Airport Road, Anchorage, Alaska. 1972, 13 p.
          (Not Available).

342.   Tritt, Mary R. Johnny nahaazhrii (Translation and
          adaptation of Johnny goes hunting). Alaska
          State-Operated School System, Alaska Unorganized
          Borough School District, 650 International
          Airport Road, Anchorage, Alaska. 1972, 31 p.
          (Not Available).

343.   _____. Moses va'ai (Translation and adaptation
          of Tendi's snowshoes). Alaska State-Operated
          School System, Alaska Unorganized Borough School
          District, 650 International Airport Road,
          Anchorage, Alaska. 1972, 8 p. (Not Available).

KUTCHIN - NOT KNOWN

344.   Mueller, Richard. Kutchin literacy workbook. Summer
          Institute of Linguistics/Wycliffe Bible Trans-
          lators, Box 329, Fort Yukon, Alaska. 1973,
          60 p. (Not Available).

345.   Pulu, Tupou and Katherine Peter. Gwandaii Juk
          neehiniidal (Animal, fish and birds). Alaska
          State-Operated School System, 650 International
          Airport Road, Anchorage, Alaska. 1974. (Not
          Available).

346.   Wycliffe Bible Translators. Scripture cards.
          (Selected portions from the Gospel of Mark).
          Wycliffe Bible Translators, Box 329, Fort Yukon,
          Alaska. 1971, 8 cards. (Not Available).

347.   _____. Tr'ihiʒ'e' naii gooawitr'it k'it (Acts
          of the Apostles). Wycliffe Bible Translators,
          Box 329, Fort Yukon, Alaska. 1974, 254 p. (Not
          Available).

KWAKIUTL - BILINGUAL

       Dall, W.H. et al. Languages of the tribes of the
          extreme Northwest - The Aleutians and adjacent
          territories. Shorey Book Store, Seattle, Wash-
          ington. 1970, 47 p. (Reprint from Contributions to
          American Ethnology, Vol. 1, Washington, D.C.
          1877).

       See under INDIANS OF SUBARCTIC

KWAKIUTL - BILINGUAL cont'd

> Pilling, James Constantine. Bibliography of the
> Wakashan languages. AMS Press, New York. 1973,
> 70 p.
>
> See Pilling under GENERAL LANGUAGES

LAKE MIWOK

> See MIWOK

LAKOTA

> See SIOUX

LOWER KOYUKON

> See KOYUKON

LUISEÑO - BILINGUAL

348. Bright, William. A Luiseño dictionary. University
      of California Publications in Linguistics, #51,
      Berkeley, California. 1968. (Not Available).

349. Hyde, Villiana. An introduction to the Luiseño
      language. Malki Museum Press, Banning, Califor-
      nia. 1971, 236 p.

> A linguistically accurate, simple and readable   gram   self
> work for use by general public. Major portion   voc
> of book concerned with grammar of Luiseño.
> Each grammar chapter has several exercises and
> lessons illustrating grammatical points.
> Luiseño-English word list and English-Luiseño
> word list. More complete form of Luiseño word
> is in former list. Table of contents.

MAIDU, SOUTHERN

> See NISENAN

123

MALECITE-PASSAMAQUODDY - BILINGUAL

350. Teeter, Karl V. The main features of Malecite-
     Passamaquoddy grammar. in Jesse Sawyer
     (Editor), Studies in American Indian Languages.
     University of California Press, Berkeley,
     California. University of California
     Publications in Linguistics #65. 1973,
     pp. 191-249.

     A grammatical sketch containing phonology, verb,   phon   col
     noun and pronoun paradigms, a brief text with   gram
     detailed analysis. The work is intended for   lit
     linguists but can be useful to the nonlinguist
     with some effort.

MICMAC - BILINGUAL

351. Francis, Gordon and Kenneth Hale. Migëmeöeöögemg
     (Speaking Micmac). Big Cove Band Council,
     Rexton, New Brunswick, Canada. 1970, 34 p.

     Linguistic approach to pronunciation of Micmac.   pron   prim
     Addressed to layman. Includes extensive examples   self
     of Micmac phonemes and words containing these
     sounds.

352. Milliea, Mildred. Mic-Mac alphabets and Mic-Mac
     phonetics. Big Cove Band Council, Rexton,
     New Brunswick, Canada. ca. 1970, 13 p.

     First section presents phonemes of Micmac with   pron   self
     pronunciation guide, and examples of Micmac words   voc
     using these sounds. Second section discusses
     sounds more fully. Third section presents
     alphabetical lists of Micmac animal names,
     numbers, trees, and herbal medicines. Not
     linguistically oriented.

MINTO

See TANANA

MIWOK - BILINGUAL

353. Callaghan, Catherine. Bodega Miwok dictionary.
     University of California Publications in Linguis-
     tics, No. 60, Berkeley, California. 1970, 133 p.

     Bodega Miwok-English, English-Bodega Miwok dic-   voc   self
     tionary. Some entries in latter part refer to   phon
     root word in former part, where etymologies are   gram
     more complete. Alphabet-phonetic key and gram-
     matical synopsis. Few cross references.

124

MIWOK - BILINGUAL cont'd

354. Callaghan, Catherine   Lake Miwok dictionary. Univer-
          sity of California, Berkeley, California. 1965,
          287 p.

          Lake Miwok-English, English-Lake Miwok dictionary.   voc   self
          Introduction explains that there were at time of   phon
          writing only eight living speakers of this
          language. Alphabet and phonetic key included.
          Adequate cross references.

MOHAWK - BILINGUAL

355. Beatty, John J. Mohawk morphology. Doctoral
          Dissertation, City University of New York.
          1972, 127 p. (Not Available - Dissertation
          Abstract #72- 24,118).

          Description of Caughnawaga dialect of Mohawk as   gram col
          spoken in Quebec. Discusses and analyzes various
          classes of morphemes. Linguistically oriented.

356. Bonvillain, Nancy and Beatrice Francis. English-
          Mohawk dictionary, Parts I and II. University
          of New York, State Education Department, Albany,
          New York. 1971, 215 p.

          Part I of dictionary English-Mohawk, Part II   voc   self
          Mohawk-English. Each part in two sections: gram
          Noun dictionary and verb dicitonary. Noun dic-   phon
          tionaries sub-divided into 35 categories ranging
          alphabetically from "Animals" to "Weather and
          Weather Conditions." Included are 20 pages of
          prefatory material on grammar, spelling, and
          pronunciation. Few cross references. Manuscript.

357. Bonvillain, Nancy. A Grammar of Akwesasne Mohawk.
          National Museum of Man, Mercury Series, No. 8,
          Ottawa, Ontario. 1973, 249 p.

          Descriptive analysis of Akwesasne Mohawk, with   voc   col
          some ethnographic information as it relates to   gram
          language. Introduction gives general charac-
          teristics of Mohawk. Discussion of phonemics
          and morphophonemics. Majority of work deals
          with structure and use of verbs. Linguistically
          oriented.

358. Michelson, Gunther. A thousand words of Mohawk.
          National Museum of Man, National Museums of
          Canada, Mercury Series, Ethnology Division,
          Paper No. 5, Ottawa, Ontario. 1973, 186 p.

          Brief grammatical introduction followed by root   gram col
          list, Mohawk-English and English-Mohawk. A   voc
          relatively nontechnical introduction to Mohawk
          grammar.

MOHAWK - BILINGUAL cont'd

359.   Mohawk Staff of Salmon River Central School.
          Akwesasne Mohawk, book K. Salmon River Central
          School, Fort Covington, New York. ca. 1973,
          22 p.

          Mohawk/English vocabulary book with one word   voc   prim
          per page, accompanied by illustration of that
          word.

360.   _____. Akwesasne Mohawk, book One. Salmon
          River Central School, Fort Covington, New York.
          ca. 1973, 22 p.

          Mohawk/English vocabulary book with one word per   voc   prim
          page, accompanied by illustration of that word.

361.   Montour, Doris K. and Michele Brisebois-Ward.
          Caughnawaga yesterday and today. Thunderbird
          Press, P.O. Box 129, La Macaza, County Labelle,
          Quebec. 1971, 88 p.

          Second grade curriculum in Social Studies.   lit   prim
          Intended for Indians and non-Indians, it
          describes the history of the Iroquoian people,
          both ancient and recent. Includes a few songs
          in Mohawk. Illustrated.

362.   White, Emily and Ann Lewis. Akwesasne Iewennanotakwa.
          Salmon River Central School, Fort Covington, New
          York. 1973, 33 p.

          Three short stories about a present day Mohawk   lit   int
          family. English text is presented side by side   voc
          with Mohawk text and pronunciation guide to   pron
          latter. Worksheets isolate four Mohawk words
          per story. Illustrated.

MOJAVE - BILINGUAL

363.   Munro, Pamela. Mojave language notes. (Acquired
          from author, University of California, San
          Diego, Department of Linguistics, La Jolla,
          California.) 1973, 28 p.

          Intended for use in Mojave language class taught   voc   self
          by Luther Swick on Colorado River Indian Reserva-   gram
          tion. No attempt at complete account of Mojave
          grammar. Work divided by subject; e.g.,
          sentences, people and animals, giving orders,
          questions. Manuscript.

126

NAVAJO - BILINGUAL

364. Allen, Shonnie, Martha Austin, Betty Many Goats,
      Oswald Werner, and Allen Manning. Write Navajo.
      Department of Anthropology, Northwestern
      University, Evanston, Illinois. 1973, 1872
      frames.

      Programmed learning in writing Navajo, for   script   prim
      Navajo speakers.

365. Anderson, Marjorie. The Lamb and the party. Navajo
      Curriculum Center, Rough Rock Demonstration
      School, Chinle, Arizona. 1972, 15 p. (Not
      Available - Fasthorse, Supplement ABNRM, 153).

      Story about a lamb who disrupts an awéé'   lit   prim
      chi'ideelalo' party. Illustrated.

366. Begay, Eleanor. Bruce doo biʔ hóóts'iʔ idda. Navajo
      Curriculum Center, Rough Rock Demonstration
      School, Chinle, Arizona. 1971, 11 p. (Not
      Available - Fasthorse, Supplement ABNRM, 143).

      Story of a boy who goes to school and misses the   lit   int
      dog he has left at home. Navajo text with
      English translation. Illustrated.

367. Begishe, Kenneth, Linda Singer, Wanda S. Burns.
      Ni'iichiíhji binahat'á, The Way of planning
      birth. Oswald Werner, Northwestern University,
      Evanston, Illinois. 1971, 14 p.

      Discussion of planned parenthood and methods of   lit   self
      contraception in both Navajo and English. Female
      sex organs are also explained. Illustrated.
      Index.

368. Begishe, Kenneth, Jeanette Frank, Oswald Werner. A
      Programmed guide to Navajo transcription.
      Northwestern University, Department of Anthro-
      pology, Evanston, Illinois. 1967, 915 frames.
      (Not Available - Spolsky ABNRM-118).

      Programmed text for writing in Navajo. Intro-   script   prim
      duction in English.   inter

369. Blair, Robert W. Navajo basic course, final report.
      Brigham Young University, Provo, Utah. 1969,
      521 p. (ERIC ED031699).

      Thirteen units including self preparation and   pron   prim
      question-answer exchanges with instructor.   gram   self
      Introduction gives sounds of Navajo and rules
      for reading and writing.

NAVAJO - BILINGUAL cont'd

370.   Blackhorse, Berneice. Shima. Panorama Press, P.O.
           Box 15101, Rio Rancho, New Mexico. 1973, 16 p.

           Essay about mother.   lit   prim

371.   Charles, Vangie et al. assisted by William Morgan.
           Naaltsoos naalt'a'í ádadiilniíł. Panorama Press,
           P.O. Box 15101, Rio Rancho, New Mexico. 1967,
           13 p.

           Description in Navajo of building a kite. In   lit   int
           the series produced by Sanostee-Taodlena Title
           VII Project.

372.   Condie, Le Roy. The Navajo Calendar. Navajo Social
           Studies Project, College of Education, University
           of New Mexico, Albuquerque, New Mexico. 1962-
           1970. (Not Available - Spolsky ABNRM-136).

           Month names given in Navajo. In 1970 calendar   lit   self
           story of Navajo homes is pictured with short
           descriptions. Illustrated.

373.   Crowder, Jack L., Navajo translation by William
           Morgan, Sr. Haskie dóó Yé'ii Bicheii - Haskie
           and the Yé'ii Bicheii. Jack L. Crowder, Box 728,
           Bernalillo, New Mexico. 1970, 32 p. (Not
           Available - Spolsky ABNRM-112).

           Story about a young Navajo boy's experiences at   lit
           home and at school.

374.   Crowder, Jack L. Stephannie and the coyote - Stefanii
           dóó Má'ii. Jack L. Crowder, Bernalillo, New
           Mexico. 1970, 32 p.

           Story presented simultaneously in Navajo and in   lit   prim
           English. Navajo version by William Morgani, Sr.   gram
           Introduction by Wayne and Agnes Holm deals with   pron
           a little grammar and pronunciation of Navajo.
           Story is about a small Navajo girl and her
           everday life. Illustrated with color photographs.

375.   Dick, Lynda (Editor); Dollie L. Yazzie (Developer).
           Teachers Guide to accompany Navajo music.
           Navajo Curriculum Center, Rough Rock Demonstra-
           tion School, Chinle, Arizona. 1970, 51 p. (Not
           Available - Fasthorse, Supplement APNRM, #159).

           Background information on 37 Navajo stories, with   lit   self
           Navajo texts and English translations. Classi-
           fication of Navajo song types also included. To
           accompany two records of Navajo music.

NAVAJO - BILINGUAL cont'd

376.   Duncan, Homer. Victorious life. Navajo Christian
          Reading, Route 1, Box 2F, Cortez, Colorado.
          1965, 28 p.

          Sermon on leading a Christian life. Navajo and   lit   self
          English on facing page.   adv

377.   Fasthorse, Rose and Louise Benally. Supplement to
          the analytical bibliography of Navajo reading
          materials. Navajo Reading Study, University
          of New Mexico, Albuquerque, New Mexico. 1973,
          18 p.

          Bibliography of 49 entries, covering materials   bibl   self
          produced for Navajos from 1968 through 1972.
          Includes English language, Navajo and bilingual
          materials.

378.   Franciscan fathers. An ethnologic dictionary of the
          Navajo langauge. St. Michael's, Arizona. 1968,
          539 p. (Reprint of 1910 edition).

          "Dictionary" is arranged by subjects in the   desc   self
          Navajo culture. Subjects are discussed in   voc
          English, using Navajo words for specific con-
          cepts. Sometimes a small Navajo glossary
          accompanies paragraph. Illustrated with black
          and white drawings. Table of contents, index,
          and list of illustrations.

379.   Goosen, Irvy W. Haa'ishá diné bizaad deiídiiltah -
          Let's read Navajo preprimer. Northern Arizona
          Supplementary Education Center, Northern Arizona
          University, Flagstaff, Arizona. 1968, 47 p.

          Preprimer introducing letter of Navajo alphabet   script   prim
          to native speakers not literate in Navajo, sounds   pron
          of Navajo introduced in contrastive pairs of
          words, then in simple sentences. Words illus-
          trated by drawings. Page indexed Navajo/English
          glossary of 125 items appended.

380.   _____. Navajo made easier. Northland Press,
          Flagstaff, Arizona. 1968, 271 p.

          Series of 64 short lessons designed to teach   voc   prim
          Navajo to English speakers, particularly to
          teachers of English as a Second Langauge to
          Navajo children. Not a linguistic approach to
          Navajo. Introduces a basic vocabulary in
          conversational form. Audio tapes are also
          available.

NAVAJO - BILINGUAL cont'd

381.   Haile, Berard. A Manual of Navaho grammar.   AMS
          Press, New York. 1970, 324 p. (Reprint of St.
          Michael's Press, St. Michael's, Arizona. 1926).

          Introduction to structure of Navajo. Begins   pron   self
          with short section on pronunciation. Part I   gram
          deals with nouns and noun adjuncts, Part II
          with verbs and verb stems. May be used by non-
          linguist.

382.   _____. Learning Navajo, Vol. I and II. St.
          Michael's, Arizona. 1971, 223 p. (Reprint of
          1941 edition).

          Lessons designed to teach English speakers to   voc   self
          communicate with Navajo people. Phrases   pron
          presented are of practical nature. Rules of
          grammar minimal. Correct pronunciation empha-
          sized, especially through "safe and accurate
          orthography." Vocabulary presented with a
          lesson plan. Drills and exercises included.
          Table of contents and subject index.

383.   Hale, Kenneth. The Role of American Indian linguis-
          tics in bilingual education. In Paul R. Turner
          (Editor), Bilingualism in the Southwest,
          University of Arizona Press, Tucson, Arizona.
          1973, 22 p.

          Discussion of place of Native language in truly   meth   self
          bilingual curriculum. Bulk of article consists
          of games to increase knowledge of native lan-
          guage. Examples for various games are given in
          Navajo with English translations.

384.   Hale, Ken and Loraine Honie. An Introduction to the
          sound system of Navajo, part I: articulatory
          phonetics.   Massachusetts Institute of
          Technology, Department of Linguistics, Cambridge,
          Massachusetts. 1972, 175 p. (Not Available -
          Fasthorse, Supplement ABNRM, #178).

          Introduction to Navajo phonetics, including some   phon   self
          phonological rules, orthography. Each chapter   script
          has exercises for practice.

385.   Hall, Geraldine. Kee's home; a beginning Navajo-
          English reader. Northland Press, Flagstaff,
          Arizona. 1972, 103 p.

          Story of young Navajo boy and his family. Text   lit   prim
          is entirely in both English and Navajo. Only   pron
          English words "completely translatable into
          Navajo" without change of meaning were used.
          Glossary by Irvy Goosen, introduces Navajo alpha-
          bet and fundamentals of pronunciation.

NAVAJO - BILINGUAL cont'd

386. Higgins, Roger. A dialogue on the Navajo classifier.
      Massachusetts Institute of Technology, Cambridge,
      Massachusetts. ca. 1970, 65 p.

      A conversation between two friends which intro-   gram
      duces the grammar of Navajo. Akalii tries to
      teach his friend Bill some of the basics of
      speaking Navajo. Manuscript.

387. Hill, Faith. Learning to write Navajo. Rock Point
      Mission, Rock Point, Arizona. 1973, 30 p. (Not
      Available - Kari NLB, p. 18).

388. Hoijer, Harry. A Navajo lexicon. University of
      California Publications in Linguistics, No. 78.
      Berkeley, California. 1974, 314 p.

      Consists of: (1) Verb stems and bases; (2) Noun   phon   col
      stems and bases; (3) Postpositions (act the same   gram
      way as English prepositions); (4) Verbal prefixes;
      (5) Enclitics; (6) Particles; and (7) A biblio-
      graphy. Compiled by Harry Hoijer from the field
      notes of Edward Sapir.

389. _____. Patterns of meaning in Navajo. In M.
      Zamora, J.M. Mahar, H. Orenstein (Editors).
      Themes in Culture: Essays in honor of Morris E. Opler.
      Kayumangii Publishers, Quezon City, Phillipines.
      1971, pp. 227-237.

      A study centered on the Navajo verb and verbal   gram   col
      phrase. It attempts a description of patterns
      of meaning peculiar to Navajo. Patterns of
      meaning refer to the ways in which native
      speakers of Navajo select, by virture of their
      language, certain features of real situations
      and determine the interrelationships of these
      features.

390. Holm, Wayne. Navajo spelling lists. Navajo Reading
      Study, University of New Mexico, 1805 Roma,
      Northeast, Albuquerque, New Mexico. 1971, 37 p.

      Lists compiled from a computer assisted study   voc   self
      of the Navajo vocabulary of six year old Navajo
      children. Author does not claim list is exhaus-
      tive, but it should be valuable to teachers of
      beginning reading in Navajo.

NAVAJO - BILINGUAL cont'd

391. Honie, Lorraine and Ken Hale. Ał'ąą dine'é bizaad
     ałhąąh naha'iłigíi (Comparing languages).
     Massachusetts Institute of Technology, Depart-
     ment of Linguistics, Cambridge, Massachusetts.
     1972, 13 p. (Not Available - Fasthorse,
     Supplement ABNRM, 179).

     Introduction to comparative linguistics in   meth   self
     Navajo with English translation. Includes
     examples from Navajo, Hopi, San Carlos Apache
     and Sarcee.

392. _____. Diné bizaad ya'áit' bee diits'a'igíi:
     ałtse bihoo'aahigíi (The Sounds of Navajo: Part
     One). Massachusetts Institute of Technology,
     Department of Linguistics, Cambridge, Masachus-
     etts. 1972, 22 p. (Not Available - Fasthorse,
     Supplement ABNRM, 180).

     A description, in Navajo, of four positions of   phon   adv
     articulation, with phonetics game to practice
     sounds. English translation included.

393. Kari, James. Navajo language bibliography. Navajo
     Reading Study, University of New Mexico, 1805
     Roma, Northeast, Albuquerque, New Mexico. 1973,
     39 p.

     Bibliography of "all the available references   bibl   col
     that relate to the study of the Navajo language."   self
     However, Navajo curriculum materials are excluded,
     due to the recent publication of two biblio-
     graphies that list Navajo curriculum materials
     exclusively. General works, such as those on
     the Athapaskan language family, have also been
     omitted. Items arranged alphabetically by
     author and within author by publication date.
     No index.

394. Long, Albert. Gah. Navajo Curriculum Center, Rough
     Rock Demonstration School, Chinle, Arizona.
     1971, 17 p. (Not Available - Fasthorse, Supple-
     ment ABNRM, 151).

     Story about rabbits. Glossary with English   lit   prim
     translations.

395. Martin, Judy. Shaa ni. Navajo Reading Study, Univer-
     sity of New Mexico, 1805 Roma, Northeast, Albu-
     querque, New Mexico. 1972, 12 p.

     Workbook of exercises in drill stem completion   voc   prim
     in Navajo. Page is split horizontally in an
     effort to help the child teach himself. Preface
     in English, text in Navajo. Illustrated.

NAVAJO - BILINGUAL cont'd

396. Morgan, William, Sr. Bik'ehgo nánidizídí - Calendar
          for October 1974 - September 1975. Navajo
          Reading Study, University of New Mexico, 1805
          Roma, Northeast, Albuquerque, New Mexico. 1974.

          Calendar with months and days of week in Navajo,   lit   adv
          using Navajo annual cycle. Each month has
          explanation in Navajo of an event or ceremony
          which occurred or occurs in that month. Trans-
          lation of these paragraphs is on front page.
          Illustrated with drawings.

397. _____. Teaching the Navajo language. Navajo
          Studies at Navajo Community College, Many Farms,
          Arizona. 1971, pp. 83-109. (Not Available -
          Fasthorse, Supplement ABNRM, 165).

          Presents Navajo alphabet, discusses content of   script   self
          Navajo language courses at Navajo Community   meth
          College, includes a dialogue using Navajo medical
          terms.

398. Navajo Christian Reading. Born to die. Navajo
          Christian Reading, Route 1, Box 2F, Cortez,
          Colorado. ca. 1965, 8 p.

          Story of the birth of Jesus. Navajo and English   lit   adv
          on facing pages.

399. _____. The Christian and tithing. Navajo
          Christian Reading, Route 1, Box 2F, Cortez,
          Colorado. ca. 1965, 10 p.

          Explanation of the tithe in both English and   lit   adv
          Navajo.

400. _____. The Christmas story. Navajo Christian
          Reading, Route 1, Box 2F, Cortez, Colorado.
          ca. 1965, 2 p.

          The annunciation to the shepherds as given in   lit   int
          Luke 2: 8-14. English and Navajo versions on
          facing pages.

401. _____. Following the crowd. Navajo Christian
          Reading, Route 1, Box 2F, Cortez, Colorado.
          ca. 1965, 9 p.

          Story from the book of Daniel about being stead-   lit   adv
          fast in faith, in English and Navajo.

402. _____. For Christian boys and girls. Navajo
          Christian Reading, Route 1, Box 2F, Cortez,
          Colorado. ca. 1965, 4 p.

          Tract about the body as God's temple. In Navajo   lit   adv
          and English.

NAVAJO - BILINGUAL cont'd

403. Navajo Christian Reading. The Gift of God. Navajo
      Christian Reading, Route 1, Box 2F, Cortez,
      Colorado. ca. 1965, 6 p.

      Christmas tract in English and Navajo.   lit   adv

404. _____. Good news. Navajo Christian Reading,
      Route 1, Box 2F, Cortez, Colorado. ca. 1965,
      7 p.

      Quotations from scripture in English and Navajo.   lit   adv

405. _____. The Greedy monkey. Navajo Christian
      Reading, Route 1, Box 2F, Cortez, Colorado.
      ca. 1965, 5 p.

      Story about Africans trapping a monkey - an   lit   adv
      analogy of the way the devil tries to catch
      sinners. For children and young people. In
      English and Navajo.

406. _____. He died in our place. Navajo Christian
      Reading, Route 1, Box 2F, Cortez, Colorado.
      ca. 1965, 6 p.

      Explanation of the reasons for the crucifixion.   lit   adv
      Navajo and English on facing pages.

407. _____. Hell: eternal suffering. Navajo
      Christian Reading, Route 1, Box 2F, Cortez,
      Colorado. ca. 1965, 6 p.

      Bible passages about the existence of hell.   lit   adv
      English and Navajo.

408. _____. How to live for God. Navajo Christian
      Reading, Route 1, Box 2F, Cortez, Colorado.
      ca. 1965, 6 p.

      Instructional scriptural quotations presented   lit   adv
      in Navajo and English.

409. _____. Learning to read Navajo. Navajo
      Christian Reading, Route 1, Box 2F, Cortez,
      Colorado. ca. 1965, 6 p.

      Instruction for Navajo speakers who read only   script   prim
      English. Lessons in vowel and consonant sounds
      of Navajo.

410. _____. Naabeehó ashkii bijéí - A Navajo boy's
      heart. Navajo Christian Reading, Route 1, Box
      2F, Cortez, Colorado. ca. 1965, 25 p.

      Religious discussion between a Navajo boy and a   lit   adv
      missionary, resulting in the boy's conversion to
      Christianity. Navajo version precedes English
      version. Illustrated.

NAVAJO - BILINGUAL cont'd

411. Navajo Christian Reading. The Octopus. Navajo
Christian Reading, Route 1, Box 2F, Cortez,
Colorado. ca. 1965, 5 p.

Religious lesson drawn from the life of the   lit   adv
octopus. For children and young people. In
English and Navajo.

412. _____. Old Testament Bible Stories from
Genesis - Diyin God Bizaad Bee'aha'deet'a
Aɫtsehigii Hodesshzhiizh Biyi'doo Baahane'ii ɫa'.
Navajo Christian Reading, Route 1, Box 2F,
Cortez, Colorado. 1965, 100 p.

Creation story, story of Adam and Eve, the   lit   adv
Flood, the Tower of Babel, Abraham and Isaac,
Isaac's wife, Jacob and Esau, and the story of
Joseph. Navajo version of each story precedes
English version. Illustrated.

413. _____. One thing God wants you to do. Navajo
Christian Reading, Route 1, Box 2F, Cortez,
Colorado. ca. 1965, 7 p.

Tract about accepting Jesus as one's saviour.   lit   adv
In English and Navajo.

414. _____. Salvation. Navajo Christian Reading,
Route 1, Box 2F, Cortez, Colorado. ca. 1965,
2 p.

Three passages from the Bible relating to salva-   lit   int
tion. Presented in English and Navajo.

415. _____. Someday you will stand before God.
Navajo Christian Reading, Route 1, Box 2F,
Cortez, Colorado. ca. 1965, 7 p.

Quotations from the Bible in English and Navajo.   lit   adv

416. _____. Some helps for new Christians. Navajo
Christian Reading, Route 1, Box 2F, Cortez,
Colorado. ca. 1965, 4 p.

Scriptural quotations for the spiritual growth   lit   adv
of converts. In English and Navajo.

417. _____. Speckle. Navajo Christian Reading,
Route 1, Box 2F, Cortez, Colorado. ca. 1965,
6 p.

Analogy of Christ's atonement, in terms of a hen   lit   int
who gives her life for her chicks. Story for
children.

NAVAJO - BILINGUAL cont'd

418.   Navajo Christian Reading. Speckle and other stories.
            Navajo Christian Reading, Route 1, Box 2F,
            Cortez, Colorado. 1970, 35 p.

            Series of seven short stories about animals.   lit   int
            Navajo version is presented first, followed by
            English version. Illustrated.

419.   _____. Ten things God wants you to know. Navajo
            Christian Reading, Route 1, Box 2F, Cortez,
            Colorado. ca. 1965, 11 p.

            Scriptural verse in Navajo and English.   lit   adv

420.   _____. There is only one. Navajo Christian
            Reading, Route 1, Box 2F, Cortez, Colorado.
            ca. 1965, 7 p.

            Quotations from scripture, in Navajo and English.   lit   adv

421.   _____. Unto us a savior. Navajo Christian
            Reading, Route 1, Box 2F, Cortez, Colorado.
            ca. 1965, 5 p.

            Christmas tract of Bible quotations, in English   lit
            and Navajo.

422.   _____. What's the answer? Navajo Christian
            Reading, Route 1, Box 2F, Cortez, Colorado.
            ca. 1965, 6 p.

            Answers to ten questions about Christianity.   lit   int
            In English and Navajo.

423.   _____. Which church saves? Navajo Christian
            Reading, Route 1, Box 2F, Cortez, Colorado.
            ca. 1965, 12 p.

            Scriptural verses chosen to show that Jesus   lit   adv
            alone saves - not any particular church, religion
            or one's own good works. In English and Navajo.

424.   _____. Which religion is right? Navajo Christian
            Reading, Route 1, Box 2F, Cortez, Colorado.
            ca. 1965, 7 p.

            Tract about the necessity of Christ for   lit   adv
            salvation. In English and Navajo.

425.   _____. Why he loved Christ. Navajo Christian
            Reading, Route 1, Box 2F, Cortez, Colorado.
            ca. 1965, 4 p.

            Story about the faith of a Christian Indian.   lit   adv

NAVAJO - BILINGUAL cont'd

426.   The Navajo Times. The Navajo Tribe, P.O. Box 310,
          Window Rock, Arizona. Weekly issues from
          January 1974 - December 1974.

          Weekly review of national, local, and tribal   voc   ref
          news from the Navajo viewpoint. Each issue   phon
          has a page on learning the Navajo language.   pron
                                                                                   lit

427.   Platero, Paul R. Diné bizaad hazaalyé. Navajo
          Community College, Chinle, Arizona. 1969.
          (Not Available - Spolsky ABNRM-103).

          First unit in a series of lessons in Navajo.   prim

428.   _____. Diné bizaad n'anil'iih - Navajo language
          review, Vol. 1, No. 1-4. Center for Applied
          Linguistics, Arlington, Virginia. 1974, 210 p.

          Fourteen articles on Navajo linguistics. The   gram   col
          majority of the articles are in English, but   pron
          two are entirely in Navajo. The articles tend   voc
          to be technical, but are addressed to those
          involved in Navajo and bilingual education.

429.   Platero, Paul (Editor). Papers on Navajo linguistics.
          Dine Bi'ólto' Association, Incorporated. Ganado,
          Arizona. 1973, 165 p.

          Nineteen linguistic papers on Navajo, by various   gram   col
          Navajo linguists. Some are in English, some in   voc   adv
          Navajo.   phon

430.   Rough Rock Demonstration School. Arts and crafts.
          Navajo Curriculum Center, Rough Rock Demonstra-
          tion School, Chinle, Arizona. 1972, 9 p.

          Description of several crafts. Instruction for   lit   int
          construction of crafts items is primarily in
          Navajo, but sometimes also in English. Crafts
          involved are basket weaving, rug weaving, and
          bead work.

431.   Sapir, Edward and Harry Hoijer (Editors). The Origin
          of the Salt Clan. In William Slager (Editor).
          Language in American Indian Education, Bureau
          of Indian Affairs, Albuquerque, New Mexico.
          Fall 1971, pp. 88-89.

          Legend of the origin of the Salt Clan of Navajos,   lit   self
          presented first in Navajo, then in English trans-
          lation.

NAVAJO - BILINGUAL cont'd

432. Sapir, Edward and Harry Hoijer. The phonoloay and
         morphology of the Navajo language. University
         of California Publications in Linguistics, No.
         50. Berkeley, California. 1967, 124 p.

         Linguistically oriented. Contains sections on: phon   col
         (1) Phonemes; (2) Morphophonemics; (3) The Noun;   gram
         (4) Postpositions; (5) The Verb; (6) The Particle;
         and (7) Tables.

433. Saville, Muriel R. Dine bi'olta saad naaki
         yeeyalti'ii binaa hsoos t'aala'igii. Navajo-
         English curriculum guide, kinderaarten level.
         University of Texas, Austin, Department of
         Curriculum and Instruction. 1970, 383 p.
         (ERIC ED045967).

         Provides information on bilinqualism and its   meth   col
         consequences, needs of Navajo children, Navajo   self
         and English languages, methods for first and
         second language instructions for young children,
         evaluative techniques for teaching methods,
         materials and progress of students. Also gives
         specific suggestions and sample instructional
         materials for four curriculum content areas.

434. Schwanke, Jack H. (Editor). Coyote and Santa, rodeo,
         man, boy and donkey. Rough Rock Demonstration
         School, Navajo Curriculum Center, Chinle,
         Arizona. 1970, 32 p. (Not Available - Spolsky
         ABNRM-91).

         Three plays with themes compatible with Navajo   lit
         culture. First two are original, third is adap-
         tation of European folk tale.

435. Schwanke, Jack H. Hweelde, The Lona Walk. Rough
         Rock Demonstration School, Navajo Curriculum
         Center, Chinle, Arizona. 1970, 80 p. (Not
         Available - Spolsky - ABNRM-92).

         Dramatic reading of story about episode in   lit   inter
         Navajo history.

436. Son of Former Many Beads. English translation by
         Robert W. Young and William Morgan, Sr. Navaho
         Historical Series I: The Ramah Navajo -
         Tłóhchiniji Diné Kéedahat'íinii. Publications
         Service, Haskell Institute, Lawrence, Kansas.
         1967, 17 p. (Not Available - Spolsky, ABNRM-105).

         Retelling of important events from Navajo   lit   self
         viewpoint.

NAVAJO - BILINGUAL cont'd

437. Spolsky, Bernard, Agnes Holm and Penny Murphy.
      Analytical bibliography of Navajo reading
      materials. Navajo Reading Study, University
      of New Mexico, Albuquerque, New Mexico. 1970,
      106 p.

      Annotated bibliography of English, Navajo and   bibl   self
      Navajo/English materials developed for and by
      the Navajo tribe. One hundred and forty-one
      numbered entries arranged according to language
      used, and within language, by sponsoring agency.
      Each entry contains data on format, price,
      preparing and publishing agency. Covers 1940
      to 1970.

438. Spolsky, Bernard et al. A spoken word count of six-
      year-old Navajo children with supplement -
      Complete word list. Navajo Reading Study,
      University of New Mexico, 1805 Roma, Northeast,
      Albuquerque, New Mexico. 1971, 212 p.

      Navajo word list compiled from interviews of   voc   col
      over 200 Navajo six year old children. Discusses   meth
      word count and interview texts in terms of (1)
      number of sentences, (2) number of words, (3)
      number of tokens, (4) type-token ratios, and
      (5) word-length. Words are grouped in order of
      frequency.

439. Tsinnie, Lolita. Language acquisition, Vol. 1. Dine
      Biolta' Association, Language and Culture Summer
      Workshop, Rough Rock Demonstration School, Rough
      Rock, Arizona. 1973, 181 p.

      One hundred and eighty-one on-site observations   voc   prim
      of the language behavior of Navajo children
      aged one to six. English and Navajo words
      used by the children are given. Should be
      useful base information for school entry level
      language teaching.

440. Tsinnie, Lolita M. (Editor). Navajo short and long
      vowels, book I. Dine Bi'olta' Association,
      Language and Culture Summer Workshop, Rough
      Rock Demonstration School, Rough Rock, Arizona.
      1973, 250 p.

      Workbook for children on Navajo vowels. Vowels   voc   prim
      are presented in upper and lower case with   script
      instructions and space for writing them, words
      using these vowels, and various exercises in
      recognition of written forms. Illustrated.
      Introduction and content outline, including
      translation of Navajo vocabulary, in English.

NAVAJO - BILINGUAL cont'd

441. Werner, Oswald, Kenneth Y. Begishe and June Werner.
          The Anatomical atlas of the Navajo, sixth revi-
          sion of illustrations. Northwestern University
          at Tsegi, Arizona. 1968, 34 p.

          Anatomical drawings of various parts of the   voc   int
          human body, with labels in Navajo and English.
          Areas labelled are those seen as discreet areas
          by Navajo.

442. Wilson, Alan. Basic medical Navajo: an introductory
          text in communication. University of New Mexico,
          Gallup Branch, Gallup, New Mexico. 1973. (Not
          Available - Kari NLB, p. 37).

443. _____. Laughter: the Navajo way. Humorous
          stories of the people (in Navajo and English).
          Vol. 1. Alan Dennison, University of New Mexico,
          Grants Branch, Gallup, New Mexico. 1970, 130 p.
          (ERIC ED043881).

          Includes three types of humor - (1) word plays   lit   int
          in Navajo, (2) bilingual word plays between   gram   self
          Navajo and English and (3) situational stories.
          Stories are presented in Navajo with English
          gloss. Each story followed by explanations of
          text, individual words, verb paradigms, and
          cultural notes relevant to text.

444. _____. Breakthrough Navajo· an introductory
          course. University of New Mexico, Gallup Branch,
          Gallup, New Mexico. 1969, 238 p.

          Introduction to Navajo for English speakers.   pron   prim
          Emphasis on pronunciation. Author suggests   voc
          that only useful way to master language is to   gram
          use it in real life not just in classroom.
          Audio-tape available.

445. Wycliffe Bible Translators. Adam dóó Eve, Kéin dóó
          'Eibel Baa Hane' - The Story of Adam and Eve,
          Cain and Abel. Wycliffe Bible Translators,
          Incorporated, Farmington, New Mexico. ca. 1965,
          19 p.

          Two Old Testament stories. Navajo version on   lit   int
          recto, English on verso. Illustrated.

446. _____. Diyin God Bizaad Bohool'aahgo Yeenika-
          adoolwoligii - Helps for Bible Study. Wycliffe
          Bible Translators, Incorporated, Farmington,
          New Mexico. ca. 1965, 72 p.

          Essays in background to the Bible and Bible   lit   adv
          study, capsule descriptions of the books of the
          New Testament. Navajo version in first half of
          book, English version in second half of book.

NAVAJO - BILINGUAL cont'd

447.   Wycliffe Bible Translators, Hane' Ya'at'éehii Jesus
       Christ bee Yisdá'iildéehii - The Good news of
       salvation through Jesus Christ. Wycliffe Bible
       Translators, Incorporated, Farmington, New
       Mexico. ca. 1965, 81 p.

       Synopsis of the Old and New Testament. Navajo   lit   adv
       on recto, English on verso. Illustrated.

448.   _____. Ho dee yáá dą́ą' Hane 'ii - Story of
       Creation (Old Testament Stories, Book I).
       Wycliffe Bible Translators, Incorporated,
       Farmington, New Mexico. ca. 1965, 25 p.

       The creation of the world according to the Old   lit   int
       Testament. Navajo on recto, English on verso.
       Illustrated. Contains a Navajo-English
       vocabulary at end.

449.   _____. I want a job - Naanish hanishtá.
       Distributed by Bookstore, 2103 West Main
       Street, P.O. Box 1230, Farmington, New Mexico.
       ca. 1965, 16 p.

       Series of brief dialogues appropriate to (1) the   lit   prim
       employment office, (2) the gas station, and (3)   self
       the doctor's office. Navajo on recto, English
       on verso. Illustrated.

450.   _____. Learning English - Bilagáana bizaad
       bíhoo'aah. Navajo Mission's Press, P.O. Box
       1230, Farmington, New Mexico. ca. 1965, 28 p.

       Series of sentences and short dialogues with   voc   prim
       controlled vocabulary. Navajo on verso,   self
       English on recto. Followed by list of kinship
       terms.

451.   _____. Noah, Béíbel Baa Hane' (Old Testament
       Stories, Book 3). Wycliffe Bible Translators,
       Incorporated, Farmington, New Mexico. ca. 1965,
       19 p.

       Old Testament stories of Noah and the Tower of   lit   int
       Babel. Navajo version is presented on recto and
       English on verso. Illustrated.

141

NAVAJO - BILINGUAL cont'd

452. Yazzie, Dollie L. Teacher's guide to accompany
     Navajo music. Diné Bi'ólta Association,
     Incorporated. Rough Rock Rural Branch, Rough
     Rock, Arizona. 1970, 54 p.

   To accompany two phonograph records of songs in   lit   int
   Navajo for cultural enrichment in Navajo class-   voc
   rooms. Songs include traditional songs, new
   songs to traditional tunes and familiar English
   tunes with Navajo lyrics. Each song is annotated
   as to type and cultural background. Lyrics are
   given, and specific vocabulary items are isolated
   and defined in English.

453. Young, Robert W. and William Morgan. The Navaho
     language; the elements of Navaho grammar with
     a dictionary in two parts containing basic
     vocabularies of Navaho and English. Publication
     of the Education Division, United States Indian
     Service, Salt Lake City, Utah. 1972. Varied
     paging. (Reprint of 1943 edition.)

   This work is in three parts - outline of Navajo   voc   self
   grammar, Navajo-English vocabulary, and English-   gram
   Navajo vocabulary. Also a brief section on the   phon
   Navajo sound system. Navajo-English portion of
   the vocabulary is largest element in book.
   Index.

NAVAJO - MONOLINGUAL, NAVAJO

454. American Bible Society. God Bizaad, Pee'aha'deet'á
     Ałtséhígíí - Genesis, Exodus, Joshua, Ruth,
     Psalms, Jonah. Distributed by Navajo Missions,
     Incorporated, Box 1230, Farmington, New Mexico.
     1966, 780 p. (Not Available - Spolsky ABNRM-56).

   Six books of the Old Testament in Navajo.   lit   self

455. _____. Nihi bóhólníihii dóó Visdánihiiniiłii
     aniidiii. The New Testament. American Bible
     Society, New York. 1966, 809 p.

   Entire New Testament presented in Navajo.   lit   self

456. Atcitty, Marlene. Da'iidá. Navajo Reading Study,
     University of New Mexico, Albuquerque, New
     Mexico. 1973, 8 p.

   Story in Navajo explaining various ways of   voc   prim
   saying someone is eating; e.g. "She is eating"
   said differently from "They are eating."
   Illustrated by Caryl McHarney.

NAVAJO - MONOLINGUAL, NAVAJO cont'd

457. Atcitty, Marlene and Richard Johnsen. Deezbaa'.
      Navajo Reading Study, University of New Mexico,
      1805 Roma, Northeast, Albuquerque, New Mexico.
      ca. 1970, 8 p. (Not Available).

458. Atcitty, Marlene. Mósiʔgai. Navajo Reading Study,
      University of New Mexico, Albuquerque, New
      Mexico. 1971, 6 p.

      Story about the adventures of a cat.   lit   int

459. Begay, Eleanor. Hand Chart Book to accompany Bruce
      doo Biʔ Hóóts 'íid da. Navajo Curriculum Center,
      Rough Rock Curriculum Center, Chinle, Arizona.
      1971, 33 p. (Not Available - Fasthorse,
      Supplement ABNRM, 144).

      Vocabulary charts for Navajo text, illustrated   voc   int
      by Navajo school children.

460. Begay, Lorene. Naaldlooshii baa hane'. Navajo
      Curriculum Center, Rough Rock Demonstration
      School, Chinle, Arizona. 1972, 35 p. (Not
      Available - Fasthorse, Supplement ABNRM, 152).

      Descriptions of nineteen animals.   lit   int

461. Begay, Rodger. Álástsii'. Navajo Reading Study,
      University of New Mexico, Albuquerque, New
      Mexico (For Sanostee-Toadlene Title VII Project,
      United States Bureau of Indian Affairs). 1974,
      8 p.

      Story in Navajo about seeds.   lit   int

462. Belone, Nora. Naadáá haleehgi baa hane'. Navajo
      Reading Study, University of New Mexico,
      Albuquerque, New Mexico. 1974, 8 p.

      Story of Indian corn from planting to harvesting.   lit   prim
      Illustrated.

463. Benally, Louise and Rose Fasthorse. Johnny dóó Willie.
      Navajo Reading Study, University of New Mexico,
      Albuquerque, New Mexico. 1973, 11 p.

      Story of an Indian cowboy and the work he does.   lit   int
      Illustrated.

464. Blackhorse, B.A. Hilda. Navajo Reading Study, Uni-
      versity of New Mexico, Albuquerque, New Mexico.
      1974, 12 p.

      Story of a Navajo girl's life at school and at   lit   int
      home. Illustrated.

NAVAJO - MONOLINGUAL, NAVAJO cont'd

465. Dennison, Johnson. Télii Yázhí. Navajo Curriculum
     Center, Rough Rock Demonstration School, Chinle,
     Arizona. 1971, 10 p. (Not Available - Fasthorse
     Supplement ABNRM, 145).

     Story about a little donkey who gets separated   lit   prim
     from his mother and makes some interesting dis-
     coveries. Illustrated.

466. Dick, Galena. Ats'íís. Navajo Curriculum Center,
     Rough Rock Demonstration School, Chinle, Arizona.
     1972, 21 p. (Not Available - Fasthorse,
     Supplement ABNRM, 150).

     Gives Navajo terms for various body parts.   voc   prim
     Illustrated.

467. Dick, Lynda A. and Lorene Begay. Na'niłkaadii
     bilééchąą'í hazlįį'. Navajo Curriculum Center,
     Rough Rock Demonstration School, Chinle,
     Arizona. 1972, 21 p. (Not Available - Fasthorse
     Supplement ABNRM, 149).

     Story of a new sheep dog who causes trouble with   lit   int
     the flock of sheep.

468. Dine Biolta Association. Ałk' idą́ą' jiní. Dine
     Biolta Association, Rough Rock, Arizona. 1971,
     66 p.

     Series of short articles by various authors.   lit   adv
     Illustrated.

469. Dotson, Rebecca. Kii. Rough Rock Demonstration
     School, Navajo Curriculum Center, Chinle,
     Arizona. 1970, 24 p. (Not Available - Spolsky
     ABNRM-86).

     Story of a Navajo family, written and illustrated   lit   prim
     by Navajo children.

470. Enochs, J.B. Little Man's Family, Diné Yázhí
     Ba'ałchini, Reader. Paul Platero, Navajo
     Community College, Chinle, Arizona. 1969, 39 p.
     (originally published bilingual, 1950).
     (Not Available - Spolsky ABNRM-104).

     Story of typical Navajo family's life. Illus-   lit   prim
     trated.

471. Hale, Benny. Baa'. Navajo Reading Study. Univer-
     sity of New Mexico, 1805 Roma, Northeast,
     Albuquerque, New Mexico. 1972, 8 p.

     Story of a day in the life of a Navajo girl   lit   prim
     named "Baa'."

144

NAVAJO - MONOLINGUAL, NAVAJO cont'd

472.   Harvey, Frank. Saad t'áá aanii wójíhígíí (The Words
           that have their true meaning). Rock Point
           Community School, Chinle, Arizona. 1974, 86 p.

           Thirteen chapters, each focusing on one word -   voc   adv
           its meaning, its use in sentences, etc. Words
           discussed are - watermelon, car, sundown and
           sunrise, greetings and howdy, rainbow, earth,
           corn pollen, fire poker, house, weed, dog and
           poodle, butterfly and buffalo. Illustrated.

473.   Harvey, Judy. Hastiin ch'ahii. Navajo Reading Study,
           University of New Mexico, 1805 Roma, Northeast,
           Albuquerque, New Mexico. 1972, 24 p.

           Book in Navajo about different hats that suit   lit   prim
           different types of people.

474.   _____. Hastói táá. Navajo Reading Study, Uni-
           versity of New Mexico, 1805 Roma, Northeast,
           Albuquerque, New Mexico. 1972, 8 p. (Not
           Available - Fasthorse, Supplement ABNRM, 185).

           Comic story of a blind man, a deaf man and a   lit   int
           crippled man. Illustrated.

475.   _____. Na'ahoohaidi. Navajo Reading Study,
           University of New Mexico, 1805 Roma, Northeast,
           Albuquerque, New Mexico. 1972, 8 p.

           Story in Navajo of a Navajo girl and her horse.   lit   prim
           Illustrated by Paul Wilson.

476.   _____. Pábíi dóó Másí. Navajo Reading Study,
           University of New Mexico. 1805 Roma, Northeast,
           Albuquerque, New Mexico. 1972, 16 p.

           Story about a cat and a dog playing with a ball.   lit   prim
           Illustrated.

477.   _____. Shaani. Navajo Reading Study, University
           of New Mexico, 1805 Roma, Northeast, Albuquerque,
           New Mexico. 1972, 13 p.

           Exercises with use of appropriate verb stem.   gram   prim
           Illustrated.

478.   Henderson, Jerry. Łįį'baa hane'. Navajo Reading
           Study, University of New Mexico, Albuquerque,
           New Mexico. 1974, 16 p.

           Description of a horse - its behavior, use and   lit   int
           the parts of its body. Illustrated.

145

NAVAJO - MONOLINGUAL, NAVAJO cont'd

479. Martin, Judy Harvey. Haalá wolyé. Navajo Reading
          Study, University of New Mexico, 1805 Roma,
          Northeast, Albuquerque, New Mexico. 1972. (Not
          Available - Fasthorse, Supplement ABNRM, 189).

      A riddle book.   lit   int

480. Mitchell, Charlie. Ałk'idą́ą́ ádahóót ijdii
          heeháaniihigíí baa hane' (The Story of what
          happened a long time ago, as remembered).
          Navajo Reading Study, University of New Mexico,
          1805 Roma, Northeast, Albuquerque, New Mexico.
          1974, 26 p.

      A description of the grievances the Navajos have   lit   adv
      experienced at the hands of other Indian tribes
      and of Anglos. Illustrated.

481. _____. Łįį'hazlįį'dą́ą'hane' (Story of when the
          horse arrived). Navajo Reading Study, University
          of New Mexico. 1805 Roma, Northeast, Albuquerque,
          New Mexico. 1974, 11 p.

      Description of how the horse first came to the   lit   adv
      Navajo, how the Navajo adapted to the horse and
      how the horse changed Navajo life. Illustrated.

482. Nahkai, Ray C. Bahi baahane.   Panorama Press, P.O.
          Box 15101, Rio Rancho, New Mexico (for Sanostee-
          Toadlena Title VII Project). 1973, 12 p.

      Story in Navajo about a Navajo boy named Bahi's   lit   int
      life at school and at home. Illustrated.

483. _____. Hooghadi ádaa'áháyá. Navajo Reading
          Study, University of New Mexico, Albuquerque,
          New Mexico. 1974, 23 p.

      Tells about the causes of accidents in the home -   lit   int
      playing with matches, etc. Illustrated.

484. Navajo Christian Reading. Jesus baahane'. Navajo
          Christian Reading, Route 1, Box 2F, Cortez,
          Colorado. 1967, 16 p.

      Story of the life of Jesus of Nazareth, in comic   lit   self
      book form. Color illustrations.

146

NAVAJO - MONOLINGUAL, NAVAJO cont'd

485. Navajo Reading Study. Tł'ohchiniji Diné Kéédahat'iinii
baa hane' (The story of the people of Ramah).
Navajo Reading Study, University of New Mexico,
1805 Roma, Northeast, Albuquerque, New Mexico.
1973, 28 p.

A description of Navajo life in times past in   lit   adv
the eastern part of the Navajo reservation.
Also a discussion of the archaeologists who came
to the area to study ancient dwellings in the
area. Illustrated.

486. _____. Tsé nikání hoolyéegi hóóchi' yéę baa hane'
(The Trouble at Round Rock). Navajo Reading
Study, University of New Mexico, 1805 Roma,
Northeast, Albuquerque, New Mexico. 1973, 48 p.

Description of conflicts between Anglos and   lit   adv
Navajos in the Round Rock area as a result of
the introduction of railroads and schools.
Illustrated.

487. Platero, Paul R. Ayóo honishyoi. Navajo Community
College, Chinle, Arizona. 1968, 16 p. (Not
Available - Spolsky ABNRM-102).

Aimed at giving the Navajo student a sense of   lit   inter
self-identity.

488. _____. Diné bizaad bibeeha záanii. Dine Bi'olta'
Association, Navajo Linguistics Workshop,
Massachusetts Institute of Technology, Depart-
ment of Linguistics, Cambridge, Massachusetts.
1972, 62 p. (Not Available - Fasthorse,
Supplement ABNRM, 1974).

Introduction to Navajo syntax for Navajo   synt   adv
speakers.

489. Preston, Scott. 'Ał'ąą dadine'é (Different tribes).
Navajo Reading Study, University of New Mexico,
1805 Roma, Northeast, Albuquerque, New Mexico.
1973, 7 p.

Discussion of Navajo relations with other tribes   lit   adv
of Indians, including exchange of goods and ideas
with Apaches, Comanches, Utes and Pueblos.
Illustrated.

490. _____. Ałki'dą̹ą' 'oozéé' asdjid jiní (It was
told that the Hopi tribe was extinct). Navajo
Reading Study, University of New Mexico, 1805
Roma, Northeast, Albuquerque, New Mexcio. 1973,
7 p.

Retelling of a legend about a Navajo raid upon   lit   adv
Hopi in which all Hopi men were killed and the
women and children were joined to the Navajo
tribe.

NAVAJO - MONOLINGUAL, NAVAJO cont'd

491. Rock Point Bilingual Education Project. Saad hee ahaa
      nitsáhákeesígíí (Words of encouragement, memories
      and thoughts). Rock Point Community School,
      Chinle, Arizona. 1974, 12 p.

      Short writings by various authors, telling about   lit   adv
      how they react to friendship, loneliness, and
      life. Illustrated.

492. Rough Rock Demonstration School. Navajo alphabet
      cards; consonants. Navajo Curriculum Center,
      Rough Rock Demonstration School, Chinle,
      Arizona. 1972.

      Set of 31 letters or letter combinations and   script   prim
      three glottal stops ('), to be used with
      primary grades as introduction to Navajo
      alphabet. On cardboard.

493. Sandoval, Chic. Naabeeho 'at' a a dadine'ii. Navajo
      Reading Study, University of New Mexico, 1805
      Roma, Northeast, Albuquerque, New Mexico. 1973.

      Nine book series in Navajo about different   lit   int
      districts within the reservations. Print is   self
      small. Few illustrations, varying pagination.

494. Sanostee-Toadlena Title VII Project Staff.
      Ádaa'áháyá. Navajo Reading Study, University
      of New Mexico, Albuquerque, New Mexico. 1974,
      16 p.

      Story about all the accidents that befall a   lit   int
      careless and thoughtless young man and the
      people he comes across. Illustrated.

495. _____. Chizh dóó tsin. Navajo Reading Study,
      University of New Mexico, Albuquerque, New
      Mexico. 1973, 10 p.

      Story about gathering and using wood for building   lit   prim
      and for fuel, on the Navajo reservation.

496. _____. Daan Náhásdįį'. Panorama Press, P.O. Box
      15101, Rio Rancho, New Mexico. 1973, 11 p.

      Story about the land and some daily activities   lit   int
      of the Navajo. Illustrated.

497. _____. Ma'ii dóó náshdói baa hane'. Sanostee-
      Toadlena Title VII Project, Panorama Press,
      P.O. Box 15101, Rio Rancho, New Mexcio. 1973,
      11 p.

      Story in Navajo of a coyote and a bobcat. As   lit   int
      usual in coyote stories, the coyote here ends
      up the loser. Illustrated by Jerry Henderson.

NAVAJO - MONOLINGUAL, NAVAJO cont'd

498.   Sanostee-Toadlena Title VII Bilingual Education
        Project Staff. The Navajo alphabet. Title VII
        Bilingual Education Project, Sanostee Boarding
        School, Shiprock, New Mexico. 1973, 34 p.

        Presentation of Navajo alphabet, one letter per   script   prim
        page, with a word illustrating use of that letter   voc
        and a drawing. There are 34 characters in the
        Navajo alphabet.

499.   Sanostee-Toadlena Title VII Project Trainees.
        Na'ahoohaił chi'í. Sanostee-Toadlena Title VII
        Project Trainees, Panorama Press, P.O. Box 15101,
        Rio Rancho, New Mexico. 1973, 28 p.

        Story in Navajo of the "Little Red Hen" who   lit   prim
        wanted help while she made bread. Cat, dog,   int
        pig and goat refuse to help, but then want to
        eat the finished product. Hen won't give them
        any. Illustrations by Jack Schwanke.

500.   Schwanke, Jack H. and Ethelou Yazzie. Behe (Orphan
        lamb). Navajo Curriculum Center, Rough Rock
        Demonstration School, Chinle, Arizona. 1970,
        24 p. (Not Available - Spolsky ABNRM-90).

        Story of a lamb in search of a foster mother.   lit   prim
        Produced in conjunction with a class of 8 year
        old Navajo students. Illustrated with photo-
        graphs.

501.   Silentman, Irene. Chidiłtsooí dóó gólízhii. Navajo
        Reading Study, University of New Mexico, 1805
        Roma, Northeast, Albuquerque, New Mexico. 1973,
        16 p.

        Story in Navajo about a school bus that picks   lit   int
        up its passengers on the way to school -
        including a skunk.

502.   _____. Dah díniighaazh. Navajo Reading Study,
        University of New Mexico, 1805 Roma, Northeast,
        Albuquerque, New Mexico. 1972, 12 p.

        Story in Navajo of a young man who takes some   lit   int
        fry bread that his mother has made. Another
        boy takes it from him, and a dog takes it from
        the second boy.

503.   _____. Jasper. Navajo Reading Study, University
        of New Mexico, 1805 Roma, Northeast, Albuquerque,
        New Mexico. 1971, 5 p.

        Story in Navajo about a boy and his basketball.   lit   prim
        Illustrated by Caryl McHarney.

NAVAJO - MONOLINGUAL, NAVAJO cont'd

504.   Silentman, Irene. Shilééchąą'i. Navajo Reading
          Study, University of New Mexico, 1805 Roma,
          Northeast, Albuquerque, New Mexico. 1973, 8 p.

          Story in Navajo of a pet dog who chases rabbits,   lit   prim
          prairie dogs, birds, and cats, but who is
          frightened by coyotes. Illustrated by Caryl
          McHarney.

505.   Sisco, Wilfred. Deestsin. Panorama Press, P.O. Box
          15101, Rio Rancho, New Mexico. 1973, 20 p.

          Story about the pinon tree and the different   lit   int
          uses of its products, i.e., lumber, fuel, nuts.
          List of words used at back of book. Illustrated.

506.   Southern Baptist Convention. Haa'isha'da 'iidiiltah
          (Let's Read Navajo). Southern Baptist Conven-
          tion Home Mission Board, Atlanta, Georgia.
          1969, 44 p. (ERIC ED035856).

          Beginning text in Navajo. Introduces symbols   voc   prim
          for sounds, words and simple sentences.   script
          Illustrated.

507.   Tsinajinnie, Leroy. Has tįį ts'ó sí. Navajo
          Reading Study, University of New Mexico,
          Albuquerque, New Mexico. 1973, 20 p.

          Humorous story about a horse, a Navajo and a   lit   prim
          coyote. Illustrated.

508.   Tsinajinnie, Stella. Aa' aa'. Navajo Reading
          Study, University of New Mexico, Albuquerque,
          New Mexico. 1974, 28 p.

          Humorous illustrations of words using the   lit   prim
          sound aa'. Illustrated.

509.   _____. Ałk'idáá' bisóodi shiłįį' nít'ee'.
          Navajo Reading Study, University of New Mexico,
          Albuquerque, New Mexico. 1974, 20 p.

          Story of a Navajo girl and her pet pig.   lit   int
          Illustrated.

510.   _____. Bits'áá dóó ho sé lįį í gíí. Navajo
          Reading Study, University of New Mexico, 1805
          Roma, Northeast, Albuquerque, New Mexico (for
          Rock Point Community School, Chinle, Arizona).
          1973, 7 p.

          Description in Navajo of relationship and   lit   prim
          kinship terms.   voc

150

NAVAJO - MONOLINGUAL, NAVAJO cont'd

511. Viers, Gerald. Zhiní yinishyé. Ramah Navajo School
          Board, Incorporated, P.O. Box 248, Ramah, New
          Mexico. 1965, 9 p.

          Story about a little black lamb who finds a   lit   prim
          friend in a sheep dog. Illustrated.

512. Wallace, Laura and Jack H. Schwanke. Akalii choii
          (Sloppy cowboy). Navajo Curriculum Center,
          Rough Rock Demonstration School, Chinle,
          Arizona. 1970, 80 p. (Not Available -
          Spolsky ABNRM-93).

513. _____. Awee chideeldlo (Baby's first laugh).
          Navajo Curriculum Center, Rough Rock Demon-
          stration School, Chinle, Arizona. 1970, 24 p.
          (Not Available - Spolsky ABNRM-94).

          Story of a Navajo baby's first laugh party.   lit   inter
          Illustrated.

514. Wallace, Laura and Dottie Hobsen. Gai bichei. Navajo
          Curriculum Center, Rough Rock Demonstration School,
          Chinle, Arizona. 1971. 15 p. (Not Available -
          Fasthorse Sup. ABNRM, 146).
                                                                  lit   int
          Story about a little Navajo boy who takes
          strange things to school. Illustrated.

515. Wallace, Laura. Navajo alphabet and letter sounds.
          Rough Rock Demonstration School, Navajo
          Curriculum Center, Chinle, Arizona. 1970,
          45 p. (Not Available - Spolsky ABNRM-95).

          Picture alphabet with illustrations of familiar   script   prim
          Navajo objects.

516. Watchman, John. Ałk'idáá' diné yee dahináanii baa
          hane' (The Navajo of Long Ago and their Sources
          of Survival). Navajo Reading Study, University
          of New Mexico, 1805 Roma, Northeast, Albuquerque,
          New Mexico. 1974, 10 p.

          Discussion of seven major sources of food and   lit   adv
          material for Navajos of the past - wild
          animals; corn; pinon; alfalfa, apricots and
          prunes; sheep and cattle, milk, and weaving.
          Illustrated.

517. Wilson, Paul. Tsé nitsaa deez'áhí hoolyéedi tsé
          holónigíí (The names of all the historical
          Buttes in Standing Rock, Arizona). Navajo
          Reading Study, University of New Mexico, 1805
          Roma, Northeast, Albuquerque, New Mexico.
          1974, 24 p.

          Description of the buttes in the vicinity of   lit   adv
          Standing Rock, and their names as related to
          their appearances. Illustrated.

NAVAJO - MONOLINGUAL, NAVAJO cont'd

518.   Yazzie, Emma Jean. Naaldlooshii baa hane. Panorama
          Press, P.O. Box 15101, Rio Rancho, New Mexico
          (for Sanostee-Toadlena Title VII Project).
          ca. 1970, 21 p.

          Book in Navajo about animals. Each animal is   lit   int
          pictured on the recto and a paragraph about
          the animal is on the verso.

519.   _____. Shila'. Navajo Reading Study,
          University of New Mexico, 1805 Roma, Northeast,
          Albuquerque, New Mexico (for Sanostee-Toadlena
          Title VII Project, Navajo Area Office, Bureau
          of Indian Affairs). 1974, 12 p.

          Discussion, in Navajo, of hands and fingers.   lit   prim
          Illustrated with photographs of a child's
          hands.

520.   Yazzie, Etta M. and Paul Yazzie. Ashdla'go shibee
          ákohwiinidzinii. Navajo Reading Study,
          University of New Mexico, 1805 Roma, Northeast,
          Albuquerque, New Mexico (for Sanostee-Toadlena
          Title VII Project, Navajo Area Office, Bureau
          of Indian Affairs). 1974, 12 p.

          Title can be translated as "My five senses."   lit   prim
          Illustrations are pictures of Navajo girl
          investigating her senses. Authors hope this
          work will help Navajo children know the
          importance of the senses in their daily lives.

521.   Yazzie, Etta M. K'os. Panorama Press, P.O. Box
          15101, Rio Rancho, New Mexico. 1973, 16 p.

          Story about clouds. Illustrated.   lit   int

522.   Yazzie, Paul J. Ał'aa' át'éego ádaalya. Panorama
          Press, P.O. Box 15101, Rio Rancho, New Mexico.
          1967, 19 p.

          Discussion in Navajo of shapes of different   lit   prim
          items. Illustrated. Product of Sanostee-
          Toadlena Title VII Project.

523.   Yazzie, Paul J. and Etta. Jóhonaa'éí dóó
          Nahasdzáán. Navajo Reading Study, University
          of New Mexico, Albuquerque, New Mexico. 1974,
          16 p.

          Description of the earth and its place in the   lit   prim
          solar system. Illustrated in color.

NAVAJO - MONOLINGUAL, NAVAJO cont'd

524. Zim, Herbert, S. Translated by Kenneth Y. Pegishe.
      Ha'át'íisha' shighi' hóló ? Navajo Curriculum
      Center, Rough Rock Demonstration School,
      Chinle, Arizona. 1968, 30 p.

      Introduction to anatomy, using Navajo terms   lit   int
      and Navajo models. Illustrated

NAVAJO - MONOLINGUAL, ENGLISH

525. Aragon, Claude, Wallace Cathey. Dan and his pets,
      Books One through Five. Shiprock Independent
      School District, No. 22, New Mexico. 1969,
      227 p. (ERIC ED034635).

      Reading series aimed at acquainting Navajo   voc   elem
      child with basic spelling patterns in English.
      Background of Navajo reservation is used to
      increase reader interest. Illustrated.

526. _____. Dan and his pets, Teacher's manual.
      Shiprock Independent School District, No. 22,
      New Mexico. 1968, 174 p. (ERIC ED034636).

      Teaching procedures to accompany books one   meth   col
      through three of the Dan and his pets series.
      Emphasis on spelling patterns with most
      commonly used consonants and 'short' vowels.

527. Atcitty, Marlene et al. Preparing reading materials
      in Navajo. Navajo Reading Study, University
      of New Mexico, Albuquerque, New Mexico. 1971,
      26 p.

      Discussion of the processes involved in   meth   col
      preparing pilot materials aimed at enabling   theor   self
      Navajo children to read their native language.
      Results of some of experimental use of
      materials.

528. Bureau of Indian Affairs. English as a second
      language on the Navajo reservation; a teacher-
      training program. Bureau of Indian Affairs,
      Department of Interior, Washington, D.C.
      ca. 1968, 16 p.

      Established program explained through lectures   theor   col
      by specialists in related fields - linguistics,   meth
      ESL, psychology, speech, and education.
      Program largely project of Dr. Gina P. Harvey
      and English Department at Colorado State
      University.

NAVAJO - MONOLINGUAL, ENGLISH cont'd

529.   Bureau of Indian Affairs. Enrichment material for
           first and second year language laboratory
           program for "A course in spoken English for
           Navajos." Bureau of Indian Affairs, Brigham
           City, Utah, Instructional Service Center.
           1968, 240 p. (ERIC ED074804).

           Intended for Navajos with a third to seventh   pron   int
           grade reading achievement level. Table of   gram
           contents.   lit

530.   _____. Helpful hints for new BIA teachers.
           Bureau of Indian Affairs, Window Rock, Arizona.
           1969, 54 p. (ERIC ED034601).

           Suggested lesson plans for ESL instruction.   meth   col
           Also contains a discussion of reading diffi-   self
           culties and means of using ESL in reading
           instruction.

531.   Callaway, Sydney M., Gary Witherspoon, et al.
           Grandfather stories of the Navajo. DINE,
           Incorporated, Board of Education, Rough Rock
           Demonstration School, Navajo Curriculum
           Center, Chinle, Arizona. 1968, 77 p. (Not
           Available - Spolsky ABNRM-13).

           Deals with Navajo culture.   lit   int

532.   Carlson, Vada and Gary Witherspoon. Black Mountain
           Boy; a story of the boyhood of John Honie.
           Navajo Curriculum Center, Rough Rock Demon-
           stration School, Chinle, Arizona. 1968, 81 p.

           Story of events that occurred during the child-   lit   int
           hood of a highly respected medicine man. Work
           is intended for use by Navajo students.
           Positive self-image of Indian child is stressed.

533.   Cathey, Wallace. Joe and his happy family, Book
           one and two. Shiprock Independent School
           District No. 22, New Mexico. 1968, 58 p.
           (ERIC ED034637).

           Readers aimed at increasing reading interest   voc   elem
           and English vocabulary among Navajo children.
           Book one depicts life on the reservation, book
           two moves to a town and uses abstract words.

534.   Center for Applied Linguistics. Conference on
           Navajo Orthography. Center for Applied
           Linguistics, English for Speakers of Other
           Languages Program, 1717 Massachusetts Avenue,
           Northwest, Washington, D.C., 1969 16 p. (Not
           Available - Spolsky ABNRM-117).

           Conference proceedings and recommendations   script   col
           on Navajo Orthography.   meth   self

NAVAJO - MONOLINGUAL, ENGLISH cont'd

535.   Center for In-Service Education. But it can't wear
         glasses. Center for In-Service Education,
         P.O. Box 754, Loveland, Colorado. 1974. (Not
         Available).

         Reader designed to illustrate "can-can't"   voc   prim
         distinction. Written and illustrated by
         Navajo students in Tuba City. For grades 1-4.

536.   _____. I am bigger than. Center for In-Service
         Education, P.O. Box 754, Loveland, Colorado.
         1974. (Not Available).

         Reader designed to teach comparisons. Written   gram   prim
         and illustrated by Navajo students in Tuba
         City. For grades 1-4.

537.   CITE, Inc. Bilingual-bidialectal switching strand.
         CITE, Inc., 1081 Gayley, Los Angeles,
         California. 1972, 78 p.

         Ten detailed lesson plans for first grade   pron   prim
         Navajo students. Aim is to show child the   meth
         distinctions among Navajo and two dialects
         of English - formal English (classroom
         English) and the more informal English used
         by Navajo children among themselves (playground
         English). Only English dialogue is provided.
         Methodology included.

538.   _____. Reader: Coyote and Doe. CITE,
         Incorporated, 1081 Gayley, Los Angeles,
         California. 1973, 8 p.

         Navajo tale about coyote being outwitted by   lit   int
         a doe. Illustrated.

539.   _____. Reader: Coyote and Horned Toad. CITE,
         Incorporated, 1081 Gayley, Los Angeles,
         California. 1973, 10 p.

         Navajo story about a horned toad teaching   lit   int
         coyote a lesson.

540.   _____. Reader: Coyote and Crow. CITE,
         Incorporated, 1081 Gayley, Los Angeles,
         California. 1973, 6 p.

         Navajo tale about a crow outwitting coyote.   lit   int
         Illustrated.

NAVAJO - MONOLINGUAL, ENGLISH cont'd

541. CITE, Inc. Reading Strand, Level B, Navajo Unit.
        CITE, Inc., 1081 Gayley, Los Angeles, California.
        1973, 28 p.

        Three detailed lesson plans focusing on three   meth   prim
        traditional Navajo stories. First grade   voc
        reading level.

542. _____. Spelling Book: Comparative of
        Adjectives. CITE, Inc., 1081 Gayley,
        Los Angeles, California. 1974, 19 p.

        Workbook with rules for forming comparisons,   script   int
        spaces for writing comparative forms of given   gram   int
        adjectives, etc. Answers provided at back of
        book. Text discusses Navajo life and land.
        Second grade level.

        For the rest of the CITE materials, see Appendix.

543. Cook, Mary J. and Margaret A. Sharp. Problems of
        Navajo speakers in learning English. Language
        Learning, Vol. 16. 1966, p. 21-29.

        A discussion of the phonological and grammatical   phon   col
        aspects of English most difficult for young   gram   self
        Navajos, with reference to the differences   meth
        between the two languages. Should be of
        considerable use to teachers of ESL.

544. Correll, J. Lee, Editha Watson, and David M. Brugge.
        Navajo bibliography with subject index.
        Navajo Parks and Recreation Research Section.
        Window Rock, Arizona (Revised edition) 2
        volumes. 1969, 394 p.

        A comprehensive, although unannotated,   bibl   self
        bibliography. Subsequent updating planned.
        Subject index compiled from those subjects
        suggested by citation titles and has many
        cross references.

545. _____. Navajo bibliography with subject index.
        Supplement No. 1. Research Report No. 2,
        Research Section, Museum and Research Section,
        The Navajo Tribe, Window Rock, Arizona.
        1973, 122 p.

        First supplement to above bibliography.   bibl   self
        Citations arranged alphabetically by author;
        good subject index.

NAVAJO - MONOLINGUAL, ENGLISH cont'd

546.   Davis, Bertha M. Teaching reading to the bilingual
          child; motivational techniques. Sharing Ideas,
          Vol. 7, No. 6, Arizona State Department of
          Education, Phoenix, Arizona. 1970, 69 p.

       Description of techniques used in teaching   meth   col
       reading of English to Navajo children in   self
       grades K-8. Gives activities and techniques
       for each grade level.

547.   Davis, Ruth et al. A Curriculum guide for beginning
          non-English speaking children. Shiprock -
          Independent School District No. 22, New Mexico.
          1969, 66 p. (Not Available - Nafziger, p. 56).

       Created for the specific needs of the Navajo   meth
       child. Curriculum presents teacher and
       student objectives in five language areas -
       oral English, listening skills, cognitive
       processes, writing readiness and formal
       reading readiness; as well as social studies,
       numbers, science, health and safety, physical
       education and expressive arts. Suggestions are
       given for learning activities, instructional
       materials, and methods of presentation.

548.   Denunzio, Vincent. A Course in spoken English for
          Navajo: first year program. Language
          Laboratory No. I, Bureau of Indian Affairs,
          Washington, D.C. 1967, 559 p. (ERIC ED074803).

       Manual concentrates on phonics and increasing   pron   prim
       skills in spoken English. Prose and poetry are
       incorporated for cultural enrichment. Plans
       for work in language laboratory included.

549.   _____. A Course in spoken English for
          Navajos: second year program. Language
          Laboratory No. II, Bureau of Indian Affairs,
          Washington, D.C. 1967, 429 p. (ERIC ED074802).

       A review of difficult English sounds,   gram   int
       conversational dialogues, and grammar. Prose   pron
       and poetry are included for cultural enrich-
       ment. Plans for work in language laboratory
       included.

550.   Dzilth-Na-O-Dith-Hle Boarding School. Teacher-Aide
          for Navajo Area. Dzilth-Na-O-Dith-Hle
          Boarding School, Bloomfield, New Mexico.
          1970, 219 p. (ERIC ED049844).

       Developed from a workshop for teachers and   meth   self
       aides in Navajo schools. Includes fingerplays,
       songs and games for teaching English as a
       second language, and four original stories to
       teach reading.

NAVAJO - MONOLINGUAL, ENGLISH cont'd

551.   Glendon, Mary Troy. The curious kid. Navajo
          Curriculum Center, Rough Rock Demonstration
          School, Chinle, Arizona. 1971, 16 p. (Not
          Available - Fasthorse, Supplement ABNRM, 156).

          Story of a young goat who learns which things   lit   prim
          he should eat. Illustrated.

552.   _____. Hand Chart Book to accompany The curious
          kid. Navajo Curriculum Center, Rough Rock
          Demonstration School, Chinle, Arizona. 1971,
          22 p. (Not Available - Fasthorse, Supplement
          ABNRM, 157).

          Chart reviewing vocabulary and structure of   voc   prim
          the reader, The Curious Kid. Illustrated.

553.   Gorman, Howard, Scott Preston. Navajo history,
          Vol. I. Navajo Curriculum Center, Rough Rock
          Demonstration School, Chinle, Arizona and
          Navajo Community College Press. 1970, 250 p.
          (Not Available - Spolsky ABNRM-15).

          History of the Navajo people and their lives   lit   self
          in the first, second and third worlds and
          emergence into the present fourth world.
          Illustrated with photographs and drawings.

554.   Hale, Kenneth. Navajo linguistics: Part I, II,
          and III. Massachusetts Institute of Technology,
          Cambridge, Massachusetts. ca. 1965.

          Author believes that Navajo linguistics should   meth   col
          be taught to native speakers of Navajo. He
          feels that introduction of Navajo linguistics
          to Navajo-speaking students early in their
          education "will serve as a means of introducing
          the scientific method to students and will,
          thereby, contribute significantly to their
          educational development." He discusses some
          elements of scientific study of Navajo
          language and suggests how a curriculum of
          Navajo linguistics might be developed.
          Manuscript.

555.   Hoffman, Virginia. Lucy learns to weave:
          gathering plants. Rough Rock Demonstration
          School, Navajo Curriculum Center, Chinle,
          Arizona. 1969, 46 p. (Not Available -
          Spolsky ABNRM-16).

          Controlled vocabulary reader for beginning   lit   elem
          students. Each page illustrated.

NAVAJO - MONOLINGUAL, ENGLISH cont'd

556.   Hoffman, Virginia, Broderick H. Johnson. Navajo
          biographies. DINE, Incorporated and Rough Rock
          Demonstration School, Navajo Curriculum Center,
          Chinle, Arizona. 1970, 342 p. (Not Available -
          Spolsky ABNRM-17).

          Biographies of fifteen Navajo leaders from the
          eighteenth century to present.   hist   self
                                                                          int

557.   Holm, Wayne S. Some aspects of Navajo orthography.
          Doctoral dissertation, University of New
          Mexico. 1972, 370 p. (Not Available -
          Dissertation Abstract #73-870).

          Discussion of written Navajo, the difficulty   pron   col
          native speakers have in reading and writing   script   self
          the language, and the possibility that these
          difficulties might be alleviated by omission
          of all diacritical marks - without loss of
          comprehension.

558.   Intermountain School. Language arts curriculum.
          Intermountain School, Brigham City, Utah.
          1972, 54 p. (ERIC ED079758).

          ESL program for Navajo students. Three levels -   gram   prim
          Low (first to third grade), Medium (fourth to   pron   int
          sixth) and High (seventh and above). Academic   lit
          year broken into quarters, quarters into units
          on grammar, writing, speaking and listening,
          reading and literature.

559.   Kane, Katy. The Language arts portion of the CITE
          curriculum. CITE, Inc., 1081 Gayley, Los
          Angeles, California. 1973, 14 p.

          A description of the various language arts,   meth   self
          strands of the CITE materials, their relation-   theor
          ship to each other, and their contribution to
          the child's education. See entries under CITE,
          Incorporated.

560.   Kari, James. Some suggestions for a university
          program in Navajo linguistics. Navajo Reading
          Study, University of New Mexico, 1805 Roma,
          Northeast, Albuquerque, New Mexico. 1972, 15 p.

          Author discusses literature on the subject of   theor   col
          native speakers of languages as "para-linguists"   meth   self
          in a mutually beneficial relationship between
          a professional linguist and his informant. A
          relationship defined by Kenneth Hale as a
          "reciprocal tutorial". Author hopes this is
          the direction an expanded Navajo program at
          the University of New Mexico will take.
          Manuscript.

NAVAJO - MONOLINGUAL, ENGLISH cont'd

561. Kluckhohn, Clyde and Katherine Spencer. A
          bibliography of the Navajo Indians. A.M.S.,
          New York, 1972, 93 p. (Reprint of J.J.
          Augustin, New York, 1940).

      Precursor of the Correll bibliography above.   bibl   col
      Makes no effort to be comprehensive in each   self
      subject area but provides indexes of many
      government documents. Intended primarily as
      bibliography for anthropologists, so coverage
      of anthropological works is more extensive than
      that of other areas.

562. National Association for the Education of Young
          Children. A Kindergarten curriculum guide for
          Indian children: A bilingual-bicultural
          approach. National Association for the
          Education of Young Children, Washington, D.C.
          1968, 14 p. (Not Available - Nafziger, p. 25).

      A curriculum using the familiar aspects of   meth   prim
      Navajo life, while broadening students'
      experience of larger American culture.
      Curriculum covers language development,
      social interaction, math, music, foods and
      health and safety. Appendices and biblio-
      graphy include enrichment materials.

563. Ohannessian, Sirarpi. Conference on Navajo
          orthography, Albuquerque, New Mexico, May 2-3,
          1969. Center for Applied Linguistics,
          Washington, D.C. 1969, 18 p. (ERIC ED044668).

      Report of a meeting to agree on an orthography   script   self
      for Navajo. Includes recommended script,   col
      discussion of purposes for Navajo writing
      system, and lists of various Navajo alphabets.

      _____. Teaching English to speakers of Choctaw,
      Navajo, and Papago; a contrastive approach.
      Prepared at the Center for Applied Linguistics
      for the Bureau of Indian Affairs. Center for
      Applied Linguistics, Washington, D.C. 1969,
      138 p.

      See under GENERAL/ESL

564. Roessel, Robert A. and Dillon Platero. Coyote stories
          of the Navajo people. Navajo Curriculum Center,
          Rough Rock Demonstration School, Chinle, Arizona.
          1968, 141 p.

      Collected stories from the traditional Navajo   lit   int
      myths about coyote. These stories are only to
      be told during the winter months. Designed for
      use by Navajo children. Illustrated.

NAVAJO - MONOLINGUAL, ENGLISH cont'd

565. Rough Rock Demonstration School. Curriculum guide-
          lines for the skills of English. Rough Rock
          Demonstration School, Chinle, Arizona. 1969,
          133 p. (ERIC ED036389).

      Curricula for preschool, elementary and   prim
      secondary levels, including English skills,   int
      mathematics, social studies, Navajo language,
      and science.

566. Sawyer, Marileta. C and Sid. Navajo Curriculum
          Center, Rough Rock Demonstration School, Chinle,
          Arizona. 1971, 16 p.

      Illustration of sibilant and vowel sounds.   pron   prim
      Short story and page of comprehension ques-
      tions with blanks for answers. Simple illus-
      trations by Troy Glendon.

567. _____. The gink. Navajo Curriculum Center,
      Rough Rock Demonstration School, Chinle,
      Arizona. 1971, 11 p.

      Story introduces "ink" sounds and words that   pron   prim
      use it. On several pages, child is required
      to fill in the desired "-ink" word. Compre-
      hension questions are included. Illustrated
      by Troy Glendon.

568. _____. Mr. Goat's new hogan. Navajo Curriculum
      Center, Rough Rock Demonstration School, Chinle,
      Arizona. 1971, 24 p. (Not Available - Fast-
      horse, Supplement ABNRM, 155).

      Story about a goat who convinces several parties   lit   int
      to help him build his hogan. Sentences are
      carefully structured. Illustrated.

569. _____. Super grape and the ape. Navajo
      Curriculum Center, Rough Rock Demonstration
      School, Chinle, Arizona. 1971, 12 p.

      Short story based on the word "ape" and words   pron   prim
      that rhyme with it. Comprehension questions
      are included. Illustrated by Troy Glendon.

570. Schwanke, Jack H. Close up things. Navajo
          Curriculum Center, Rough Rock Demonstration
          School, Chinle, Arizona. 1970, 24 p. (Not
          Available - Spolsky ABNRM-21).

      Photographic essay on small objects. Simple   lit   elem
      English text.

161

NAVAJO - MONOLINGUAL, ENGLISH cont'd

571. Schwanke, Jack H. Kinalda. Navajo Curriculum Center,
          Rough Rock Demonstration School, Chinle, Arizona.
          1970, 93 p. (Not Available - Spolsky ABNRM-22).

     Story of a Navajo girl's coming of age ceremony.   lit   elem

572. _____. Navajo pottery. Navajo Curriclum Center,
     Rough Rock Demonstration School, Chinle, Arizona.
     1970, 22 p. (Not Available - Spolsky ABNRM-24).

     Describes procedure for making Navajo pottery.   lit   elem
     Illustrated with photographs.

573. _____. Navajo wedding. Navajo Curriclum Center,
     Rough Rock Demonstration School, Chinle, Arizona.
     1970, 60 p. (Not Available - Spolsky ABNRM-25).

     Story of a traditional Navajo wedding.   lit   elem
     Illustrated.

574. Shiprock Independent School District No. 22. Phillip
          and his family. Shiprock Independent School
          District No. 22, New Mexico. 1968, 243 p.
          (ERIC ED035488).

     Teacher's guide for an oral English program   voc   elem
     for non-English speaking pupils. Uses the   gram
     social setting of the Navajo child as a basis   pron
     of discussion and instruction. Bibliography
     of enrichment materials.

575. Shumway, Cherie. Hello, tree. Navajo Curriculum
          Center, Rough Rock Demonstration School, Chinle,
          Arizona. 1971, 19 p. (Not Available -
          Fasthorse, Supplement ABNRM, 154).

     A girl talks to a tree, imagining the things   lit   prim
     she could do with it. Illustrated.

576. Sisco, Wilfred. Mother Nature at work. Center
          for In-Service Education, P.O. Box 754,
          Loveland, Colorado. 1974. (Not Available).

     Reader for grades 1-5. Illustrated.   lit   int

577. _____. My uncle. Center for In-Service
     Education, P.O. Box 754, Loveland, Colorado.
     1974. (Not Available).

     Reader about life on the reservation. For   lit   int
     grades 1-5. Illustrated.

NAVAJO - MONOLINGUAL, ENGLISH cont'd

    Slager, William R. (Editor). Language in American
        Indian education: A newsletter of the Office
        of Education Programs, Bureau of Indian Affairs,
        United States Department of the Interior,
        Albuquerque, New Mexico. Fall 1971, 92 p.

    See under GENERAL/ESL

578. Southern Baptist Convention. Charts and teaching
        helps for Haa'isha'da'iidiiltah (Let's Read
        Navajo) based upon techniques developed by
        Frank C. Lauback. Southern Baptist Convention
        Home Mission Board, Atlanta, Georgia. 1969,
        44 p. (ERIC ED035855).

    Guide for teaching first six lessons of   meth   self
    Haa'isha'Da'Iidiiltah (which see). Notes on
    teaching writing. For use by teachers trained
    in Lauback literacy program and teaching tech-
    niques. See under NAVAJO, Haa'isha'Da'Iidiiltah.

579. Tefft, Virginia J. A physical education guide with
        English language practice drills for teachers
        of Navajo Kindergarten and primary school
        children. University of New Mexico, Albuquerque,
        New Mexico. 1969, 461 p. (ERIC ED038192).

    ESL combined with enjoyable physical exercises.   voc   prim
    Prescribed sentences and vocabulary to
    accompany activities. Report on use of materials
    and evaluation of field study as well as actual
    teaching guides.

580. Trueba, Antonio de. The fox and the wolf. Navajo
        Curriculum Center, Rough Rock Demonstration
        School, Chinle, Arizona. 1970, 18 p.

    Spanish folk tale adapted by Troy Glendon.   lit   int
    Tale of how fox outwits wolf. Intended for
    student with some facility in reading English.
    Illustrated by Andy Tsinajinnie.

581. Wilson, Robert D. Assumptions for bilingual
        instruction in the Primary Grades of Navajo
        Schools. CITE, Incorporated, 1081 Gayley,
        Los Angeles, California. 1973, 38 p.

    A description for the rationale behind the   meth   self
    CITE curriculum. Deals with general questions theor
    of education, the problems of the bilingual/
    bicultural child, and the particular problems
    of the Navajo child. See entries under CITE,
    Incorporated.

NEZ PERCE - BILINGUAL

582. Aoki, Haruo. Nez Perce grammar. University of
        California Publications in Linguistics,
        Berkeley, California. 1970, 168 p.

        An analysis of the "surface structure" of Nez   phon   col
        Perce with sections on Phonology, morphology,   gram
        and syntax. Linguistically oriented.

NIKOLAI

        See UPPER KUSKOKWIM

NISENAN - BILINGUAL

583. Uldall, Hans Jorgen and William Shipley. Nisenan
        texts and dictionary. University of California
        Publications in Linguistics #46, Berkeley,
        California. 1966, 282 p.

        Work begun by Uldall and completed by Shipley.   lit   self
        Seventy-one stories are presented. Each text   voc
        appears in Nisenan and in English. Dictionary
        is Nisenan-English and English-Nisenan, with
        longer and more complete entry under former.

OJIBWA - BILINGUAL

584. Baraga, Friedrich. A Dictionary of the Otchipwe
        language, explained in English. Ross and
        Haines, Incorporated, Minneapolis, Minnesota,
        1966, 422 p. (Reprint of publication by
        Beauchemin and Valoris, Montreal, 1878).

        First section is English/Ojibwa, second section   phon   self
        Ojibwa/English. Note original date of   voc
        publication.   bibl

585. Minnesota State Department of Education. Ojibwe
        language: a course for elementary schools,
        plus visual aids. State of Minnesota, Department
        of Education, Division of Instruction, Elementary
        and Secondary Section, Foreign Language Unit,
        St. Paul, Minnesota. 1974, 114 p. and 70
        pictures.

        Lesson plans to accompany audio tapes in   voc   prim
        beginning Ojibwa. Divided into three levels: pron   int
        Grades 1-2, Grades 3-4, Grades 5-6. Drawings
        provided to illustrate lessons. Progresses
        from single words to short conversations.

OJIBWA - BILINGUAL cont'd

586. The Nishnawbe News. Organization of North American
          Indian Students, Editorial Offices, Room 140,
          University Center, North Michigan University,
          Marquette, Michigan. Monthly issues from
          November 1973 - Fall 1975.

      Monthly review of national, local and tribal   voc   self
      news from the Indian students at North Michigan
      University. Each issue includes an article on
      learning the Ojibwa-Ottawa language.

587. Todd, Evelyn M. A Grammar of the Ojibwa language:
          The Severn dialect. Ph.D. dissertation,
          University of North Carolina at Chapel Hill.
          1970, 308 p. (Not Available - Dissertation
          Abstract #71-3606).

      Linguistic analysis of a dialect spoken in the   gram   col
      interior of northwestern Ontario. Paper also   desc
      includes a general description of this dialect
      and its relationship to the other dialects of
      Ojibwa.

588. Wilson, Edward Francis. Ojebway language: a manual
          for missionaries and others employed among the
          Ojebway Indians. Indian Affairs and Northern
          Development, Ottawa. 1970, 412 p. (Reprint of
          publication by Roswell and Hutchinson for the
          Venerable Society for Promoting Christian
          Knowledge, London, 1874).

      A manual of grammar with paradigms, dialogues,   gram   self
      and exercises, with a large English-Ojebway   voc
      dictionary. Note intended audience and original
      date of publication. Cross references.

OJIBWA - MONOLINGUAL, OJIBWA

589. Ontario Region, DIAND. Ocipe tipačimohin (Trans-
          literated from Ojibwa syllabary by KLA)   Lake-of-
          the-Woods dialect .   Ontario Region Department
          of Indian and Northern Affairs, Toronto
          Ontario. 1973, 32 p. (Not Available).

      A book of stories for beginning readers.

OJIBWA

      see also CHIPPEWA

OMAHA - BILINGUAL

590. Thompson, James D. and Elmer Blackbird. The Omaha-
        Ponca language in writing: suggestions for a
        practical orthography. Manuscript, Department
        of Linguistics, University of Kansas, Lawrence,
        Kansas. 1974, 27 p.

Attempt to develop a practical means of writing these two closely related Siouan languages. Includes a rationale for the need of writing a language, detailed description of phonology. Suggested orthography is presented with Omaha-Ponca words using each sound and English equivalents where available. A sample text in Omaha-Ponca with English translation included. Appendices include a list of linguistic terms used, lexicon of words in sample text.	script self phon col voc

ONONDAGA - BILINGUAL

591. Chafe, Wallace L. A semantically based sketch of
        Onondaga. Indiana University Publications in
        Anthropology and Linguistics, Memoir #25,
        1970, 91 p. (Not Available).

OTTAWA

    See OJIBWA

PATUANEK

    See CHIPEWYAN

PAIUTE

    Pietroforte, Alfred. Songs of the Yokuts and Paiutes.
        Naturegraph Publishers, Healdsburg, California.
        1965, 63 p.

    See under YOKUTS

PAPAGO - BILINGUAL

592. Alvarez, Albert. Appendix to a new perspective on
          American Indian linguistics. New Perspectives
          on the Pueblos, School of American Social
          Research Book, University of New Mexico Press,
          Albuquerque, New Mexico. 1972, pp. 111-133.

       Discussion of various grammatical aspects of   gram   col
       Papago. Article is aimed at linguists and/or   self
       people with some knowledge of the Papago
       language. Could be very helpful for those who
       are trying to learn the finer points of
       distinction in Papago speech.

593. Alvarez, Albert with Kenneth Hale. ?O?edham Ñé?oki
          ha-káidag (The Sounds of Papago). Manuscript.
          1969, 111 p. (Not Available - CAILC Newsletter,
          Vol. I, No. 2, p. 13).

594. Mathiot, Madeleine. A dictionary of Papago usage,
          Vol. 1 B-K. Research Center for the Language
          Sciences, Indiana University, Bloomington,
          Indiana. 1973, 504 p.

       Dialect used as basis of dictionary is Totoguañ,   voc   self
       but variant forms from other dialects are   gram   (col)
       included as they were available to author.
       Included are a grammar of Papago and a Papago-
       English dictionary covering letters B through K.
       Introduction explains how to use dictionary.
       Dictionary is intended for non-native speakers
       of Papago, without linguistic background.
       However, text is rather dense and demands a
       high level of competency in English.

595. Pancho, Jose and Madeleine Mathiot. Coyote and the
          Quails. In William Slager (Editor), Language
          in American Indian Education, Bureau of Indian
          Affairs, Albuquerque, New Mexico. Spring 1972,
          pp. 106-109.

       Story about coyote being hoodwinked by some   lit   adv
       quail. Papago version presented on verso with
       English translation on recto. Text is presented
       in numbered sentences for ready comparison to
       translation.

PAPAGO - BILINGUAL cont'd

596.   Saxton, Dean and Lucille Saxton. Dictionary: Papago
       and Pima to English, O' odham - Mil- gahn -
       English. University of Arizona Press, Tucson,
       Arizona. 1969, 191 p.

           In addition to the dictionaries there are five   voc   self
           appendices: Appendix I discusses alphabet of   script
           Papago and Pima, Appendix II discusses use of   gram
           dictionary, Appendix III discusses grammar of   desc
           Papago and Pima, Appendix IV lists some technical
           terms and illustrations (calendars, medical and
           sociological terms), and Appendix V discusses
           different dialects of Papago and Pima as well
           as related languages. Detailed entries in
           dictionaries with cross references.

597.   Saxton, Dean and Lawrence Hogan (Compilers). Our
       book T-O'hana Nuesto libro and vocabulary.
       San Xavier Mission School, Tucson, Arizona.
       1969, 14 p. (Not Available - Nafziger, p.39).

           Stories about everyday life situations written   lit   prim
           in Papago, Spanish and English by first and   voc
           second grade students at San Xavier Mission
           School. Vocabulary section gives English
           translation of Papago and Spanish words.
           Illustrated.

PAPAGO - MONOLINGUAL, ENGLISH

       Ohannessian, Sirarpi. Teaching English to speakers
       of Choctaw, Navajo, and Papago; a contrastive
       approach. Prepared at the Center for Applied
       Linguistics for the Bureau of Indian Affairs.
       Center for Applied Linguistics, Washington, D.C.
       1969, 138 p.

       See under GENERAL ESL

PASSAMAQUODDY - MONOLINGUAL, PASSAMAQUODDY

 598. Wabnaki Bilingual Education Program. Akonutomuwin
       (Tell me a story). Wabnaki Bilingual Education
       Program, Indian Township, Maine. 1974, 12 p.
       (Not Available).

           Four traditional Passamaquoddy stories.   lit
           Illustrated.

PASSAMAQUODDY - MONOLINGUAL, PASSAMAQUODDY cont'd

599. Wabnaki Bilingual Education Program. Amucalu (The
      Fly). Wabnaki Bilingual Education Program,
      Indian Township, Maine. 1973, 8 p.

      Traditional story of an encounter between a fly   lit   prim
      and an elderly woman. Illustrated with drawings
      and photographs.

600. _____. Ehem (The Hen). Wabnaki Bilingual
      Education Program, Indian Township, Maine.
      1973, 8 p. (Not Available).

      Short story, illustrated.   lit

601. _____. Opan opu aponok (The bread is in the
      oven). Wabnaki Bilingual Education Program,
      Indian Township, Maine. 1973, 8 p. (Not
      Available).

      Short story, illustrated.   lit

602. _____. Neqt, tapu, sis: 1, 2, 3 (Numbers book).
      Wabnaki Bilingual Education Program, Indian
      Township, Maine. 1974, 24 p. (Not Available).

603. _____. Mus naka wikuwossol (The moose and his
      mother (The Earth)). Wabnaki Bilingual Education
      Program, Indian Township, Maine. (Not Available).

      Traditional Passamaquoddy story. Illustrated.   lit

604. _____. Mali naka tahahsumol (Mary and her
      horse). Wabnaki Bilingual Education Program,
      Indian Township, Maine. 1973, 8 p. (Not
      Available).

      Short story, illustrated   lit

605. _____. Mahtoqehs naka Malsom (Rabbit and Wolf).
      Wabnaki Bilingual Education Program, Indian
      Township, Maine. 1974, 10 p.

      Traditional animal story, illustrated with   lit   adv
      drawings.

606. _____. Kukec (The game warden). Wabnaki
      Bilingual Education Program, Indian Township,
      Maine. 1974, 12 p. (Not Available).

      Short story, illustrated.   lit

607. _____. Espons ali ehemuhke (The Racoon goes
      chickening). Wabnaki Bilingual Education
      Program, Indian Township, Maine. 1973, 8 p.
      (Not Available).

      Short story, illustrated.   lit

PASSAMAQUODDY - MONOLINGUAL, PASSAMAQUODDY cont'd

608. Wabnaki Bilingual Education Program. Eli
        posonutekhotimok (How they make baskets).
        Wabnaki Bilingual Education Program, Indian
        Township, Maine. 1973, 8 p. (Not Available).   lit

609. _____. Ehtaste likotok (Every year - seasonal
        activities). Wabnaki Bilingual Education
        Program, Indian Township, Maine. 1974, 20 p.
        (Not Available).

        Description of Passamaquoddy food, crafts and   lit
        oral tradition. Illustrated.

610. _____. Ehpit (The Woman). Wabnaki Bilingual
        Education Program, Indian Township, Maine.
        1973, 8 p. (Not Available).

        Short story, illustrated.   lit

611. _____. Sisqeyal (Eyeglasses). Wabnaki
        Bilingual Education Program, Indian Township,
        Maine. 1974, 16 p. (Not Available).

        Short story, illustrated.   lit

612. _____. Skinuhsis naka sipsis (The Boy and the
        bird). Wabnaki Bilingual Education Program,
        Indian Township, Maine. 1973, 8 p. (Not
        Available).

        Short story, illustrated.   lit

613. _____. Susehp naka kohusumol (Joseph and his
        cow). Wabnaki Bilingual Education Program,
        Indian Township, Maine. 1973, 8 p. (Not
        Available).

        Short story, illustrated.   lit

614. _____. Tan ktolomolsin? (How do you feel?).
        Wabnaki Bilingual Education Program, Indian
        Township, Maine. 1974, 28 p. (Not Available).

        Stories to finish, for practice in writing
        Passamaquoddy.

615. _____. Wonakine (Let us rise - Passamaquoddy
        songs for dancing). Wabnaki Bilingual
        Education Program, Indian Township, Maine.
        1974, 12 p. (Not Available).

        Words and music to Passamaquoddy songs.   lit
        Illustrated.

PASSAMAQUODDY

See also MALECITE-PASSAMAQUODDY

PAWNEE - BILINGUAL

616.   Densmore, Frances. Pawnee music. Reprint Da Capo
        Press, New York. 1972, 129 p. (Reprint of
        publication by U.S. Government Printing Office,
        Washington, D.C., 1929).

        Transcription of eighty-six songs, including   lit   self
        game songs, ceremonial songs, and society songs.
        Text explains context of songs. Lyrics are
        given in Pawnee with literal English translation.

PIMA - BILINGUAL

617.   Bahr, Donald, Juan Gregorio, David Lopez and Albert
        Alvarez. Piman shamanism and staying sickness.
        University of Arizona Press, Tucson, Arizona.
        1974, 332 p.

        Anthropological text on Piman theory of   lit   self
        sickness and curing. Contains texts of several   col
        curing rituals presented in Pima and English.
        Introduction gives pronunciation guide to Pima
        texts.

        Saxton, Dean and Lucille Saxton. Dictionary: Papago
        and Pima to English, O' odham - Mil-ghan; English
        to Papago and Pima, Mil-gahn - English.
        University of Arizona Press, Tucson, Arizona.
        1969, 191 p.

        See under PAPAGO

POMO - BILINGUAL

618.   Moshinsky, Julius B. Southeastern Pomo grammar.
        Ph.D. dissertation, University of California,
        Berkeley, California. 1970, 253 p. (Not
        Available - Dissertation Abstracts #71- 15,846).

        Grammatical sketch in two sections - one a   phon   col
        phonology of Pomo, the other a morphological   gram
        analysis of the language. Linguistically
        oriented.

PONCA - BILINGUAL

Thompson, James D. and Elmer Blackbird. The Omaha-
Ponca language in writing. Manuscript,
Department of Linguistics, University of Kansas,
Lawrence, Kansas. 1974, 27 p.

See under OMAHA

SALISH - BILINGUAL

619.   Carlson, Barry F. A Grammar of Spokan: A Salish
language of eastern Washington. Doctoral
Dissertation, University of Hawaii. 1972,
164 p. (Not Available - Dissertation Abstract
#72- 31,052).

Linguistic description of the language spoken   phon   col
on the Spokane Indian reservation. Includes   gram
phonology, morphophonemics and grammar.

620.   Kruege, John R. Miscellanea Selica IV; an interim
Moses' Columbia (Wenatchee) Salishan vocabulary.
Anthropological Linguistics, Indiana University,
Bloomington, Indiana. 1967, Vol. 9, Part 2,
p. 5-11.

Brief list of words in the Wenatchee Salishan   voc   self
dialect. Words are arranged by category, e.g.
human society, animals. English version
precedes Salishan word.

Pilling, James Constantine. Bibliography of the
Salishan languages. AMS Press, New York.
1973, 86 p.

See under Pilling under GENERAL LANGUAGES

621.   Snyder, Warren A. Southern Puget Sound Salish:
phonology and morphology. Sacramento Anthropological Society Publication #8, Sacramento
State College, California. 1968, 83 p.

Linguistic study of sound system and word   phon   col
formation in this dialect of Salish.

SALISH - BILINGUAL cont'd

622. Snyder, Warren A. Southern Puget Sound Salish
         texts, place names, and dictionary. Sacramento
         Anthropological Society Publication #9,
         Sacramento State College, Sacramento,
         California. 1968, 199 p.

         Twenty stories presented in both Salish and   lit   self
         English. Paragraphs numbered with Salish   voc
         version on verso, English on recto. This
         section comprises bulk of work. Suquamish
         place names are presented in eight page section,
         including map of this area of Washington. Last
         Section is Salish-English, English-Salish
         dictionary with most complete entries in former.

623. Thompson, Laurence and M. Terry Thompson. Clallum:
         a preview. In Studies in American Languages,
         Jesse Sawyer (Editor), University of California
         Publications in Linguistics No. 65. 1971,
         p. 251-294.

         Description of a local dialect of Straits   phon   col
         Salish. Includes phonology, morphophonemics,   gram
         syntax and morphology. Linguistically oriented.

SAULTEAUX - BILINGUAL

624. Gallerneault, Bob and Les Cook. Elementary Saulteaux.
         Indian and Northern Curriculum Resources Center,
         University of Saskatchewan, Saskatoon,
         Saskatchewan, Canada. ca. 1972. (Not Available).

         Pictures of animals and other items with Saulteaux   voc   prim
         and English labels. Designed for young children.

SEMINOLE - BILINGUAL

     Pilling, James Constantine. Bibliography of the
         Muskogean languages. AMS Press, New York.
         1973, 114 p.

     See Pilling under GENERAL LANGUAGES

625. Seminole Bilingual Project. Estowen netty momen nere
         tekvpihoc vhvks. (How night and day were divided).
         Seminole Bilingual Project, East Central
         University, Ada, Oklahoma. 1973, 11 p.

         Seminole legend presented in Seminole at the   lit   int
         top of each page, with English version at bottom
         of the page. Illustrated as a coloring book.

173

SEMINOLE - BILINGUAL cont'd

626.   Seminole Bilingual Project. Nakcokv yvlunkv enhake,
        Seminole phonics I. Seminole Bilingual Project,
        East Central University, Ada, Oklahoma. 1974,
        25 p.

        Introduces written phonemes of Seminole with   phon   prim
        words using these sounds and pictures illus-   script
        trating these words. Instructions in English.

627.   _____. Seminole calendar. Seminole Bilingual
        Project, East Central University, Ada,
        Oklahoma. Published annually, 24 p.

        Names of months, days of week and holidays in   lit   self
        Seminole, with some English translations.
        Illustrated.

SEMINOLE - NOT KNOWN

628.   Seminole Bilingual Project. Cokv eskerretv semvhayetv
        svhokkolat, Seminole phonics II. Seminole
        Bilingual Project, East Central University,
        Ada, Oklahoma. 1974, 30 p. (Not Available).

629.   _____. Cufe horkopv, Why the rabbit is a
        thief. Seminole Bilingual Project, East Central
        University, Ada, Oklahoma. 1973, 16 p. (Not
        Available).

        Coloring book.

630.   _____. Locv, eco tentokorkvtes, The Terrapin
        race. Seminole Bilingual Project, East Central
        University, Ada, Oklahoma. 1973, 32 p. (Not
        Available).

        Coloring book.

631.   _____. Ohhonvyetv cokv. Seminole Bilingual
        Project, East Central University, Ada,
        Oklahoma. 1973, 16 p. (Not Available).

        Second grade reader.   prim

632.   _____. Ohhonvyetv cokv svtuteenat. Seminole
        Bilingual Project, East Central University,
        Ada, Oklahoma. 1973, 14 p. (Not Available).

        Third grade reader.   int

633.   _____. Seminole ahunkvtkv semhayetv, Number
        readiness workbook I. Seminole Bilingual
        Project, East Central University, Ada,
        Oklahoma. 1973, 21 p. (Not Available).

SEMINOLE - NOT KNOWN cont'd

634. Seminole Bilingual Project. Lesson plans for
      kindergarten through third grade, Vol. 1-4.
      Seminole Bilingual Project, East Central
      University, Ada, Oklahoma. 1973-1974, 38 p.
      (Not Available).

635. _____. Seminole haiku. Seminole Bilingual
      Project, East Central University, Ada,
      Oklahoma. 1974. (Not Available).

636. _____. Seminole songbook. Seminole Bilingual
      Project, East Central University, Ada,
      Oklahoma. 1974. (Not Available).

637. _____. Vpuekv. Seminole Bilingual Project,
      East Central University, Ada, Oklahoma. 1973,
      16 p. (Not Available).

      First grade reader.   prim

SEMINOLE

    See also MUSKOGEAN

SENECA - BILINGUAL

638. Blueye, Esther. Seneca language· Oh' - Kwe-O-Weh-Kha.
      Tonowanda Indian Reservation, Basom, New York.
      1970.

      No title page, but attributed to Ms. Blueye in   voc   prim
      Jones' bibliography of the Seneca language (see
      below). Several pictures of objects with Seneca
      word for each object below picture. Manuscript.

639. _____. Seneca today: a contemporary language
      textbook and cultural reader. Developed under
      the auspices of the Chief Council at the
      Tonowanda Indian Reservation, Basom, New York.
      ca. 1970, 17 p.

      Explanation of phonology and grammar of dialect   phon
      of Seneca spoken on the Tonowanda Reservation.   gram

SENECA - BILINGUAL cont'd

640. Chafe, Wallace L. Seneca morphology and dictionary.
        Smithsonian Press, Washington, D.C. (For sale
        by Superintendent of Documents, United States
        Government Printing Office). 1967, 126 p.

        Basically "an extended description of the   desc   self
        structure of words in the Seneca language.   voc
        Expressed purpose is to make available a Seneca   gram
        dictionary. Introduction contains paragraphs
        about grammar of Seneca. Dictionary is
        arranged from Seneca to English, with an
        English index.

641. Sanders, Jean (Editor). Talking Smoke. Seneca
        Tribal Council, Oncheota, New York. Weekly
        issues from January 1, 1971 - December 30, 1974.

        Weekly review of national, local and tribal   lit   self
        news, from Seneca viewpoint. Each issue
        includes at least one article in Seneca.

SENECA - MONOLINGUAL, ENGLISH

        Hale, Horatio Emmons (Editor). Iroquois book of
            rites. University of Toronto Press, Toronto,
            Second edition. 1965, 222 p.

        See under IROQUOIS

642. Jones, Helen Bimmer. Bibliography: Seneca language.
            1972, 2 p.

        Manuscript prepared for CED 108, Comparative   bibl   self
        Native Languages, taught in Winter Quarter of
        1972 at UCLA. Council on Educational
        Development.

SERRANO - BILINGUAL

643. Hill, Kenneth. A grammar of the Serrano language.
            Doctoral dissertation, Linguistics, University
            of California at Los Angeles. 1967, 283 p.

        Detailed linguistic description of the structure   morph   col
        of the language. Unfortunately, Serrano is
        spoken by fewer than a dozen people at present.

SHOSHONE - BILINGUAL

644. Crapo, Richley H. Language Variation Among the
        Duckwater Shoshoni. Ph.D. dissertation,
        University of Utah. 1970, 103 p. (Not
        Available - Dissertation Abstract #71-923).

        Discusses the large amount of phonetic and   voc   col
        grammatical variation among individual speakers   phon
        of Shoshone, and possible causes for these   gram
        differences. Possibly of use to non-speaker of
        Shoshone who is disconcerted by encountering
        these variations.

645. Miller, Wick R. Newe natekwinappeh: Shoshoni stories
        and dictionary. University of Utah Press, Salt
        Lake City. 1972, 172 p.

        Stories written in English and in Shoshoni.   lit   self
        Shoshoni stories are written in a "non-technical"   voc
        alphabet (as opposed to a phonetic alphabet),   gram
        to assure that the Indian reader will find this   phon
        work understandable and useful. Dictionary is
        from Shoshoni to English with a brief English
        index. Introductory paragraphs contain some
        detail about the Shoshoni alphabet, sound
        system and grammar.

646. Pabweena, Rosie. Two-Headed Antelope. In William
        Slager (Editor), English for American Indians,
        Bureau of Indian Affairs. Washington, D.C.
        1971, pp. 69-71.

        Legend of ancient times presented first in   lit   adv
        Shoshone then in English.

647. Tidzump, Malinda. Shoshone thesaurus. Summer
        Institute of Linguistics, University of North
        Dakota, Grand Forks, North Dakota. 1970, 52 p.

        A word list compiled to help young Shoshones   voc   self
        relearn their native language. Words are listed   pron
        by subject: e.g., world, plants, animals, body.
        Format is Shoshone-English. List of "handy
        phrases" at end of book. Pronunciation guide
        precedes word list. Not linguistically oriented.

SHUSWAP - BILINGUAL

648. Gibson, James Albert. Shuswap grammatical structure.
      Doctoral dissertation. University of Hawaii.
      1973, 144 p. (Not Available - Dissertation
      Abstract #73- 28, 799).

      Linguistic description of language spoken on   phon   col
      Naskanlith Reserve in British Columbia.   gram
      Description is presented in four parts:
      phonology, morphophonemics, morphology and
      syntax.

SIBERIAN YUPIK - MONOLINGUAL, YUPIK

649. Apassingok/Imingan/Omwari/Toolie/Badten. Ayumiim
      ungipaghaatangi I (Stories of long ago I).
      University of Alaska, Alaska Native Language
      Center, Fairbanks, Alaska. 1972, 33 p. (Not
      Available).   adv

650. Badten, L. Atightughyuggaaghusit (First reader).
      University of Alaska, Alaska Native Language
      Center, Fairbanks, Alaska. 1974, 30 p. (Not
      Available).   prim

651. _____. Atightuusim aallghi (Second (Another)
      reader). University of Alaska, Alaska Native
      Language Center, Fairbanks, Alaska. 1974, 67 p.
      (Not Available).   prim

652. Kaneshiro, V. Ayumiim ungipaghaatangi II (Stories
      of long ago II). University of Alaska, Alaska
      Native Language Center, Fairbanks, Alaska.
      1974, 38 p. (Not Available).   adv

653. _____. Lataput (Our letters). University of
      Alaska, Alaska Native Language Center, Fairbanks,
      Alaska. 1973, 24 p. (Not Available).   prim

654. _____. Naatvamun pilghiit (Going to the lake).
      University of Alaska, Alaska Native Language
      Center, Fairbanks, Alaska. 1974, 26 p. (Not
      Available).   prim

655. _____. Pingayut kaviighhaat (The three little
      foxes). University of Alaska, Alaska Native
      Language Center, Fairbanks, Alaska. 1973,
      17 p. (Not Available).   adv

SIBERIAN YUPIK - MONOLINGUAL, YUPIK cont'd

656. Kaneshiro, V. Qungluk liillghii pugimammeng
         (Qungluk learns to swim). University of
         Alaska, Alaska Native Language Center,
         Fairbanks, Alaska. 1974, 50 p. (Not Available).   . prim

657. _____ Unkusequlghiik (Going to see the fox
         traps). University of Alaska, Alaska Native
         Language Center, Fairbanks, Alaska. 1974, 21 p.
         (Not Available).   prim

658. Oozevaseuk, E. and E. Apatiki. Sivuqam neghyugnall-
         ghan yataaghqellghan igii (St. Lawrence Island
         delicacy recipe book). University of Alaska,
         Alaska Native Language Center, Fairbanks,
         Alaska. 1973, 10 p. (Not Available).   adv

659. Otayahak, J. and L. Badten. Otayahuk Ungazimi
         (Otayahuk in Ungaziq). University of Alaska,
         Alaska Native Language Center, Fairbanks,
         Alaska. 1973, 14 p. (Not Available).   adv

SIBERIAN YUPIK - NOT KNOWN

660. Badten, Adelina (Translator). Analgaam qikmii.
         Alaska Native Language Center, University
         of Alaska, Fairbanks, Alaska. 1973, 20 p.
         (Not Available).

661. Badten, Adelina. Atightumerq liinnagellghet I, II.
         Alaska State Language Center, University of
         Alaska, Fairbanks, Alaska. 1973. (Not
         Available).

662. Badten, Adelina (Translator). Ayumiim ungipaghaatangi
         I. Alaska Native Language Center, University
         of Alaska, Fairbanks, Alaska. 1972, 33 p.
         (Not Available).

663. Badten, Adelina. Goldilock sallu pingayutlu kaynget.
         Alaska State Language Center, University of
         Alaska, Fairbanks, Alaska. 1972, 50 p. (Not
         Available).

664. Badten, Adelina (Translator). Ighsanitalghii
         afsengaq. Alaska State Language Center,
         University of Alaska, Fairbanks, Alaska. 1972,
         22 p. (Not Available).

665. _____. Kulusiinkut. Alaska State Language
         Center, University of Alaska, Fairbanks, Alaska.
         1972, 28 p. (Not Available).

SIBERIAN YUPIK - NOT KNOWN cont'd

666. Badten, Adelina (Translator). Kulusiq. Alaska State
         Language Center, University of Alaska, Fairbanks,
         Alaska. 1972, 18 p. (Not Available).

667. _____. Sallghet. Alaska State Language Center.
         University of Alaska, Fairbanks, Alaska. 1972,
         25 p. (Not Available).

668. Gologergen, Ora (Translator). Qepgh aghaqukut
         naghaaghaqukut. Alaska State Language Center,
         University of Alaska, Fairbanks, Alaska. 1972,
         25 p. (Not Available).

669. Kaneshiro, Vera, Sharon Orr and David Shinen.
         Atightumum liinnaqusit. Alaska State Language
         Center, University of Alaska, Fairbanks, Alaska.
         1973. (Not Available).

670. Kaneshiro, Vera and David Shinen. Pata, ama ilangi.
         Summer Institute of Linguistics, P.O. Box 1028,
         Fairbanks, Alaska. 1973. (Not Available).

671. _____. Patankut (Pata and others). Summer
         Institute of Linguistics, P.O. Box 1028,
         Fairbanks, Alaska. 1973. (Not Available).

672. Oozeva, Elinor and David Shinen, translators.
         Kiyahta7ha Jesus Christ-m (The life of Jesus
         Christ). Eibel-mission, Dr. Kurt Koch, 7502
         Berghausen, Germany. 1970, 91 p. (Not
         Available - Kraus, CTL, p. 1353).

673. Shinen, David and Marilene Shinen. Yopigun atihtoosi
         (Workbook). Summer Institute of Linguistics,
         P.O. Box 1028, Fairbanks, Alaska. 1966. (Not
         Available).

674. Shinen, Marilene R. and David C. Shinen. Yopiguston
         momihkokat ilagaatut (Hymnal). Fairbanks, 1969,
         56 p. (Not Available - Kraus, CTL, p. 1359).

SIBERIAN YUP'IK

      See also YUP'IK AND ESKIMO

SIOUAN

    see WINNEBAGO, CROW, OMAHA, SIOUX

    Pilling, James C. Bibliography of the Siouan
        languages. AMS Press, New York. 1973, 87 p.

        See Pilling under GENERAL LANGUAGES

SIOUX - BILINGUAL

675. Buechel, Eugene. A dictionary of the Teton Sioux
       language (Lakota dialect). Red Cloud Indian
       School, Pine Ridge, South Dakota. 1970, 820 p.

       Basically a Lakota-English, English-Lakota   voc   self
       dictionary. Also included is a short sketch of   desc
       the Sioux tribe, a guide to use of dictionary,   gram
       grammar summary and some appendices dealing
       with the Sioux nation.

676. Bushotter, George. Ghost story number one (Lakota
       dialect). In William Slager (Editor), Language
       in American Indian Education, Bureau of Indian
       Affairs, Albuquerque, New Mexico. Fall 1971,
       p. 81-83.

       Explanation of relations between living people   lit   self
       and ghosts. Story is presented first in Lakota   adv
       then in English.

677. Densmore, Frances. Teton Sioux music. Da Capo Press,
       New York. 1972, 561 p. (Reprint of publication
       of Smithsonian Institution, Bureau of American
       Ethnology, Bulletin 61, 1918).

       Analysis of the music of the Teton Sioux and   lit   self
       its place in the Teton culture. Considerable
       ethnographic information. Songs are presented
       with musical scoring and words in Lakota.
       English translation is provided. Illustrated
       with photographs.

678. Grant, Paul Warcloud. Sioux Indian dictionary
       (Dakota dialect). State Publishing Company,
       303 East Sioux, Pierre, South Dakota. 1971,
       192 p.

       Aim of work is to preserve language for native   voc   self
       speakers and to provide information for non-   pron
       speakers. Format is English-Dakota, with Lakota
       variants given where known to author. Explana-
       tion of phonetic system employed precedes word
       list. Lists of Dakota months, bands, and names
       of other tribes follow. Not linguistically oriented.

SIOUX - BILINGUAL cont'd

679. Karol, Joseph S. (Editor). Everyday Lakota: an
        English-Sioux dictionary for beginners (Lakota
        dialect). Nebraska Curriculum Development
        Center, University of Nebraska, Lincoln. 1971,
        123 p.

        Dictionary developed to help English speakers   voc   prim
        learn Lakota. Written for teachers of bilingual/   gram   self
        bicultural programs. "Conversation Guide" with
        phrases and idioms such as months of years,
        numbers. Also short section on grammar of Lakota.

680. Oglala Sioux Culture Center. Ehanni ottunkakan.
        Curriculum Materials Resource Unit, Red Cloud
        Indian School, Incorporated, Pine Ridge, South
        Dakota; Black Hills State College, Spearfish,
        South Dakota. 1973, 197 p. (ERIC ED073860).

        Instructional material for ninth grade Oglala   lit   adv
        Sioux. Three sets of stories - (1) Creation
        stories, (2) Stories of ancient times, (3)
        Historical stories. Stories are lessons in
        manners, religion, social behavior.

681. Paige, Harry W. The songs of the Teton Sioux.
        Westernlore Press, Los Angeles. 1970, 201 p.

        Presents a brief history of the Sioux, followed   lit   self
        by chapters on the purpose and nature of song in   gram
        a "primitive" society. Different chapters
        discuss individual's songs, ceremonial songs
        and modern songs. Songs are presented within
        text, with Lakota version beside English trans-
        lation. First appendix given an extremely
        cursory sketch of Lakota grammar.

682. University of Colorado. Lahkota project.
        University of Colorado, Boulder, Colorado.
        1972, 121 p.

        Series of five lessons, plus a summary and   voc   col
        review for the beginning learner of Lahkota.   pron   prim
        Pronunciation drills, an introduction to grammar   gram
        and vocabulary are covered. Meant to be used
        with a tape and/or an instructor.

683. Working Indians Civil Association. An English-Dakota
        dictionary. Wascium ka Dakota riska wowape
        (Dakota dialect). Fort Pierre, South Dakota.
        1969, 264 p.

        Dictionary "to aid all people in their quest of   voc   self
        Indian Culture in its true form and practice."   gram
        The introductory pages present Dakota alphabet,   script
        grammar of Dakota and its parts of speech.

SIOUX - MONOLINGUAL, ENGLISH

684. Damron, Rex. An Educational model for planned inter-
      vention in language development. Black Hills
      State College, Spearfish, South Dakota. 1971,
      15 p. (ERIC ED084060).

      Description of a psycholinguistic program in   meth   col
      language learning conducted in kindergarten
      classes of Sioux children. Evaluation and
      suggestions for use included.

      Minnesota Historical Society. Chippewa and Dakota
      Indians; a subject catalog of books, pamphlets,
      periodicals, and manuscripts in the Minnesota
      Historical Society. St. Paul, Minnesota. 1969.

      See under CHIPPEWA

685. Powers, William K. The Language of the Sioux. In
      William Slager (Editor), Language in American
      Indian Education, Bureau of Indian Affairs,
      Albuquerque, New Mexico. Spring 1972, pp. 1-21.

      Description of the differences among the various   desc   self
      Sioux dialects. Also provided is a bibliography   bibl
      of books and articles about the Sioux and in
      Sioux.

686. Webster, Loraine. The Creation of stories and
      beginning reading material for preschool Indian
      children in South Dakota. Final Report. South
      Dakota University, Vermillion, South Dakota.
      1972, 48 p. (ERIC ED062080).

      Report on two sets of simple books - "Read Aloud   meth   self
      Stories" and "Rebus Reading Book Series,"   bibl   col
      designed to improve children's command of English.
      Includes overview of the books and their
      preparation, evaluation of the books, lists of
      resource materials and bibliographies used in
      book preparation.

687. _____. Rebus reading book series: A product of
      a project to create stories and beginning
      reading material for preschool Indian children
      in South Dakota. South Dakota University,
      Vermillion, South Dakota. 1972, 178 p. (ERIC
      ED062082).

      Series of ten booklets, each containing a story   lit   prim
      adapted from an Indian folk tale. Books are   voc
      intended for use as supplementary readers.
      Illustrated.

SLAVEY - BILINGUAL

> Canada, Department of Information. Elementary
> education in the Northwest Territories; A
> handbook for Curriculum development.
> Curriculum Division, Department of Education,
> Northwest Territories, Canada. ca. 1970, 313 p.
>
> See under GENERAL/ESL

SPOKANE - BILINGUAL

688. Carlson, Barry F. At Colville: A story in the
      Spokane language. Rawhide Press, The Spokane
      Tribal Council, Box 652, Wellpinit, Washington.
      January 1974, Vol. IV, No. 9, p. 8-9.

      A story about the raising of children in the   lit   self
      Spokane language and translated into English.
      Includes a pronunciation key.

689. Reulhlinger (Editor). Rawhide Press. Spokane Tribal
      Council, Box 652, Wellpinit, Washington. Monthly
      issues from August 1975 - December 1975.

      Monthly review of local and tribal news from   voc   self
      the Spokane viewpoint. Each issue includes one   phon
      article on learning the Spokane language.

SPOKANE

   see also SALISH

SQUAMISH - BILINGUAL

690. Kuipers, Aert Hendrik. The Squamish language, Vol. I
      and Vol. II, Mouton, The Hague, Netherlands.
      1967, 1969, 515 p.

      Includes grammatical breakdown of Squamish,   voc   col
      Squamish/English dictionary, and Squamish texts   gram
      presented in native language and in translation.   lit
      Linguistically oriented.

      Snyder, Warren A. Southern Puget Sound Salish texts,
      place names and dictionary. Sacramento
      Anthropological Society, Sacramento State
      College, Sacramento, California. 1968, 199 p.

      See under SALISH

TANACROSS

    See TANANA

TANAINA - BILINGUAL

691. Kalifornsky, P. and J. Kari. Ch'enlahi sukdu (The
        Gambling story). University of Alaska, Alaska
        Native Language Center, Fairbanks, Alaska.
        1974, 10 p. (Not Available).

        English text interlinear with Tanaina text.   lit   adv

TANAINA - NOT KNOWN

692. Kalifornsky, Peter and James Kari. K'eła sukdu
        (Mouse Story). Alaska Native Language Center,
        Center for Northern Educational Research,
        University of Alaska, Fairbanks, Alaska. 1974.
        (Not Available).

693. Kari, James. Kenai Tanaina noun dictionary. Alaska
        Native Language Center. Center for Northern
        Educational Research, University of Alaska,
        Fairbanks, Alaska. 1974. (Not Available).

TANANA - BILINGUAL

694. The River Times. Fairbanks Native Association,
        Fairbanks Native Center, 102 Lacey Street.
        Monthly, January 1972, Vol. III, No. 1, p. 10.

        This issue of the newspaper contains an untitled   voc   self
        article in the Upper Tanana language.

695. _____. Fairbanks Native Association, Fairbanks
        Native Center, 102 Lacey Street. Monthly,
        March 12, 1974, Vol. III, No. 1, p. 4.

        This issue contains an untitled article on the   voc   self
        Minto dialect of Tanana.   lit

TANANA - NOT KNOWN

696. Denny, Annie and Mildred Jonathan. Medenildiy (Touch
        it) (Tanacross dialect). Summer Institute of
        Linguistics, P.O. Box 1028, Fairbanks, Alaska.
        1973. (Not Available).

TANANA - NOT KNOWN cont'd

697. Jimerson, Shirley David   Diphthongs in Upper Tanana
     (Flashcards) (Upper Tannana dialect). Alaska
     Native Education Board, 4510 International
     Airport Road, Anchorage, Alaska. 1974. (Not
     Available).

698. _____. Vowels in Upper Tanana (Flashcards)
     (Upper Tanana dialect). Alaska Native Education
     Board, 4510 International Airport Road,
     Anchorage, Alaska. 1974. (Not Available).

699. McLellan, Kathy and Annie Denny. Gah gaay ch'etnel' i̧
     (Little Rabbit hiding) (Tanacross dialect).
     Summer Institute of Linguistics, P.O. Box 1028,
     Fairbanks, Alaska. 1973. (Not Available).

700. McRoy, Nancy. Gah nt'ih (Tanacross dialect). Alaska
     Native Language Center, Center for Northern
     Educational Research, University of Alaska,
     Fairbanks, Alaska. 1973. (Not Available).

701. Milanowski, Paul G. Uusii dinaht·l'aa' I (Reader I)
     (Upper Tanana dialect). Summer Institute of
     Linguistics, P.O. Box 1028, Fairbanks, Alska.
     1965. (Not Available).

702. _____. Uusii dinaht·l'aa' II (Reader II) (Upper
     Tanana dialect). Summer Institute of Linguistics,
     P O. Box 1028, Fairbanks, Alaska. 1965. (Not
     Available).

703. Milanowski, Paul and Fred Demit. Gah kol (Trans-
     lation and adaptation of Gah kol) (Upper Tanana
     dialect). Summer Institute of Linguistics,
     P.O. Box 1028, Fairbanks, Alaska. 1974. (Not
     Available).

704. _____. Gah ndee? (Translation and adaptation
     of Gah nt'ih?) (Upper Tanana dialect). Summer
     Institute of Linguistics, P.O. Box 1028,
     Fairbanks, Alaska. 1974. (Not Available).

705. Milanowski, Paul and Alfred John. Billy Aanda
     (Translation and adaptation of Nuk'ankut)
     (Upper Tanana dialect). Summer Institute of
     Linguistics, P.O. Box 1028, Fairbanks, Alaska.
     1972. (Not Available).

706. _____. Nts'ąą' duhdii̧' (Translation and adapta-
     tion of Cacirkat) (Upper Tanana dialect).
     Summer Institute of Linguistics, P.O. Box 1028,
     Fairbanks, Alaska. 1972. (Not Available).

TANANA - NOT KNOWN cont'd

707. Milanowski, Paul, Jessie Ervin and Rosa Charlie.
      Ts'eht'uudn dinaht/'aa' (Bird book) (Upper
      Tanana dialect). State-Operated School System,
      650 International Airport Road, Anchorage,
      Alaska. 1973. (Not Available).

TEWA - BILINGUAL

708. Speirs, Randall H. Report on Tewa portion of
      trilingual program at San Juan Elementary
      School, 1971-72. 1972, 9 p. (ERIC ED069447).

      Guides for teaching oral and written Tewa to   meth   prim
      native grades 1-6. Includes evaluation of   eval
      program's effectiveness and suggestions for
      future programs.

TLINGIT - BILINGUAL

      Dall, W.H. et al. Languages of the tribes of the
      extreme Northwest - the Aleutians and adjacent
      territories. Shorey Book Store, Seattle,
      Washington. 1970, 47 p. (Reprint from
      Contributions to American Ethnology, Vol. 1,
      Washington, D.C. 1877).

      See under INDIANS OF SUBARCTIC

709. Dauenhauer, Nora (Editor). Doo goojee yéenaadei
      (Tlingit language workshop reader). Tlingit
      Readers, Box 25, Alaska Methodist University,
      Anchorage, Alaska. 1972, 59 p.

      Explanation in English of how to use the Tlingit   lit   adv
      writing system, followed by a series of short
      Tlingit speeches and stories, and translations
      of English poetry and religious texts.

710. Davis, Henry A. Kéet. Sitka Printing Company, Sitka,
      Alaska. 1973, 14 p.

      Tlingit legend of the creation of the killer   voc   int
      whale, told in English with Tlingit words as   lit
      captions to illustrations.

711. _____. Kéet, Teaching Unit. Tlingit Readers,
      Sheldon Jackson College, Sitka, Alaska. 1973,
      23 p.

      Teaching unit to accompany reader - Kéet.   voc   int
      Includes Tlingit language lessons with teacher-
      student dialogues, and science lessons about
      killer whales.

TLINGIT - BILINGUAL cont'd

712. Hoonah High School Students. Woosh yáx yaa datúwch -
      Tlingit math book. Tlingit Readers, Incorporated,
      Sheldon Jackson College, Sitka, Alaska. 1973,
      19 p.

      Arithmetic workbook with word problems in Tlingit.   voc   int
      Glossary of Tlingit words used with English   lit
      translation at end of book. Illustrated.

713. James, Susie (transcribed by Nora Dauenhauer). Sít
      kaa káx Kana.áa (Glacier Bay history). Tlingit
      Readers, Box 25, Alaska Methodist University,
      Anchorage, Alaska. 1973. 28 p.

      Text in Tlingit, including several songs. Note   lit   adv
      in English follows, explaining some of the phonic   phon
      variations in the songs.

714. Johnson, Frank (transcribed by Nora Dauenhauer).
      Dukt'ootl' (Strong man). Tlingit Readers,
      Box 25, Alaska Methodist University, Anchorage,
      Alaska. 1973, 28 p.

      Text in Tlingit, followed by brief explanation   lit   adv
      of sound system, with examples in English and   phon
      Tlingit (with English translation). Also a   voc
      list of words in Tlingit for reading practice.

715. Peter, Tom. Xóotsx X'ayakuwdligadee Shaawát (Bear
      Husband). Tlingit Readers, Eskimo, Indian and
      Aleut Printing Company, Fairbanks, Alaska.
      1973, 32 p.

      Text in Tlingit, followed by brief explanation   lit   adv
      of sound system, with examples in English and   phon
      Tlingit. Also list of words in Tlingit for   voc
      reading practice.

716. Story/Naish. Tlingit verb dictionary. University of
      Alaska, Alaska Native Language Center, Fairbanks,
      Alaska. 1973, 386 p. (ERIC ED113932).

      English-Tlingit, Tlingit-English verb dictionary.   voc   self
      Tlingit-English section is arranged alphabetically   gram
      by Tlingit verb stem, with verbal expressions
      including that stem following. Appendix contains
      grammar sketch concentrating on verb morphology.

TLINGIT - MONOLINGUAL, TLINGIT

717. Zuboff, Robert. Transcribed by Henry Davis and
        Students at Sheldon Jackson . Kudatan kahidee
        (The Salmon box). Tlingit Readers, Box 25,
        Alaska Methodist University, Anchorage, Alaska.
        1973, 17 p.

        Story and song.   lit   int

718. _____. Transcribed by Richard Dauenhauer .
        Táax'aa (Mosquito). Tlingit Readers, Box 25,
        Alaska Methodist University, Anchorage, Alaska.
        1973, 14 p.

        Story.   lit   int

TLINGIT - MONOLINGUAL, ENGLISH

719. Krause, Aurel. Translated by Erna Gunther. The Tlingit
        Indians; results of a trip to the northwest
        coast of American and the Bering Straits.
        University of Washington, Seattle. 1970, 310 p.
        (Original date of publication, 1885).

        Chapter 14 of this work discusses the language   voc   self
        of the Tlingit. There are several pages on the   pron
        alphabet, pronunciation, dialects. literature   desc
        in the Tlingit language, nouns, pronouns, verbs,
        adjectives, numbers and time reckoning. There
        is a vocabulary list and names of specific
        animals, plants, birds, etc.

TLINGIT - NOT KNOWN

720. Dauenhauer, Richard. Tlingit spelling book. Tlingit
        Readers, Box 25, Alaska Methodist University,
        Anchorage, Alaska. 1974. (Not Available).

721. Florendo, Nora and Richard Dauenhauer. First year
        Tlingit I-VI. Alaska State Language Center,
        University of Alaska, Fairbanks, Alaska.
        1972-73, 80 p. (Not Available).

TONKAWA - BILINGUAL

722.   Hoijer, Harry. Tonkawa texts. University of
           California Press, Berkeley, California. 1972,
           106 p.

       Collection of myths and tales in English and in   lit   self
       Tonkawa. They are divided into two parts: night
       stories and old stories. Text appears fist in
       Tonkawa and second in English.

TUSCARORA - BILINGUAL

723.   Fickett, Joan. The phonology of Tuscarora. in
           Studies in Linguistics, Southern Methodist
           University, Dallas, Texas. 1967, Vol. 19,
           pp. 33-57.

       A linguistic study of the Tuscarora sound system.   phon   col
       At the end of the article is a brief English-   voc   self
       Tuscarora word list, and a bibliography of   bibl
       printed materials on Tuscarora.

724.   Williams, Marianne Mithun. A grammar of Tuscarora.
           Doctoral dissertation, Yale University. 1974,
           310 p. (Not Available - Dissertation Abstract
           #74- 26,360).

       Linguistic discussion of Iroquoian language of   phon   col
       western New York state. Description covers   gram
       phonology and morphology, but concentrates on
       grammar.

UPPER KUSKOKWIM - BILINGUAL

725.   The River Times. Fairbanks Native Association,
           Fairbanks Native Center, 102 Lacey Street,
           Fairbanks, Alaska. Monthly, March 1974, Vol.
           III, No. 3, p. 4.

       This issue of the newspaper contains an untitled   voc   self
       article on the Upper Kuskokwim language.   lit

UPPER KUSKOKWIM - MONOLINGUAL, UPPER KUSKOKWIM

726. Alaska State-Operated School System. Yada uzaze⁄ts'on
(What can you hear?) (Nikolai dialect). Alaska
State-Operated School System, 650 International
Airport Road, Anchorage, Alaska. 1974, 34 p.

Series of answers to the title question, using   voc   prim
sounds from the Alaskan environment, e.g.,
snowmobile, goose. Workbook section in back
of book. Illustrated.

727. _____. Yada uzaze⁄ts'on? (What can you hear?)
(Nikolai dialect). Alaska State-Operated School
System, 650 International Airport Road,
Anchorage, Alaska. 1974, 72 p.

Twelve short stories about sounds two   lit   int
Athabaskan boys hear. Illustrated.

UPPER KUSKOKWIM - NOT KNOWN

728. Collins, Raymond and Sally Jo Collins. Dinak'i.
Summer Institute of Linguistics, Box 1028,
Fairbanks, Alaska. 1966. (Not Available).

729. _____. Dinak'i ch'its'utozre 1 (Reader 1).
Summer Institute of Linguistics, Box 1028,
Fairbanks, Alaska. 1966. (Not Available).

730. _____. Dinak'i chi'its'utozre 2 (Reader 2).
Summer Institute of Linguistics, Box 1028,
Fairbanks, Alaska. 1970. (Not Available).

731. _____. Dinak'i chi'its'utozre 3 (Reader 3).
State-Operated School System, 650 International
Airport Road, Anchorage, Alaska. 1973. (Not
Available).

732. _____. Nen⁄an hineyash ch'uzaze⁄ts'on (Initial
consonants of Upper Kuskokwim Athabaskan).
State-Operated School System, 650 International
Airport Road, Anchorage, Alaska. 1973. (Not
Available).

733. _____. Sam (Translation and adaptation of
Nuk'ankut). State-Operated School System, 650
International Airport Road, Anchorage, Alaska.
1972. (Not Available).

UPPER KUSKOKWIM - NOT KNOWN cont'd

734. Collins, Raymond L., Sally Jo Collins and the Nikolai
        Bilingual Teachers. Duhtot'il (Things you can
        do, translation and adaptation of Cacirkat).
        State-Operated School System, 650 International
        Airport Road, Anchorage, Alaska. 1973. (Not
        Available).

735. Dennis, Helen. Dotron' nonot'ok (Translation and
        adaptation of Raven gets fooled). State-
        Operated School System, 650 International
        Airport Road, Anchorage, Alaska. 1973. (Not
        Available).

736. _____. Tok'e shisr (Translation and adaptation
        of the Three bears). State-Operated School
        System, 650 International Airport Road,
        Anchorage, Alaska. 1973. (Not Available).

737. Petruska, Betty. Aesop kwnja' (Translation and
        adaptation of the Frog and the mouse and Why
        the bear has a short tail). State-Operated
        School System, 650 International Airport Road,
        Anchorage, Alaska. 1973. (Not Available).

738. Petruska, Betty and Mary Ellen Petruska. Tinde
        hwkwnja (Translation and adaptation of Tendi's
        canoe). State-Operated School System, 650
        International Airport Road, Anchorage, Alaska.
        1973. (Not Available).

UPPER TANANA

    See TANANA

UTE - BILINGUAL

739. Green, John (Translator). A Trip to the Sundance.
        In William Slager (Editor), Language in American
        Indian Education, Bureau of Indian Affairs,
        Albuquerque, New Mexico. Fall 1971, p. 86-87.

        Brief description of a trip to an intertribal   lit   self
        Sundance. Presented first in Ute, then in
        English.

UTE - BILINGUAL cont'd

740. Wardie, Hazel. Uncompahgre Ute words and phrases.
      Western History Center, University of Utah,
      Salt Lake City, Utah. 1969, 34 p.

      Basically a vocabulary of Ute words. Some   voc   self
      pronunciation symbols are given as a preface   pron
      to English-Uncompahgre Ute dictionary.   lit
      Appendices list animals, birds, colors, family
      relationships, food and some parts of speech.
      There also are some conversational phrases listed,
      and a short section on stories and legends.
      The work is amateur and should be used with care.

UTO-AZTECAN - MONOLINGUAL, ENGLISH

741. Grimes, J. Larry. A bibliography of the Uto-Aztecan
      languages. University of Texas Press, Austin,
      Tecas. 1966, 32 p.

      Bibliography of documents in English and Spanish   bibl   self
      from as early as 1732 and up to 1965. Of parti-
      cular interest are specific sections dealing
      with various aspects of specific languages
      such as Hopi and Shoshoni. No index.

UTO-AZTECAN

      see also CAHUILLA, LUISENO, HOPI, SHOSHONE, UTE

WALAPAI - BILINGUAL

742. Redden, J.E. Walapai I: phonology. International
      Journal of American Linguistics. 1966, Vol. 32,
      p. 1-16.

      Linguistic analysis of sound system of this   phon   col
      Yuman language.

743. Winter, Werner. Yuman languages II: Wolf's son - A
      Walapai text. International Journal of American
      Linguistics. 1966, Vol. 32, No. 1, p. 17-40.

      A brief outline of Walapai phonology and   lit   col
      morphophonemic changes is followed by the
      text - with Walapai version presented line by
      line, broken into morphological units. Each
      line of text is followed by literal English
      translation.

WAPPO - BILINGUAL

744.   Sawyer, Jesse O. English-Wappo dictionary.
         University of California Publications in
         Linguistics #43, Berkeley, California, 1965,
         128 p.

         At time of publication there were only four   voc   self
         native speakers of Wappo. Introductory para-
         graphs explain some of sounds of Wappo. Author
         lists Wappo-English affixes needed for analyzing
         sequences of Wappo words.

WINNEBAGO - BILINGUAL

745.   Radin, Paul. The Winnebago tribe. University Press,
         Lincoln, Nebraska, 1971, 511 p. (Reprint of
         publication by Bureau of American Ethnology,
         Washington, D.C.   1923).

         Work contains some examples of Winnebago   voc   self
         language, but little explanation of grammar or
         usage. Textual material that is in Winnebago
         deals with "clan war-bundle feasts." Large part
         of book is devoted to history and social organi-
         zation of the Winnebago Indians.

WISHRAM - BILINGUAL

         Pilling, James Constantine. Bibliography of Chinookan
           languages. AMS Press, New York. 1973, 81 p.

         See Pilling under GENERAL LANGUAGES

746.   Sapir, Edward   Wishram texts. AMS Press, New York.
         1974, 235 p. (Reprint of publication by
         E.J. Bull, Leyden. 1909).

         Collection of myths, descriptions of cultural   lit   self
         activities, letters and narratives. Wishram
         and English on facing pages. In 1909 there
         were 150 living speakers of the Upper Chinnokan
         dialect. Texts are preceded by a key to
         phonetic system employed in transcribing
         Wishram.

YAKIMA - BILINGUAL

747. Pandosy, Reverend M.C. Grammar and dictionary of the
          Yakima language. AMS Press Incorporated, New
          York. 1970, 59 p. (Reprint of publication by
          Cramoisy Press, New York. 1962).

          Grammatical sketch of Yakima language, including   voc   self
          verb paradigms. Lord's prayer in Yakima, and a   gram
          song composed in Yakima by the author, are   lit
          followed by a brief English to Yakima dictionary.
          Note original date of publication.

YAQUI - BILINGUAL

748. Lindenfeld, Jacqueline. Yaqui syntax. University
          of California Publications in Linguistics #76,
          University of California Press, Berkeley,
          California. 1973, 162 p.

          Linguistic study of Yaqui, intended for use by   synt   col
          linguists, but likely to be of some help to   gram
          non-linguist with some knowledge of Yaqui.

YOKUTS - BILINGUAL

749. Newman, Stanley. Yokuts. Lingua, 1967. Vol. 17,
          p. 182-199.

          Linguistic sketch of this California language.   morph   col
          Focuses on morphology and grammar.

750. Pietroforte, Alfred. Songs of the Yokuts and
          Paiutes. Naturegraph Publishers, Healdsburg,
          California. 1965, 63 p.

          English text with musical notation and phonetic   lit   self
          transcription of native langauge lyrics to
          24 songs. Songs are not translated.

YUMAN

      See DIEGUENO and WALAPAI

YUP'IK - BILINGUAL

751.   Afcan, Paschal, Irene Reed and Eskimo Language
         Workshop. Ella iquilnguq (The Universe)
         (Central dialect). Eskimo Language Workshop,
         Department of Linguistics and Foreign Languages,
         University of Alaska, Fairbanks, Alaska. 1972,
         37 p.

         Discussion in Yup'ik of climate, weather and   lit   int
         cosmology. Has Yup'ik-English glossary at
         back of book. Illustrated.

752.   Reed, E. Irene (Compiler). List of materials
         developed by the Eskimo Language Workshop,
         Department of Linguistics and Foreign Languages,
         University of Alaska, Fairbanks, Alaska. 1974,
         10 p. (ERIC ED093184).

         Materials for levels kindergarten through third   bibl   self
         in Yup'ik and English. List includes teachers'
         handbooks, instructional materials and teaching
         aids.

753.   Travers, Ruth et al. Iqalluanek iqsalriit (Smelt
         fishing) (Twin Hills dialect). Alaska State-
         Operated Scnools, Anchorage, Alaska. 1974,
         32 p.

         Reader prepared by third and fourth grade Yup'ik   lit   int
         students. Yup'ik text is beside illustration,
         English translation on reverse side of picture
         page.

YUP'IK - MONOLINGUAL, YUP'IK

754.   Afcan, Paschal. Avelngayagaq kameksiigka-llu (The
         Little mouse and my boots) (Central dialect).
         Eskimo Language Workshop, University of Alaska,
         Fairbanks, Alaska. 1972, 21 p.

         Two short whimsical stories. Illustrated.   lit   int

755.   _____. Iqmik Ingaq Paymyuq'Llu (Snuffy, Eye-
         patch and Tail) (Central dialect). Eskimo
         Language Workshop, University of Alaska,
         Fairbanks, Alska. 1972, 44 p.

         Stories about three dogs. Illustrated.   lit   int

756.   _____. Napam cuyaa (Tree-leaf) (Central dialect).
         Eskimo Language Workshop, University of Alaska,
         Fairbanks, Alaska. 1972, 13 p.

         Story about a tree and the life of one leaf on   lit   int
         that tree as the seasons pass. Illustrated.

YUP'IK - MONOLINGUAL, YUP'IK cont'd

757. Afcan, Paschal. Qimalleq (Central dialect). Eskimo
      Language Workshop, University of Alaska,
      Fairbanks, Alaska. 1972, 20 p.

      Translation and adaptation of Peter Rabbit,   lit   int
      illustrated.

758. _____. Uqumeyak (Pesky little mouse) (Central
      dialect). Eskimo Language Workshop, University
      of Alaska, Fairbanks, Alaska. 1971, 15 p.

      Story about an adventurous and mischievous mouse.   lit   int
      Illustrated.

759. Afcan, Paschal and Marie Blanchett (Translators and
      adapters). Angulan Kegeluneq-llu (Peter and the
      Wolf) (Central dialect). Eskimo Language
      Workshop, University of Alaska, Fairbanks,
      Alaska. 1972, 21 p.

      Russian story of Peter and the Wolf adapted to   lit   int
      Eskimo culture and environment. Illustrated.

760. Afcan, Paschal L. and Irene Reed. Qaneryarat
      ayagnerita nepait (The Sounds that begin words)
      (Central dialect). Eskimo Language Workshop,
      Department of Linguistics and Foreign Languages,
      University of Alaska, Fairbanks, Alaska. 1972,
      68 p.

      Letters beginning words are introduced on recto   voc   prim
      with illustrations of words beginning with that
      letter. Words themselves are on verso.

761. Afcan, Paschal, Irene Reed and Eskimo Language
      Workshop Staff. Cat anerteqellriit; unguvalriit
      naunraat-llu (Living things; animals and plants)
      (Central dialect). Eskimo Language Workshop,
      Department of Linguistics and Foreign Languages,
      University of Alaska, Fairbanks, Alaska. 1972,
      39 p.

      Discussion of various classes of living things   int
      including birds, mammals, plants. English
      glossary at end of book. Illustrated.

762. Andersen, Hans Christian. Translated and adapted by
      Martha Teeluk. Kumluc'kaq (Little Thimble)
      (Central dialect). Eskimo Language Workshop,
      University of Alaska, Fairbanks, Alaska. 1973,
      32 p.

      Story of Thumbelina retold in an Eskimo   lit   int
      environment. Illustrated.

YUP'IK - MONOLINGUAL, YUP'IK cont'd

763. Breiby, John. Translated by Paschal Afcan and Marie
     Nick. Taqukaq qanganaq-llu(The Bear and the
     squirrel) (Central dialect). Eskimo Language
     Workshop, Department of Linguistics and Foreign
     Languages, University of Alaska, College, Alaska.
     1971, 50 p.

     Whimsical animal story about a very human bear   lit
     and his squirrel neighbors. Illustrated.

764. Eastman, P.D.   Translated and adapted by Paschal
     Afcan. Aanakamken-qaa? (Are you my mother?)
     (Central dialect). Eskimo Language Workshop,
     University of Alaska, College, Alaska. 1971,
     57 p.

     Amusing story about a baby bird who hatches,   lit   prim
     falls from his nest and goes out looking for
     his mother. Illustrated.

765. Eskimo Language Workshop Members. Yuarutet (Central
     dialect). Eskimo Language Workshop, Department
     of Linguistics and Foreign Languages, University
     of Alaska, Fairbanks, Alaska. 1972, 22 p.

     Various familiar songs (Happy Birthday, Three   lit   self
     Blind Mice, etc.) in Central Yup'ik with musical
     scoring and guitar chords.

766. Joe, Anna Rose. Tukutukuaraller (The Common snipe)
     (Central dialect). Eskimo Language Workshop,
     University of Alaska, College, Alaska. 1971,
     22 p.

     Traditional Eskimo story about a snipe.   lit   int
     Illustrated.

767. Kein, Geri. Translated by Paschal Afcan. Qanganacuar
     (Little squirrel) (Central dialect). Eskimo
     Language Workshop, University of Alaska,
     Fairbanks, Alaska. 1973, 19 p.

     Whimsical story about a squirrel who gathers   lit   int
     pine cones at great risk. Illustrated.

768. Mather, Elsie. Qessanquq avelngaq (The Lazy mouse)
     (Central dialect). Eskimo Language Workshop,
     University of Alaska, Fairbanks, Alaska. 1973,
     18 p.

     Story about a field mouse's adventure inside a   lit   int
     house. Illustrated.

YUP'IK - MONOLINGUAL, YUP'IK cont'd

769. Teeluk, Martha. Translated by Marie N. Blanchett.
      Naaqiyugngaunga cali (I can read) (Central
      dialect). Eskimo Language Workshop, University
      of Alaska, Fairbanks, Alaska. 1973, 67 p.

      Series of five short stories about children's   lit   int
      lives in the arctic. Included are games, food
      gathering activities. Illustrated.

770. Teeluk, Martha. Nuk'ankut (Nuk'aq's family) (Central
      dialect). Eskimo Language Workshop, University
      of Alaska, College, Alaska. 1971, 23 p.

      Story about a young Eskimo boy, his family and   lit   prim
      their daily activities. Illustrated.

771. Teeluk, Martha and Marie N. Blanchett. Nuk'aq (Central
      dialect). Eskimo Language Workshop, University
      of Alaska, College, Alaska. 1971, 13 p.

      Story about an Eskimo boy and his dog.   lit   prim
      Illustrated.

772. Toyukak, Mary. Qangqiirenkuk iggiayuli-llu (The
      Ptarmigan and the owl) (Central dialect).
      Eskimo Language Workshop, University of Alaska,
      Fairbanks, Alaska. 1972, 10 p.

      Dialogue between a partridge and an owl.   lit   prim
      Illustrated.

YUP'IK - NOT KNOWN

773. Afcan, Paschal. Alrakum qupai (The four seasons).
      Eskimo Language Workshop, University of Alaska,
      Fairbanks, Alaska. 1971, 64 p. (Not Available -
      Kraus, CTL, p. 1329).

774. _____. Amirlucuar (Little cloud). Eskimo
      Language Workshop, University of Alaska,
      Fairbanks, Alaska. 1971, 24 p. (Not Available).

775. _____. Angalgaam qimugtai (Pat's dogs). Eskimo
      Language Workshop, University of Alaska,
      Fairbanks, Alaska. 1971, 25 p. (Not Available).

776. _____. Canek amllernek nallunritua (I know
      many things). Eskimo Language Workshop,
      University of Alaska, Fairbanks, Alaska. 1971,
      14 p. (Not Available).

YUP'IK - NOT KNOWN cont'd

777. Afcan, Paschal. Cat assikek'nganka (The things I
        like). Eskimo Language Workshop, University
        of Alaska, Fairbanks, Alaska. 1971, 30 p. (Not
        Available).

778. _____. Cikemyaq (Blinky). Eskimo Language
        Workshop, University of Alaska, Fairbanks,
        Alaska. 1972, 26 p. (Not Available).

779. _____. Egacuyiit Kenurraita Tanqiit (The Twinkle
        of the Little Spirits lights). Eskimo Language
        Workshop, University of Alaska, Fairbanks,
        Alaska. 1974, 34 p. (Not Available).

780. _____. Erenerput (Our day). Eskimo Language
        Workshop, University of Alaska, Fairbanks,
        Alaska. 1971, 28 p. (Not Available - Kraus,
        CTL, p. 1330).

781. Afcan, Paschal (Translator). Goldilocksaaq pingayun-
        llu taqukaat (Goldilocks and the three bears).
        Eskimo Language Workshop, University of Alaska,
        Fairbanks, Alaska. 1971, 46 p. (Not Available).

782. _____. Kameksagka (My mukluks). Eskimo
        Language Workshop, University of Alaska,
        Fairbanks, Alaska. 1971, 10 p. (Not Available -
        Kraus, CTL, p. 1330).

783. Afcan, Paschal (Translator and adapter). Kavirliq
        Nacacuar (Little Red Riding Hood). Eskimo
        Language Workshop, University of Alaska,
        Fairbanks, Alaska. 1972, 20 p. (Not Available).

784. Afcan, Paschal (Translator). Kul'tilakessaaq
        pingayun'llu taqukaat. Eskimo Language
        Workshop, University of Alaska, Fairbanks,
        Alaska. 1974. (Not Available).

785. _____. Nayirculeriik (Seal hunt). Eskimo
        Language Workshop, University of Alaska,
        Fairbanks, Alaska. 1971, 10 p. (Not Available -
        Kraus, CTL, p. 1330).

786. _____. Nunamtni (In our village). Eskimo
        Language Workshop, University of Alaska,
        Fairbanks, Alaska. 1971, 52 p (Not Available -
        Kraus, CTL, p. 1330).

200

YUP'IK - NOT KNOWN cont'd

787. Afcan, Paschal (Translator). Pingayun qimugkauyaraat
      (The three little puppies). Eskimo Language
      Workshop, University of Alaska. 1971, 30 p.
      (Not Available - Kraus, CTL, p. 1330).

788. Afcan, Paschal. Pit'eqarraalria (The First catch).
      Eskimo Language Workshop, University of Alaska,
      Fairbanks, Alaska. 1974, 46 p. (Not Available).

789. _____. Qanemcicuaraak angalgaam (Two short
      stories by Pat). Eskimo Language Workshop,
      University of Alaska, Fairbanks, Alaska. 1973,
      21 p. (Not Available).

790. _____. Upsankut (Upsaq and his family). Eskimo
      Language Workshop, University of Alaska,
      Fairbanks, Alaska. 1971, 17 p. (Not Available).

791. Afcan, Paschal, John Angaiak, Martha Teeluk, and Irene
      Reed. Qunguturaq naruyayagaq (The little pet
      seagull). Eskimo Language Workshop, University
      of Alaska, Fairbanks, Alaska. 1971, 29 p. (Not
      Available).

792. Afcan, Paschal and Irene Reed. Caucium piniun'llu
      (Matter and energy). Eskimo Language Workshop,
      University of Alaska, Fairbanks, Alaska. 1973,
      40 p. (Not Available).

793. _____. Nunarpak (The Earth). Eskimo Language
      Workshop, University of Alaska, Fairbanks,
      Alaska. 1973, 48 p. (Not Available).

794. _____. Yuum temiin elpeksuutai (The Senses of
      the human body). Eskimo Language Workshop,
      University of Alaska, Fairbanks, Alaska. 1973,
      28 p. (Not Available).

795. Alakayak, Anecia. Qaillun irniaruat piurtellrat
      (How dolls came about). Eskimo Language
      Workshop, University of Alaska, Fairbanks,
      Alaska. 1974, 16 p. (Not Available).

796. Alexie, Joe. Iralankuk akerta-llu (The moon and the
      sun). Eskimo Language Workshop, University of
      Alaska, 1971, 15 p. (Not Available - Kraus,
      CTL, p. 1331).

797. American Bible Society. Kanearakgtar (New Testament)
      (Kuskokwim dialect). American Bible Society,
      New York. 1967, 627 p. (Not Available - Kraus,
      CTL, p. 1342).

YUP'IK - NOT KNOWN cont'd

798. Andrew, Annie. Uugnar ayalleq (The Mouse that went
         away). Eskimo Language Workshop, University of
         Alaska, Fairbanks, Alaska. 1973, 20 p. (Not
         Available).

799. Andrew, George and Sophie Parks. Elitnauram Ayuqucia
         (report card). Eskimo Language Workshop,
         University of Alaska, Fairbanks, Alaska. 1973.
         (Not Available).

800. Andrew, Helen. Ciutiim qavanqua (Ciutiq's dream).
         Eskimo Language Workshop, University of Alaska,
         Fairbanks, Alaska. 1974, 18 p. (Not Available).

801. Andrew, Maxie. Qugyucullrem kanaqlangellra (How
         Qugyucullaq got muskrats). Eskimo Language
         Workshop, University of Alaska, Fairbanks,
         Alaska. 1974, 12 p. (Not Available).

802. Angaiak, John. Maketacuaraanka (My little book).
         Eskimo Language Workshop, University of Alaska,
         Fairbanks, Alaska. 1971, 62 p. (Not Available -
         Kraus, CTL, p. 1332).

803. Blanchett, Marie Nick. Cetugpak (Long-nails). Eskimo
         Language Workshop, University of Alaska,
         Fairbanks, Alaska. 1972, 22 p. (Not Available).

804. Blanchett, Marie N. (Translator). Kaukaq
         naucetaarpak-llu (Jack and the beanstalk).
         Eskimo Language Workshop, University of Alaska,
         Fairbanks, Alaska. 1973. (Not Available).

805. Blanchett, Marie N. Uqsuqaq mecaq'amek at'lek (A
         Mallard named "Splash"). Eskimo Language
         Workshop, University of Alaska, Fairbanks,
         Alaska. 1973, 23 p. (Not Available).

806. Blanchett, Marie (Translator). Waniwa Cinq'aq (Here's
         Jack). Eskimo Language Workshop, University of
         Alaska, Fairbanks, Alaska. 1973, 24 p. (Not
         Available).

807. Blanchett, Marie N. and Martha Teeluk. Caliluta
         aquiluta-llu (We work and we play). Eskimo
         Language Workshop, University of Alaska,
         Fairbanks, Alaska. 1973, 20 p. (Not Available).

808. _____. Nuk'aq ilai-llu (Nuk'aq's family).
         Eskimo Language Workshop, University of Alaska,
         Fairbanks, Alaska. 1973, 21 p. (Not Available).

202

YUP'IK - NOT KNOWN cont'd

809. Coolidge, Joseph. Al'ankut qimugtait (Al'aq's family's dogs) Eskimo Language Workshop, University of Alaska, Fairbanks, Alaska. 1973, 12 p. (Not Available).

810. _____. Igaryaraq II (Worksheets). Eskimo Language Workshop, University of Alaska, Fairbanks, Alaska. 1973, 71 p. (Not Available).

811. _____. Kegguterpalek (Big-teeth). Eskimo Language Workshop, University of Alaska, Fairbanks, Alaska. 1972, 10 p. (Not Available).

812. Coolidge, Joseph and Marie Blanchett (Translators and adaptors). Wangnek tamalkurma (All about me). Eskimo Language Workshop, University of Alaska, Fairbanks, Alaska. 1972, 59 p. (Not Available).

813. Dart, Diane. Angnilria asriq issuriyagaq (The playful little seal). Eskimo Language Workshop, University of Alaska, Fairbanks, Alaska. 1973, 22 p. (Not Available).

814. Dart, Diane. Translated by Paschal Afcan. Aseriyagaq issuriyagaq (Little mischief). Eskimo Language Workshop, University of Alaska, Fairbanks, Alaska. 1971, 21 p. (Not Available - Kraus, CTL, p. 1330).

815. Enoch, Lincoln. Uugnar angun-llu (The Mouse and the man). Eskimo Language Workshop, University of Alaska, Fairbanks, Alaska. 1973, 10 p. (Not Available).

816. Eskimo Language Workshop Staff. Cacirkat (Things to do). Eskimo Language Workshop, University of Alaska, Fairbanks, Alaska. 1972, 22 p. (Not Available).

817, _____. Elluarrlua wangnek auluklerkaga (The ways I take care of myself). Eskimo Language Workshop, University of Alaska, Fairbanks, Alaska 1973, 15 p. (Not Available).

818. _____. Igaryaraq I (Worksheets). Eskimo Language Workshop, University of Alaska, Fairbanks, Alaska. 1971, 200 p. (Not Available).

819. _____. Naaqut'liuryarat caliarkait (Mathematics worksheets). Eskimo Language Workshop, University of Alaska, Fairbanks, Alaska. 1972, 100 p. (Not Available).

YUP'IK - NOT KNOWN cont'd

820. Forshaug, Jean and Marie Nick (Translators). Kavirelit
        kalikanka (My red book). Eskimo Language
        Workshop, University of Alaska, Fairbanks,
        Alaska. 1971, 26 p. (Not Available - Kraus,
        CTL, p. 1353).

821. Fulton, Sylvia and Kathleen Breckman. Translated by
        Marie Nick. Waniwa cinglaq (Here's Jack).
        Eskimo Language Workshop, University of Alaska,
        Fairbanks, Alaska. 1971, 25 p. (Not Available -
        Kraus, CTL, p. 1353).

822. Gautier, Dora. Pataaskaarrluunkuk negair-llu
        (Pataaskaarluk and the spider). Eskimo
        Language Workshop, University of Alaska,
        Fairbanks, Alaksa. 1974, 20 p. (Not Available).

823. Gloko, Michael and Moses White. Arnaq pingayun-llu
        angutet and tutgara'urluq arnassagaq-llu (The
        woman and the three men and the grandson and
        the old woman). Eskimo Language Workshop,
        University of Alaska, Fairbanks, Alaska. 1973.
        (Not Available).

824. Jack, Noah. Elluarlua auluklerkaga wangnek (Health
        unit). Eskimo Language Workshop, University of
        Alaska, Fairbanks, Alaska. 1971, 15 p. (Not
        Available - Kraus, CTL, p. 1341).

825. Keim, Geri (Adaptor). Caurluq (a version of
        Cinderella). Eskimo Language Workshop,
        University of Alaska, Fairbanks, Alaska. 1973,
        60 p. (Not Available).

826. Keim, Geri. Kaviaq angniilnguq (The sad little fox).
        Eskimo Language Workshop, University of Alaska,
        Fairbanks, Alaska. 1973, 21 p. (Not Available).

827. Kipnuk Bilingual Team. Nuk'aq Ilai'llu caliarkaput
        (Our workbook for Nuk'aq Ilai-llu). Eskimo
        Language Workshop, University of Alaska,
        Fairbanks, Alaska. 1974, 21 p. (Not Available).

828. Lande, Winifred, Marie N. Blanchett and Martha
        Teeluk. Handbook for teachers of primary
        reading of the Yup'ik language. Eskimo
        Language Workshop, University of Alaska,
        Fairbanks, Alaska. 1972, 44 p. (Not Available).

829. Lomack, Mary Ann. Acsiyalriit (The berrypickers).
        Eskimo Language Workshop, University of Alaska,
        Fairbanks, Alaska. 1971, 18 p. (Not Available).

YUP'IK - NOT KNOWN cont'd

830. Lupie, Henry. Maqaruaq, tan'gerliq, usvituli-llu
(The rabbit, black bear and wise owl). Eskimo
Language Workshop, University of Alaska,
Fairbanks, Alaska. 1974, 24 p. (Not Available).

831. Meyoryuk students. Translated by Marie Blanchett.
Neqa Piitam itaqesciigatellra (The fish that
Pete could not catch). Eskimo Language
Workshop, University of Alaska, Fairbanks,
Alaska. 1973, 61 p. (Not Available).

832. Miyaoka, Osahito, et al. Yupik Eskimo classroom
grammar. University of Alaska, Fairbanks,
Alaska. 1969-1970. (Not Available - Kraus,
CTL, p. 1352).

833. Morack, Kathy. Translated by Paschal Afcan.
Anuqlirtuq (It's windy). Eskimo Language
Workshop, University of Alaska, Fairbanks,
Alaska. 1973, 26 p. (Not Available).

834. Napoleon, Dorothy. Translated by Martha Teeluk.
Wiinguuq (It's me). Eskimo Language Workshop,
University of Alaska, Fairbanks, Alaska. 1971,
16 p. (Not Available - Kraus, CTL, p. 1361).

835. Neck, Moses. Qanganaq meqsartulria (A squirrel
going for water). Eskimo Language Workshop,
University of Alaska, Fairbanks, Alaska. 1973,
23 p. (Not Available).

836. Nick, Marie. Cetugpak (Long nails). Eskimo Language
Workshop, University of Alaska, Fairbanks,
Alaska. 1971, 12 p. (Not Available - Kraus,
CTL, p.1353).

837. Nick, Marie (Translator). Ciukam yupiim qalangesaa
(The story of Papik, an Eskimo boy). Eskimo
Language Workshop, University of Alaska,
Fairbanks, Alaska. 1971, 51 p. (Not Available -
Kraus, CTL, p. 1353).

838. _____. Nasaaq (Cinderella). Eskimo Language
Workshop, University of Alaska, Fairbanks,
Alaska. 1971, 33 p. (Not Available - Kraus,
CTL, p. 1353).

839. Nick, Marie and students at Mekoryuk. Neqa Piitam
pitaqesciigalra (The fish that Pete could not
catch). Eskimo Language Workshop, University
of Alaska, Fairbanks, Alaska. 1971, 61 p.
(Not Available - Kraus, CTL, p. 1353).

YUP'IK - NOT KNOWN cont'd

840.   Nolte, Nancy. Translated by Anna Alexie and
          Elizabeth Worm. Uutacugluar angun (The
          gingerbread man). Eskimo Language Workshop,
          University of Alaska, Fairbanks, Alaksa. 1971,
          18 p. (Not Available - Kraus, CTL, p. 1331).

841.   Nolte, Nancy. Translated by Paschal Afcan. Yuguaq
          kelipaq (The gingerbread man). Eskimo Language
          Workshop, University of Alaska, Fairbanks, Alaska.
          1971, 23 p. (Not Available - Kraus, CTL, p.
          1331).

842.   Reed, Irene and Diane Dart. Translated by Paschal
          Afcan. Ayugenerilenguut yuut (Different kinds
          of people). Eskimo Language Workshop,
          University of Alaska, Fairbanks, Alaska. 1971,
          35 p. (Not Available - Kraus, CTL, p. 1330).

843.   Rey, H.A. Translated by Paschal Afcan. Paqnatareli
          Cuucicuar (Curious George). Eskimo Language
          Workshop, University of Alaska, Fairbanks,
          Alaska. 1971, 26 p. (Not Available - Kraus,
          CTL, p. 1330).

844.   Teeluk, Martha. Caarkat Goldilocksaamek (Workbook
          for Goldilocks). Eskimo Language Workshop,
          University of Alaska, Fairbanks, Alaska. 1971,
          35 p. (Not Available - Kraus, CTL, p. 1361).

845.   _____. Caarkat upsankunek (Workbook for Upsankut,
          20). Eskimo Language Workshop, University of
          Alaska, Fairbanks, Alaksa. 1971, 21 p. (Not
          Available - Kraus, CTL, p. 1361).

846.   _____. Igareyarat (Writing). Eskimo Language
          Workshop, University of Alaska, Fairbanks,
          Alaska. 1971, 40 p. (Not Available - Kraus,
          CTL, p. 1361).

847.   _____. Ilanka (My family). Eskimo Language
          Workshop, University of Alaska, Fairbanks,
          Alaska. 1973, 23 p. (Not Available).

848.   _____. Kaviarem kavirillra (How the fox turned
          red). Eskimo Language Workshop, University of
          Alaska, Fairbanks, Alaska. 1972, 24 p. (Not
          Available).

849.   _____. Kuk'uq (Little dog). Eskimo Language
          Workshop, University of Alaska, Fairbanks,
          Alaska. 1973, 13 p. (Not Available).

YUP'IK - NOT KNOWN cont'd

850.   Teeluk, Martha. Tan'gurraq nervallalleq (The boy who
            ate too much). Eskimo Language Workshop,
            University of Alaska, Fairbanks, Alaska. 1973,
            15 p. (Not Available).

851.   _____   Wii makut pikanka (These belong to me,
            human anatomy) Eskimo Language Workshop,
            University of Alaska, Fairbanks, Alaska. 1971,
            95 p. (Not Available - Kraus, CTL, p. 1361).

852.   Teeluk, Martha and the children at Chesterfield Inlet.
            Inupiat ayuquciat (Eskimo's way of living).
            Eskimo Language Workshop, University of Alaska,
            Fairbanks, Alaska. 1971, 46 p. (Not Available -
            Kraus, CTL, p. 1361).

853.   Thoburn, Tina and Betty Lou Hedges. Translated by
            Martha Teeluk, Marie Nick and Paschal Afcan.
            Qanemcika wangnek (My story about me). Eskimo
            Language Workshop, University of Alaska,
            Fairbanks, Alaska. 1971. (Not Available -
            Kraus, CTL, p. 1361).

854.   Toyukak, Mary. Qangpiiyaaq tulukaruk angayyagaq-llu
            (The Ptarmigan, the crow and the shrew). Eskimo
            Language Workshop, University of Alaska,
            Fairbanks, Alaska. 1971, 14 p. (Not Available).

YUP'IK

    See also SIBERIAN YUP'IK, ESKIMO

YUROK - BILINGUAL

855.   Robins, R.H. The Mourning dove. In William Slager
            (Editor), English for American Indians, Bureau
            of Indian Affairs, Washington, D.C. 1971,
            pp. 78-79.

        Legend about the way the mourning dove came to   lit   adv
        mourn.

ZUNI - BILINGUAL

856.   Newman, Stanley Steward. Zuni grammar. University
            of New Mexico Press, Albuquerque, New Mexico.
            1965, 77 p.

        Grammar of Zuni language presented in technical   gram   col
        orthography.   self

GENERAL BILINGUAL EDUCATION

857.   Anderson, Theodore and Mildred Boyer. Bilingual
          schooling in the United States, Vol. II.
          Southwest Educational Development Laboratory,
          Austin, Texas. 1970. (Available through
          Government Printing Office, Washington, D.C.).

          Concerned with individual minority groups and   hist   col
          their efforts at bilingual education. One   meth   self
          chapter deals with Indians, Eskimos and Aleuts.   theor
          Purpose of work to "reveal the promise of
          bilingual education and to serve as a guideline
          for those planning bilingual programs."

858.   Bureau of Indian Affairs. A Kindergarten curriculum
          guide for Indian children: A bilingual-bicultural
          approach. Bureau of Indian Affairs, Washington,
          D.C. 1970, 395 p. (ERIC ED065236).

          A reference work for the development of curricula.   meth   self
          Includes material on early childhood education,   bibl   col
          creation of a learning environment and supporting
          services. Also includes bibliography of relevant
          materials.

859.   Dissemination Center of Bilingual Bicultural
          Education. Cartel: annotated bibliography of
          bilingual bicultural materials, cumulative
          issue - 1973. Dissemination Center for
          Bilingual Bicultural Education, 6504 Tiracor
          Lane, Austin, Texas. 1973, 207 p.

          Most entries deal with Spanish/English bilingual   bibl   self
          instruction, but several are developed for or by
          Native North American groups. Information on
          availability of material is included.

860.   _____. CARTEL: annotated bibliography of
          bilingual bicultural materials, No. 18. Dissemi-
          nation Center for Bilingual Bicultural Education,
          6504 Tiracor Lane, Austin, Texas. 1974, 32 p.

          This issue of CARTEL is devoted to American   bibl   self
          Indian bilingual/bicultural materials. The
          majority of entries are English language books
          about American Indians written for children and/
          or adults. Native language materials in Navajo,
          Cherokee and Seminole are discussed briefly.

GENERAL BILINGUAL EDUCATION cont'd

861. Education Journal. The ABC's of Indian bilingual
        education. Education Journal of the Institute
        for the Development of Indian Law, Washington,
        D.C., September 1973, Vol.2, No. 2, 20 p.

        Various articles on Indian bilingual education,   meth   self
        including a list of ESEA Title VII Projects   theor
        serving Indians and Eskimos.

862. Guide to Title VII ESEA bilingual bicultural
        projects 1973-1974. Dissemination Center for
        Bilingual Bicultural Education, 6504 Tracor
        Lane, Austin, Texas. April 1974.

        Annotated list of bilingual/bicultural projects   desc   self
        in United States and possessions. Projects are   bibl
        arranged by state but some states have several
        entries. Addresses of project directors are
        given for ease in contacting workers in the field.

863. Holzmueller, Diana Lynn. Multi-media resource list:
        Indian and Eskimo culture in the North. Center
        for Northern Educational Research, University of
        Alaska, College, Alaska, in collaboration with
        the Institute of Social, Economic, and Government
        Research. 1973, 59 p.

        List of annotated citations arranged by age   bibl   self
        group of students. After each section, a list
        of sources with addresses is given. No index.

864. Jessen, Mariana. A kindergarten curriculum guide
        for Indian children; a bilingual-bicultural
        approach. United States Bureau of Indian
        Affairs, Washington, D.C. 1970, 204 p.

        Object of work is to enable child to "become   theor   self
        deeply involved and self-directive in his   meth   col
        learning, acquire a positive image of himself
        as a person and as a learner, and grow in terms
        of his intellectual function, his ego strength,
        initiative, and his inventiveness, his
        relatedness to people and his coping capacity
        both in adapting to his culture and eventually
        to help in shaping it." Work includes mainly
        English works, with suggestion that teachers
        translate these to Native tongues for reading
        to their children.

GENERAL BILINGUAL EDUCATION cont'd

865.   Rebert, Robert J. Bilingual Education for American
          Indians. Bureau of Indian Affairs, Washington,
          D.C. 1971, 102 p. (ERIC ED061789).

          Divided into three parts. Part one includes a   meth   col
          review of past and present bilingual education,   bibl   self
          history of language instruction in American
          Indian schools, and the effect of bilingual
          education on the American Indian. Part two
          describes preparation for teaching bilingual
          students and presents a program for Navajo
          children. Part three includes a bibliography,
          glossary of relevant terms and linguistic
          principles for describing North American Indian
          and Eskimo bilingual educational materials.

866.   Valencia, Alilano. Bilingual/bicultural education -
          an effective learning scheme for first grade
          Spanish speaking, English speaking, and American
          Indian children in New Mexico. A Report of
          Statistical Findings and Recommendations for
          the Grants Bilingual Education Project, Grants,
          New Mexico. Southwestern Cooperative Educational
          Laboratory, Albuquerque, New Mexico. 1970,
          46 p. (ERIC ED043418).

          Program for introducing native language of   meth   col
          student into first grade curriculum. Includes
          description of program, evaluation design,
          statistical analysis and author's recommenda-
          tions.

GENERAL ESL

          Alaska State-Operated School System. What can you
             hear? Alaska State-Operated School System, 650
             International Airport Road, Anchorage, Alaska.
             1974, 34 p.

          See under ESKIMO

          _____. What do you hear? Alaska State-Operated
             School System, 650 International Airport Road,
             Anchorage, Alaska. 1974, 72 p.

          See under INDIANS OF SUBARCTIC

          _____. What can you see? Alaska State-Operated
             School System, 650 International Airport Road,
             Anchorage, Alaska. 1974, 34 p.

          See under ESKIMO

GENERAL ESL cont'd

Alaska State-Operated School System. What can you
see? Alaska State-Operated School System, 650
International Airport Road, Anchorage, Alaska.
1974, 96 p.

See under ESKIMO

_____. What can you smell? Alaska State-Operated
School Sytem, 650 International Airport Road,
Anchorage, Alaska. 1974, 20 p.

See under ESKIMO

_____. What do you like to eat? Alaska
State-Operated School System, 650 International
Airport Road, Anchorage, Alaska. 1974, 33 p.

See under ESKIMO

867. Allen, T.D. and John Povey. Writing to create
ourselves; a manual for teachers of English
and creative writing in Bureau of Indian
Affairs secondary schools. Bureau of Indian
Affairs, Washington, D.C. 1969, 186 p. (Not
Available - Nafziger, p. 66).

A series of suggestions for improving written   meth   sec
English skills among Native American high school
students, by increasing motivation to write.
Specifics for improving motivation through use
of topics from the lives of the students.

868. Antell, Will and Lee Antell. American Indians: an
annotated bibliography of selected library
resources. Library Services Institute for
Minnesota Indians, University of Minnesota.
1970, 156 p.

Bibliography of English language books and non-   bibl   self
printed materials likely to give Native Americans
a positive self image. Each entry annotated as
to date of publication, price, reading level
and content. Includes fiction and nonfiction,
periodicals, films, slides, records and pictures.
Also includes list of Indian organizations and
services in Minnesota.

Aragon, Claude, Wallace Cathey. Dan and his pets.
Books one through five. Shiprock Independent
School District No. 22, New Mexico. 1969, 227 p.

See under NAVAJO

GENERAL ESL cont'd

    Aragon, Claude, Wallace Cathey. Dan and his pets,
       teacher's manual. Shiprock Independent School
       District No. 22, New Mexico. 1968, 174 p.

       See under NAVAJO

    Bear, Robert. Cree legends. Indian and Northern
       Education, University of Saskatchewan, Saskatoon,
       Saskatchewan. ca. 1965, 15 p.

       See entry under CREE

    Beauline, Antoine. Getting lime. Canarctic
       Publishing, Limited, Yellowknife, Northwest
       Territories, Canada, for Curriculum Division,
       Department of Education, Northwest Territories,
       Canada. 1973, 15 p.

       See under INDIANS OF SUBARCTIC   lit   int
                                         hist

869. Bureau of Indian Affairs Office of Education Programs.
      An annotated bibliography of young people's
      books on American Indians. Office of Education
      Programs, United States Bureau of Indian Affairs,
      Curriculum Bulletin No. 12, Washington, D.C.
      1973, 57 p.

      List of fiction and nonfiction books about   bibl   self
      Indians. Books are listed alphabetically by
      author, and are annotated as to content, tribe,
      and reading level.

870. Bureau of Indian Affairs. Basic goals for elementary
      children, beginning level and level one, Vol. 1.
      Haskell Institute, Lawrence, Kansas. 1966,
      147 p.

      Outline of behavioral goals and techniques and   meth   prim
      methods for achieving them. Language Arts   voc
      areas in English covered are Listening, Speaking,
      Reading, Writing, Literature. Bibliographies
      provided for various areas.

GENERAL ESL cont'd

871. Bureau of Indian Affairs. Basic goals for elementary
          children, levels seven and eight, Vol. IV.
          Haskell Institute, Lawrence, Kansas. 1966,
          167 p.

          Outline of behavioral goals and techniques and   meth   int
          methods for achieving them. Language Arts   bibl
          areas in English covered are Listening, Speaking,
          Reading, Writing, Literature. Bibliographies
          provided for various areas.

          _____. Helpful hints for new Bureau of Indian
          Affairs teachers. Bureau of Indian Affairs,
          Window Rock, Arizona. 1969, 54 p.

          See under NAVAJO

      Callaway, Sydney M., Gary Witherspoon et al.
          Grandfather stories of the Navajo. DINE,
          Incorporated, Rough Rock Demonstration School,
          Navajo Curriculum Center, Chinle, Arizona. 1968,
          77 p.

          See under NAVAJO

872. Canada Department of Information. Elementary
          education in the Northwest Territories, a
          handbook for curriculum development. Curriculum
          Division, Department of Education, Northwest
          Territories, Canada. ca. 1970, 313 p.

          Loose leaf binder with color coded pages, each   meth   self
          color dealing with one curriculum area.   bibl   col
          Language arts section gives language objectives,
          grade by grade, bibliography of suggested
          materials, suggested techniques, and a contras-
          tive analysis of English and Eskimo and English
          and Slavey, an Athabaskan language.

873. Canadian Department of Indian Affairs and Northern
          Development. Books for teachers and children.
          Canadian Department of Indian Affairs and
          Northern Development, Toronto, Education
          Division. 1970, 28 p. (ERIC ED037266).

          Bibliography of relevant books and periodicals   bibl   self
          published between 1951 and 1969. Materials
          under ten headings· (1) Books by and about
          Indian people, (2) General education, (3)
          Language, (4) English as a Second Language,
          (5) Reading, (6) Poetry, (7) Pre-school and
          kindergarten, (8) Disadvantaged child (9)
          Miscellaneous, and (10) periodicals. Prices
          included.

GENERAL ESL cont'd

Carlson, Vada and Gary Witherspoon. Black Mountain
Boy; a story of the boyhood of John Honie.
Navajo Curriculum Center, Rough Rock Demonstra-
tion School, Chinle, Arizona. 1968, 81 p.

See under NAVAJO

Cathey, Wallace Joe and his happy family, Book one
and two. Shiprock Independent School District
No. 22, New Mexico. 1968, 58 p.

See under NAVAJO

874. Center for Applied Linguistics. Recommendations for
language policy in Indian education. Center for
Applied Linguistics, Arlington, Virginia. 1973,
21 p.

Twenty-five recommendations for English and   meth   self
native language education. Directed to Bureau
of Indian Affairs and native groups.

Center for In-Service Education. But it can't wear
glasses. Center for In-Service Education, P.O.
Box 754, Loveland, Colorado. 1974.

See under NAVAJO

_____. I am bigger than. Center for In-Service
Education, P.O. Box 754, Loveland, Colorado.
1974.

See under NAVAJO

Chino, Galbert. My best friend. Jicarilla Apache
Cultural Awareness Program, Dulce, New Mexico.
1974, 9 p.

See under APACHE

CITE, Incorporated. Various.

See under NAVAJO and in APPENDIX

875. Colliou, Rose C. Basic oral English course for
kindergarten and grade one beginners. Education
Division, Indian Affairs Branch, Department of
Citizenship and Immigration, Ottawa. 1966, 289 p.

This course is designed as an Oral English   meth   prim
course. Methods included have been used success-   lit
fully in teaching ESL to non-English speaking   pron
beginners. Includes lessons for one year,   voc
verses and rhymes, games and activities.

214

GENERAL ESL cont'd

Davis, Bertha M. Teaching reading to the bilingual
child: motivational techniques. Sharing Ideas,
Arizona State Department of Education, Phoenix
Arizona. 1970, Vol. 7, No. 6, 69 p.

See under NAVAJO

876. Estrada, Beatrice Torres. Manual of sentence patterns
for teaching English as a second language (Book
1). Revised ed. Gallup-McKinley Schools, Gallup,
New Mexico. 1966, 227 p.

Manual designed to "present a useful and complete   meth col
method for teaching English to all non-English   self
speaking students entering school for the first
time." Twenty-two units with 183 lessons, each
lesson in four parts--review, teach, suggested
procedures, and enrichment activities.

Football, Virginia. Tesqua and the chief's son.
Curriculum Division, Department of Education,
Northwest Territories, Canada. 1972, 32 p.

See under DOGRIB

Glendon, Mary Troy. The curious kid. Navaho
Curriculum Center. Rough Rock Demonstration
School, Chinle, Arizona. 1971, 16 p.

See under NAVAJO

_____. Hand chart book to accompany the
curious kid. Navaho Curriculum Center,
Rough Rock Demonstration School, Chinle,
Arizona. 1971, 22 p.

See under NAVAJO

877. Goodner, James. Language and related characteristics
of 1968 Haskell Institute students. University
of Minnesota, Minneapolis, Minnesota. 1970, 83 p.

Study of comparison of performance in English of   theor col
Indian students from three language environments:
1) homes in which both Indian and English were
spoken, 2) homes in which only English was spoken,
3) homes in which only the Indian language was
spoken. Appendix has survey questions and
student responses.

GENERAL ESL cont'd

Gorman, Howard, Scott Preston. Navajo history, Vol. 1.
Navajo Curriculum Center, Rough Rock Demonstra-
tion School, Chinle, Arizona and Navajo Community
College Press. 1970, 250 p.

See under NAVAJO

878. Graustein, Jean McCarthy and Carol L. Jaglinski.
An annotated bibliography of young people's
fiction on American Indians. Office of Education Programs, U.S. Bureau of Indian Affairs,
1951 Constitution Avenue, NW, Washington, D.C.
1972, 55 p.

Part One is a list of fictional works by tribe,   bibl self
Part Two is an annotated list by author. Most   int
but not all of items in Part One are annotated
in Part Two. Bibliography covers period from
1933 to 1966, but is not totally comprehensive
for this period. Annotations include tribal
identification, reading level, and story synop-
sis. Should be useful in gathering outside
reading for Native American students.

879. Harkins, Arthur M. Modern Native Americans: a
selective bibliography. Minnesota University,
Minneapolis, Minnesota. 1971, 131 p. (ERIC
ED054890).

List of 1500 items published between 1927 and   bibl self
1970. One of areas covered is English as a
Second Language.

Hoffman, Virginia. Lucy learns to weave: gathering
plants. Navajo Curriculum Center, Rough Rock
Demonstration School, Chinle, Arizona. 1969,
46 p.

See under NAVAJO

Hoffman, Virginia and Broderick H. Johnson. Navajo
biographies. DINE, Inc. and Navajo Curriculum
Center, Rough Rock Demonstration School, Chinle,
Arizona. 1970, 342 p.

See under NAVAJO

GENERAL ESL cont'd

880.   Idaho State Department of Education. Books about
          Indians. Idaho State Department of Education,
          Indian Education, Boise, Idaho. 1971, 175 p.

          Bibliography of hundreds of items published from   bibl   self
          1800 to 1969. Covers popular and academic works,
          fiction and nonfiction, juvenile and adult. Items
          arranged by publisher, which makes for considerable
          duplication. Many entries are annotated as to
          content and grade level of material. Should be
          valuable resource for Native American ESL students.

        Jicarilla Apache Cultural Awareness Program. I used
          to be afraid. Jicarilla Apache Cultural Aware-
          ness Program, Dulce, New Mexico. 1974, 29 p.

          See under APACHE

        Kane, Katy. Language arts portion of the CITE cur-
          riculum. CITE, Inc. 1081 Gayley, Los Angeles,
          California. 1973, 14 p.

          See under NAVAJO

        MacDiarmid, J.A. Johnny goes hunting. Curriculum
          Division, Department of Education, Yellowknife,
          Northwest Territories, Canada. 1972, 29 p.

          See under DOGRIB

        _____. Johnny goes to Yellowknife. Curriculum
          Division, Department of Education, Yellowknife,
          Northwest Territories, Canada. 1972, 21 p.

          See under DOGRIB

        _____. Tendi goes beaver snaring. Curriculum
          Division, Department of Education, Yellowknife,
          Northwest Territories, Canada. 1972.

          See under DOGRIB

        _____. Tendi's mossbag. Curriculum Division,
          Department of Education, Yellowknife, Northwest
          Territories, Canada. 1972, 15 p.

          See under DOGRIB

GENERAL ESL cont'd

881. Marken, Jack Walter. The Indians and Eskimos of
        North America: a bibliography of books in print
        through 1972. University of South Dakota,
        Vermillion, South Dakota. 1973, 200 p.

        Bibliography of 4,050 entries, divided into   bibl self
        bibliographies, handbooks, autobiographies,
        myths and legends, and other books. Includes
        a large list of fictional works for children,
        and a list of twentieth century fiction about
        Indians.

882. Mitchell, Marjorie (Compiler). Native Indian studies
        and curriculum development programmes: a descrip-
        tive mailing list. British Columbia Intercultural
        Curriculum Project, Studies of Intercultural
        Education, University of Victoria, Victoria,
        British Columbia. 1974, 26 p. (ERIC ED108843).

        Annotated listing of 96 educational projects,   bibl self
        with mailing addresses. Items organized by Canadian
        province or United States state within four
        categories: 1) Canadian Native Indian Studies,
        2) Canadian Curriculum Development Projects, 3)
        American Native Indian Studies, 4) American
        Curriculum Development Projects.

883. Mullen, Diana. Fluency first: instructor training
        course. Training Research and Development Station,
        Prince Albert, Saskatchewan. 1972, 150 p.
        (ERIC ED082199).

        Manual for teachers of ESL to illiterate adults   meth self
        of Indian ancestry. Contents include outline   col
        notes for proposed topics and list of learning
        activities.

        _____. LEREC: learning English as a second
        language through recreation. Saskatchewan
        Newstart, Inc., Prince Albert, Saskatchewan.
        1972, 263 p.

        See under INDIANS OF SUBARCTIC

884. _____. A plan for fluency first. Saskatchewan
        Newstart, Inc. Prince Albert, Saskatchewan.
        1971, 183 p. (ERIC ED056565).

        Detailed report on program for teaching English   meth col
        as second language to adult Indians. Includes   bibl self
        annotated list of materials on language, language
        teaching, and Indian culture. Course content
        included with discussion of instructional
        arrangements and objectives.

GENERAL ESL cont'd

885. Nafziger, Alyce J. American Indian education, a
         selected bibliography, supplement no. 1. New
         Mexico State University, University Park, New
         Mexico. 1970, 132 p.

      Bibliography is divided into two parts. Part one   bibl self
      covers abstracts of 176 documents cited in "Research
      in Education" from September 1969 through September
      1970. Part two covers 81 citations from "Current
      Index to Journals in Education" from January
      1969 through June 1970.

886. Ohannessian, Sirarpi. The study of the problem of
         teaching English to American Indians. Center
         for Applied Linguistics, Washington, D.C. 1967,
         40 p.

      Report and recommendations of a study group on   meth self
      teaching English. Recommendations cover testing,   theor
      reading, adult education.

887. _____. Teaching English to speakers of Choctaw,
         Navajo, and Papago; a contrastive approach. Pre-
         pared at the Center for Applied Linguistics for
         the Bureau of Indian Affairs, Center for Applied
         Linguistics, Washington, D.C. 1969, 138 p.

      Series of articles commissioned by the Bureau of   theor col
      Indian Affairs to make available to teachers some   meth self
      of the results of a comparison of English with the   desc
      three languages involved. Articles based on work
      of linguists who have studies these languages.

      Parrish, Sidney. How sickness came to the people.
      Ya-ka-ma, Indian Education and Development, Inc.
      P.O. Box 11339, Santa Rosa, California. 1974, 16 p.

      See under INDIANS OF CALIFORNIA

      _____. The owl story. Ya-ka-ma, Indian Education
      and Development, Inc. PO Box 11339, Santa Rosa,
      California. 1974, 8 p.

      See under INDIANS OF CALIFORNIA

      _____. The slug woman. Ya-ka-ma, Indian Educa-
      tion and Development, Inc. P.O. Box 11339, Santa
      Rosa, California. 1974, 12 p.

      See under INDIANS OF CALIFORNIA

GENERAL ESL cont'd

Roessel, Robert A. and Dillon Platero. Coyote stories
of the Navajo people. Navajo Curriculum Center,
Rough Rock Demonstration School, Chinle, Arizona.
1968, 141 p.

See under NAVAJO

Rough Rock Demonstration School. Curriculum guidelines
for the skills of English. Rough Rock Demonstration
School, Chinle, Arizona. 1969, 133 p.

See under NAVAJO.

Sawyer, Marileta. C and Sid. Navajo Curriculum Center,
Rough Rock Demonstration School, Chinle, Arizona.
1971, 16 p.

See under NAVAJO

_____. The gink. Navajo Curriculum Center, Rough
Rock Demonstration School, Chinle, Arizona. 1971, 11 p.

See under NAVAJO

_____. Super grape and the ape. Navajo Curriculum
Center, Rough Rock Demonstration School, Chinle,
Arizona. 1971, 12 p.

See under NAVAJO

Schwanke, Jack H. Close up things. Navajo Curriculum
Center, Rough Rock Demonstration School, Chinle,
Arizona. 1970, 24 p.

See under NAVAJO

_____. Kinalda. Navajo Curriculum Center,
Rough Rock Demonstration School, Chinle, Arizona.
1970, 93 p.

See under NAVAJO

_____. Navajo pottery. Navajo Curriculum Center,
Rough Rock Demonstration School, Chinle, Arizona.
1970, 22 p.

See under NAVAJO

_____. Navajo wedding. Navajo Curriculum Center,
Rough Rock Demonstration School, Chinle, Arizona.
1970, 60 p.

See under NAVAJO

GENERAL ESL cont'd

888. Scoon, Annabelle R. Bibliography of Indian Educa-
        tion and curriculum innovation. Albuquerque
        Indian School, New Mexico. June 1971, 62 p.
        (ERIC ED053614).

        Bibliography of over 200 ERIC documents with   bibl self
        abstracts. Divided into three sections: 1)
        Indian education and bilingualism, 2) general
        aspects of American Indian education, 3) innova-
        tive curriculum concepts and materials.

889. Selby, Suzanne R. Bibliography on materials in the
        field of Indian education. Saskatoon Institute
        for Northern Studies, Saskatchewan. 1968, 110 p.
        (ERIC ED026180).

        Bibliography of one hundred and five annotated   bibl self
        entries, covering books, articles and pamphlets
        on Indian education published from 1956 to 1968.
        Appendix contains a list of other bibliographies,
        journals and research centers working with
        Indian and Eskimo education.

890. Shears, Brian T. Aptitude, content and method of
        teaching word recognition with young American
        Indian children. Doctoral dissertation, Univer-
        sity of Minnesota. 1970, 162 p. (Not Available -
        Dissertation Abstract #70- 20,250).

        Report of a strictly controlled reading experi-   meth col
        ment with twelve kindergarten students on Red   theor
        Lake Indian reservation. Four teaching methods
        were used - auditory method using words familiar
        to students, auditory method with basal reader
        words, visual method with words familiar to
        students, and visual method with basal reader words.
        No signifcant difference in results with visual and
        auditory. Significantly more familiar words
        learned than basal reader words.

    Shiprock Independent School District, No. 22. Phillip
        and his family. Shiprock Independent School
        District No. 22, New Mexico. 1968, 243 p.

        See under NAVAJO.

    Shumway, Cherie. Hello, tree. Navajo Curriculum
        Center, Rough Rock Demonstration School, Chinle,
        Arizona. 1971, 19 p.

        See under NAVAJO

GENERAL ESL cont'd

    Sikkuark, Nick. Book of things you will never see.
       Keewatin Region Education Office, Department
       of Education, Curriculum Division, Government
       of Northwest Territories, Yellowknife, North-
       west Territories, Canada. 1973, 25 p.

       See under INDIANS OF SUBARCTIC

       _____. What animals think. Keewatin Region
       Education Office, Department of Education,
       Curriculum Division, Government of Northwest
       Territories, Yellowknife, Northwest Territories,
       Canada. 1973, 39 p.

       See under INDIANS OF SUBARCTIC

    Sisco, Wilfred. Mother Nature at work. Center for
       In-Service Education, P.O. Box 754, Loveland,
       Colorado. 1974.

       See under NAVAJO

       _____. My uncle. Center for In-Service
       Education, P.O. Box 754, Loveland, Colorado,
       1974.

       See under NAVAJO

891. Slager, William R. (Editor). English for American
       Indians; a newsletter of the Office of Education
       Programs. Bureau of Indian Affairs, Department
       of the Interior, Washington, D.C. 1971, 85 p.

       Issue devoted to literature and creative writing   meth self
       with emphasis on teaching American Indian stu-   bibl col
       dents. Final section includes stories, legends
       and tales from Shoshoni, Nahuatl, Cherokee, Nav-
       ajo, and Yurok with English translations.

892. _____. Language in American Indian education: a
       newsletter of the Office of Education Programs.
       Bureau of Indian Affairs, Department of the
       Interior, Albuquerque, New Mexico. Fall 1971,
       92 p.

       This issue contains articles on materials for   meth self
       teaching English, bilingual reading materials,   bibl col
       language study programs. Also has section on
       specific instructional materials, particularly
       Navajo materials, and section of stories in
       several Indian languages, with English trans-
       lations.

GENERAL ESL cont'd

893. Slager, William R. (Editor). Language in American
        Indian Education: a newsletter of the Office of
        Education Programs. Bureau of Indian Affairs,
        Department of the Interior, Albuquerque, New
        Mexico. Spring 1972, 116 p.

        This issue contains a bibliographic essay on   meth self
        the Sioux language, a report on two bilingual   bibl col
        education programs, an article on evaluation
        of student progress in English. Also included
        are a Papago story and sample of Cree language
        materials.

894. Stensland, Anna L. American Indian culture and the
        reading program. Journal of Reading. 1971,
        Vol. 15, No. 1, p. 22-26.

        Brief bibliography of books appropriate for the   bibl self
        American Indian child who has difficulty reading
        English. Lists are given of fiction, biography,
        and anthologies dealing with American Indians and
        their cultures. Entries annotated with precis of
        contents. Entries chosen for their viewpoint
        and their interest, rather than degree of diffi-
        culty.

     Talaswaima, Terrance. Hopi bride at the home dance.
        Hopi Action Program, P.O. Box 178, Oraibi, Arizona.
        1974, 21 p.

        See under HOPI

     Tefft, Virginia J. A physical education guide with
        English language practice drills for teachers of
        Navajo kindergarten and primary school children.
        University of New Mexico, Albuquerque, New
        Mexico. 1969, 461 p.

        See under NAVAJO

     Trueba, Antonio de. The fox and the wolf. Navajo
        Curriculum Center, Rough Rock Demonstration
        School, Chinle, Arizona. 1970, 18 p.

        See under NAVAJO

     Unka, Helene. Working for wages. Curriculum Division,
        Department of Education, Northwest Territories,
        Canada. 1973, 19 p.

        See under INDIANS OF SUBARCTIC

GENERAL ESL   cont'd

895.   Whiteside, Don (sin a paw). Aboriginal people: a
          selected bibliography concerning Canada's first
          people. National Indian Brotherhood, Ottawa,
          Ontario. 1973, 345 p.

          Selected bibliography of works. published and   bibl   self
          unpublished. Of particular interest is section
          XVI, Formal Education. Bibliography contains
          relatively few works directly relevant to language
          education, but many that may be useful for back-
          ground, cultural, economic or political infor-
          mation. Indexed by author and subject.

GENERAL LANGUAGE

896.   Boas, Franz. Race, language and culture. Free Press
          Paperback edition, New York. 1966, 647 p. (Reprint
          of publication by Macmillan Co., New York. 1940).

          Approximately one fifth of this work is devoted   desc   self
          to American Indian languages. In addition the   col
          culture section contains several chapters on
          American Indian mythology and folktales. There
          are several useful articles on the culture of
          the Eskimo. The work has no index but the table
          of contents is quite detailed and makes the book
          easy to use. Very good background information
          provided.

897.   _____. Introduction to handbook of American
          Indian Languages. Indian linguistic families
          of America north of Mexico, by J.W. Powell.
          Preston Holder (Editor).   University of Nebraska
          Press, Lincoln, Nebraska. 1966, 221 p. (Reprint
          of publication by Boas, 1911 and Powell 1891).

          Double volume of linguistic background on native   desc   col
          North American languages. Boas's section is con-   theor self
          cerned with basic linguistic characteristics.
          Powell's section is concerned with the classifi-
          cation of languages in terms of lexical elements.
          Two works bound together because both bear on
          the problem of defining the nature of North
          American native languages.

GENERAL LANGUAGE cont'd

898. Osborn, Lynn R. A bibliography of North American Indian
      speech and spoken language. University of Kansas,
      Lawrence, Kansas. 1968, 57 p. (ERIC ED044223).

      List of approximately six hundred items published   bibl self
      between 1810 and 1967. Intended as a list of
      resource materials for students of native North
      American languages.

899. Pilling, James C. Bibliographies of the languages of
      the North American Indians. AMS Press, New York.
      1973, 3 vol. (Reprint of publications of U.S.
      Government Printing Office, Washington, D.C.
      1887-1894.)

      These volumes contain reprints of bibliographies   bibl adv
      compiled in the late 19th century from "the   self
      principal public and private libraries of the
      United States, Canada, and Northern Mexico" by
      James Pilling. Arrangement is alphabetical by
      author within language family, or by title when
      author is unknown. Volume One contains separate
      bibliographies on the following language families --
      Eskimo, Siouan, Iroquoian and Muskhogeon. Volume
      Two is comprised solely of the Algonkian biblio-
      graphy. Volume Three contains separate biblio-
      graphies on Athabascan, Chinookan, Salishan, and
      Wakashan languages.

900. Pilling, James C. Catalogue of linguistic manuscripts
      in the library of the Bureau of American ethno-
      logy. Osiris Publications, Montreal, Quebec.
      1973, 22 p. (Reprint of publication by U.S.
      Government Printing Office, Washington, D.C.
      1881.)

      Bibliography of linguistic holdings of the   bibl self
      Smithsonian Institution as of the original   col
      date of publication. Many of the items listed
      are vocabularies. No subject access to the
      list. Items arranged alphabetically by author.

      Powell, J.W. Indian linguistic families of America
      north of Mexico.

      See under Boas, Franz. Introduction to handbook
      of American Indian languages, in this section.

GENERAL LANGUAGE cont'd

901. Summer Institute of Linguistics. Reprints. Summer
         Institute of Linguistics, P.O. Box 1960, Santa
         Anna, California. 1973, 32 p.

         List of reprints of language materials offered   bibl self
         by the SIL. Some deal with native North Ameri-
         can languages. Items are listed alphabetically
         by author with title and cost. No further
         annotation.

APPENDICES

APPENDIX I

APPENDIX I

902. Bass, Willard P. and Henry G. Burger. American
       Indians and educational laboratories. Publica-
       tion No. 1-1167, Southwestern Cooperative Educa-
       tional Laboratory, Inc., 117 Richmond Drive, NE,
       Albuquerque, New Mexico. 1967, 37 p.

       Discussion of standing and problems of native   meth col
       North American student vis-a-vis Anglo school   theor self
       system. Suggested remedies include education of
       teachers in a native North American culture.
       Includes map of native North American language
       areas in the United States, proportion of native
       North American school enrollment by area, compar-
       ison of native North American census figures
       (income, life expectancy, etc.) to general
       population of United States.

903. Dudley, John Wallace. Testing American Indian per-
       ceptions of English. M.A. thesis - TESOL.
       University of California, Los Angeles. 1971,
       98 p.

       Design for a test to measure native North Amer-   test col
       cans' receptive competence in English at the   theor
       university level. Results of test administered
       to one group are included.

904. Hale, Kenneth. A new perspective on American Indian
       linguistics. New Perspectives in the Pueblos.
       School of American Research Book, University of
       New Mexico Press, Albuquerque, New Mexico.
       1972, p. 87-110.

       Argument for the continuation of American Indian   meth col
       linguistic study by native speakers of American   theor
       Indian languages. Several examples of the suc-
       cess of this method given.

905. Harris, David P. (Editor). Report of the evaluation
       of English as a second language in Navajo area
       schools. Conducted for U.S. Bureau of Indian
       Affairs by Teachers of English to Speakers of
       Other Languages (TESOL), Washington, D.C.
       1970, 54 p.

       Consensus of the TESOL team which evaluated   meth col
       English as a Second Language programs in Navajo   theor
       area schools. Purpose of evaluation was to
       provide objective professional assessment of
       ESL programs. Evaluations were product of site
       visits to each school.

227

APPENDIX I cont'd

906. Hopkins, Thomas R. Language testing of North American
          Indians. Paper delivered at Conference on Pro-
          blems in Foreign Language Testing, English Language
          Institute, University of Michigan, Ann Arbor,
          Michigan, September 28-30, 1967 (Sponsored by U.S.
          Bureau of Indian Affairs). 1968, 32 p.

      Review of research and studies on language test-   test col
      ing of North American Indians and Eskimos. Only
      standardized tests included, some of which were
      still in process of development.

907. Ohannessian, Sirarpi (Editor). Planning conference
          for a bilingual kindergarten program for Navajo
          children; conclusions and recommendations, Octo-
          ber 11-12, 1968. Center for Applied Linguistics,
          Washington, D.C. 1969, 16 p.

      Research commissioned by the Bureau of Indian   theor col
      Affairs by a committee of experts from various   meth self
      fields. Lengthy discussions of theory, policy
      and practical aspects of bilingual programs.

908. Ohannessian, Sirarpi. The study of problems of
          teaching English to American Indians: Report and
          Recommendations, July 1967. Center for Applied
          Linguistics, Washington, D.C. 1968, 40 p.

      Study commissioned by the Bureau of Indian Affairs   meth col
      to "Assess...the learning and teaching of English"   theor self
      in certain BIA schools and public schools which
      have American Indian students. Concentrated on
      four problem areas: 1) administration of boarding
      and day schools, 2) teacher performance, prepara-
      tion, recruitment and retraining, 3) student
      performance, and 4) instructional materials.
      Recommendations of the investigating committee
      are listed in the final section.

909. Powell, J.V. Pidgins as an alternative in teaching
          moribund Canadian Indian languages. Department of
          Anthropology and Sociology, University of British
          Columbia, Vancouver, British Columbia. 1973, 12 p.

      Author points out that many Canadian Indian   meth self
      languages have died or are in the process of doing   theor
      so. However, many tribes with moribund languages
      might prefer a pidgin language to no tribal lan-
      guage at all. Author proposes to teach Indian
      children a pidgin language in order to sustain
      their cultural heritage. His belief is that a
      partially bilingual program is better than a
      completely English one.

APPENDIX I cont'd

910. Sandstrom, Roy L. (Editor). Clash of cultures: report
        of the Institute on "The American Indian student
        in higher education," held at St. Lawrence Univer-
        sity, July 10-28, 1972. St. Lawrence University,
        Canton, New York. 1972, 128 p.

        Report from meeting of several high level educa-   meth self
        tors and social scientists and advocates of   theor
        native North American rights. Lectures, work-
        shops, ancillary articles. Of considerable interest
        in showing progress in field of native North
        American education at this time.

911. Spolsky, Bernard. An evaluation of two sets of mater-
        ials for teaching English as a second language
        to Navajo beginners. Consultants in Teaching
        English, Los Angeles, California. 1969, 21 p.

        Spolsky reviews assumptions behind the works   theor col
        evaluated. Also evaluates proposed methodology,   meth self
        and actual use of materials in the classroom.
        He then lists conclusions and recommendations.
        Appendix is Spolsky's "Linguistic and language
        pedagogy--applications or implications?"

912. _____. Navajo language maintenance III: acces-
        sibility of school and town as a factor in
        language shift. Navajo Reading Study, Progress
        Report No. 14, University of New Mexico, 1805
        Roma, NE, Albuquerque, New Mexico. 1971, 29 p.

        Comparison of the effects on language use of   meth col
        isolation from and proximity to speakers of   theor self
        other languages. Study showed that students of
        Bureau of Indian Affairs schools, many of them
        from remote areas of the Navajo Reservation, tend
        to speak only Navajo when they come to school.
        However, Navajo students at public schools, many
        of whom live off reservation or on the border,
        tend to be bilingual in Navajo and English.
        Author suggests latter is due to daily inter-
        action with English speakers, and that it is
        likely that some English is spoken in homes
        of Navajo public school students.

APPENDIX I cont'd

913. Spolsky, Bernard and Wayne Holm. Bilingualism in the
      six year old Navajo child. Navajo Reading Study,
      University of New Mexico, Albuquerque, New Mexico.
      1971, 15 p. (Also in Conference on Child Language,
      reprints of papers presented at conference, Chica-
      go, November 22-24, 1971, p. 225-239).

      Author contends that Navajo children generally   theor col
      speak more English by the time they reach first   self
      grade than was previously believed. Factors en-
      couraging this tendency are monolingual (English)
      schools and contacts outside reservation.

914. _____. Literacy in the vernacular: the case of
      the Navajo. Navajo Reading Study, University of
      New Mexico, Albuquerque, New Mexico. 1971, 21 p.

      Review of status of Navajo and English language   meth self
      competency among Navajo. Argument for literacy   theor
      in Navajo as means to preserve native language.
      Example of Cherokee experience with Sequoyah's
      syllabary discussed.

915. Willink, Elizabeth W. A comparison of two methods of
      teaching English to Navajo children. Ph.D.
      Dissertation, University of Arizona. 1968,
      232 p. (Not Available - Dissertation Abstracts,
      #68- 14,910).

      Comparison of traditional experiential English   meth col
      teaching to Teaching English as a Second Language.
      Using elementary grades in Navajo reservation
      schools. Standard tests showed TESL trained
      students to be more proficient in English.

916. Young, Robert W. English as a second language for
      Navajos; an overview of certain cultural and
      linguistic factors. U.S. Bureau of Indian Affairs,
      Washington, D.C. 1968, 169 p.

      Essay to "give a modicum of insight into the world-   meth col
      view of the Navajo through the window of the Nava-   theor self
      jo language, in order that better ESL materials   desc
      be developed for Navajos and other Indians."
      Premise is that teacher who understands the cul-
      ture and language of pupils is better equipped than
      teacher who knows only target language (English).

APPENDIX II

APPENDIX II

CITE (Consultants in Total Education), Inc.

These materials, while developed for the Navajo, were
intended to be general purpose ESL materials, and few
of the items are specifically concerned with Navajo
culture. The materials were developed for use in a total
CITE curriculum; however, individual strands and/or
books from these strands can be and have been used
separately from the whole.

Author and publisher of all the following materials is
CITE, Inc., 1081 Gayley Avenue, Los Angeles, California.

917. Auditory strand, Vol. I-III. ca. 1969, 468 p.

> Ninety-eight detailed lesson plans for kinder-   meth prim
> garten or first grade students. Aim is to intro-
> duce learner to rhythm and sounds of English language
> through rhymes and songs. Explanation of methodology
> included.

918. Categorization and characterization strand. 1972, 18 p.

> Aim here is to teach Navajo children to listen to   lit   prim
> spoken Navajo, ask questions in Navajo and act out
> stories in Navajo. Six sample lessons provided,
> with English dialog to be translated into Navajo
> by teacher or aide. Traditional and modern Navajo
> stories suggested for use. For kindergarten.

919. Composition strand, Vol. 1-13. 1973-1974, 1045 p.

> One hundred and fifty-three detailed lesson plans. script prim
> Aim is to teach students to generate sentences   gram
> and paragraphs in English on a given topic. Pro-
> gresses from oral generation to written. Punc-
> tuation rules and sentence arrangement included.
> For first and second grade.

920. Composition strand, teacher's guide. 1974, 29 p.

> Explains theory behind the lesson plans described theor self
> above, and methods of implementing them.   meth col

921. Critical thinking strand, Vol. 1-6. 1974, 374 p.

> Sixty-eight lesson plans. Aim is to teach stu-   meth prim
> dent to distill actual meaning from written and   gram int
> oral sentences - to spot contradictions, recog-
> nize generalizations, etc. by employing simplified
> logic diagrams. For elementary grades 1-6.

APPENDIX II cont'd

922. Critical thinking workbooks, Vol. 1-6. 1974, 921 p.

Workbooks to accompany lessons described above.   gram prim
Students are given space to diagram sentences to   int
discern meaning and application to other sentences.
Answers and correct diagrams given on following
pages.

923. Dramatization strand. 1970, 91 p.

Eighteen detailed lesson plans. Aim is to teach.   pron prim
children pronunciation and intonation of English
sounds through mimicking words using those sounds
and dramatizing situations involving those words.
For kindergarten.

924. English listening strand, Vol. 1-10. 1973, 1236 p.

Ninety detailed lesson plans. Aim is to teach   gram prim
students to distill meaning from oral English,
by applying simplified logical analysis to adap-
tations of famous stories -- Alice in Wonderland,
Gulliver's Travels, Horton Hears a Who, and the
biography of Helen Keller. Strand precedes Critical Thinking (see above) and follows Listening
(see below).

925. English listening dictionary, Vol. 1-4. 1973, 171 p.

Dictionary of words introduced in stories of   voc   prim
English Listening strand. Words are presented at
top of each page in upper and lower case type,
with definition at bottom of page. Some words
illustrated.

926. English listening, teacher's guide. 1973, 19 p.

Explains the theory behind the lesson plans desc-   theor self
cribed above, and methodology used in implementing   meth col
the theory.

927. English rhetoric strand, Vol. 1-3. 1972, 382 p.

Forty-nine lesson plans. Aim is to teach children   voc   prim
ways to express various emotions through drama-   meth
tization. Dialog is given in English, but use
in native language is also suggested. Dramatiza-
tions center on imaginary characters. For first
grade.

APPENDIX II cont'd

928. English rhetoric, Vol. 1-4. 1973, 369 p.

Twenty detailed lesson plans. Aim is to have   meth   prim
students ask questions about and dramatize real
life situations. For second grade.

929. English rhetoric, teacher's guide. 1973, 10 p.

Explains theory behind lesson plans described above   theor self
and methodology used in developing them.   meth   col

930. Introductory readings to the CITE bilingual curriculum.
1970, 57 p.

Background reading in theory and methodology for   theor col
teachers using the CITE curriculum. Includes self   meth   self
testing worksheets for readers to check their comprehension.

931. Listening strand, Vol. 1, 3-5 (Vol. 2 not available).
1972, 791 p.

Seventy-three detailed lesson plans. Aim is to   voc   prim
improve learners' comprehension of oral English
through review and analysis of short stories with
controlled vocabulary. Precedes English listening
and Critical thinking strands (see above).

932. Notes on a theory of second-language instruction. 1969,
71 p.

Collection of papers pertinent to the CITE curri-   meth   col
culum. Included are a rationale for the CITE   theor self
curriculum, instructions for planning an ESL lesson,
and a sample lesson.

933. Phonology strand, Vol. 1, 3, 7 (other volumes not available).
1972, 383 p.

Series of lessons introducing sounds of English   pron   prim
through minimal-pair words, both real and invented.
Students become familiar with distinction between
words in pair (bet/bat) by playing various games
with them. For kindergarten.

934. Pronunciation strand, Vol. 2 (Vol. 1 not available).
1972, 61 p.

Nine detailed lesson plans. Aim is to teach stu-   pron   prim
dents pronunciation of English language sounds
through mimicking teacher's pronunciation of various minimal pair words, both real and invented.
For first grade.

APPENDIX II   cont'd

935.   Reader: Ants are interesting, Parts I and II, Teacher's
          copy. 1974, 76 p.

          Factual discussion of the lives and activities of   lit   int
          ants. Illustrated. Format for this series of CITE
          readers is to present a short segment of story which
          leaves reader with a question. This question is
          stated and answered on the next page. In teacher's
          copy, question is also printed on page with text that
          precedes it.

936.   Reader: Birds are interesting, Parts I and II, Teacher's
          copy. 1974, 76 p.

          Factual discussion of birds, their anatomy, life   lit   int
          history and the various ways they survive. Illus-
          trated. See "Reader: Ants are interesting," above
          for format.

937.   Reader: A birthday party by the swamp. 1973, 11 p.

          Story about a dinosaur's birthday party.   lit   prim
          Illustrated.

938.   Reader: The bubble gum pink reading book. 1973, 48 p.

          Story of the Three Billy Goats Gruff retold. Second lit   int
          section of book consists of short series of ques-
          tions and answers about this story and others in
          the reading series.

939.   Reader: The copper penny reading book. 1973, 28 p.

          Story of Hansel and Gretel retold. Second section   lit   int
          of book consists of series of questions and answers
          about this story and others.

940.   Reader: Dogs are interesting, Parts I and II. 1974,
          70 p.

          Factual discussion of the history of dogs' com-   lit   int
          panionship and service to man. Illustrated. See
          "Reader: Ants are interesting" above for format.

941.   Reader: Early communication / Let's talk to each other,
          Teacher's copy. 1974, 79 p.

          Factual discussion of various sorts of communica-   lit   int
          tion, from cave paintings to telephones. Illustrated.
          See "Reader: Ants are interesting" above for format.

APPENDIX II cont'd

942. Reader: The egg yolk yellow reading book. 1973, 50 p.

Two short adventure stories -- one about a pair of   lit   int
twins in Tahiti, one about a boy in the French Alps.
Each story is followed by a series of questions
about that story.

943. Reader: Facts about air. 1973, 19 p.

Explanations of four simple science experiments   lit   int
which can be performed at home or in the class-
room. Illustrated.

944. Reader: Facts about animals of long ago. 1973, 37 p.

Factual descriptions of three extinct animals --   lit   int
the brontosaur, the wooly mammoth, and the dodo.
Illustrated.

945. Reader: The first reading book. 1973, 31 p.

Story of the Ugly Duckling retold. Second section   lit   int
consists of pairs of questions followed by two para-
graph stories which answer the questions.

946. Reader: Hansel and Gretel. 1973, 21 p.

The traditional fairy tale retold. Illustrated.   lit   int

947. Reader: Iffy, the boy who got his wish, Teacher's copy.
        1974, 40 p.

Fairy tale about an unhappy prince who wants to be   lit   int
a frog. Illustrated. See "Reader: Ants are interesting" above for format.

948. Reader: The ivory reading book. 1973, 44 p.

Factual discussion of the moon. Second section   lit   int
consists of series of questions and answers about
this reading material and others in the series.

949. Reader: The lemon yellow reading book. 1973, 24 p.

Story of the little red hen. Major portion of book   lit   int
consists of a series of questions and answers about
this and other stories.

950. Reader: The lion and the mouse. 1973, 11 p.

Aesop's fable about the value of even the smallest   lit   int
of friends, retold. Illustrated.

APPENDIX II   cont'd

951.   Reader: Maxine's mystery. 1973, 11 p.

A little girl makes a mystery gift for Mother's   lit   int
Day. Illustrated.

952.   Reader: The mustard gold reading book. 1973, 37 p.

Story of the Gingerbread Boy retold. Second   lit   int
portion of book consists of short series of
questions and answers about this story and others.

953.   Reader: My story book. 1973, 6 p.

Story about two thoughtless boys whose games disturb lit   int
a group of frogs. Illustrated.

954.   Reader: Nancy's dumb bird / Ralph the jacks player,
         Teacher's guide. 1974, 73 p.

Two short stories -- one about a young Japanese-   lit   int
American girl who rescues a wounded bird, and one
about a young Anglo boy who loves to play jacks.
Illustrated. See "Reader: Ants are interesting"
above for format.

955.   Reader: Nelson's dream. 1973, 13 p.

Story about a young boy who dreams he goes to   lit   int
the moon with the astronauts. Illustrated.

956.   Reader: The odd little children, Teacher's copy.
         1974, 40 p.

Story about four misfits who sail off to a place   lit   int
where they will feel less lonely. Illustrated.
See "Reader: Ants are interesting" above for
format.

957.   Reader: The old woman and her geese, Teacher's copy.
         1974, 31 p.

Folk tale about a clever old woman who solves her   lit   int
problems in a roundabout way. Illustrated. See
"Reader: Ants are interesting" above for format.

958.   Reader: Penelope's adventure / Charlie the newspaper
         boy, Teacher's copy. 1974, 82 p.

Two stories, one about an adventurous Anglo girl,   lit   int
one about an urban Black boy who wants to get a
job. Illustrated. See "Reader: Ants are interesting" above for format.

APPENDIX II   cont'd

959.   Reader: Peter plays baseball / A day in the life of
           Maribel, Teacher's copy.   1974, 80 p.

       Two stories, one about a young Anglo boy learning   lit   int
       to play baseball, one about a day in the life of
       a young Chicana farm worker.   Illustrated.   See
       "Reader: Ants are interesting" above for format.

960.   Reader: Pinocchio, Parts I and II, Teacher's copy.
           1974, 72 p.

       The traditional Italian story retold.   Illustrated.   lit   int
       See "Reader: Ants are interesting" above, for
       format.

961.   Reader: The proud peacock, Teacher's copy.   1974,
           38 p.

       Story about a peacock who learns a lesson about   lit   int
       humility.   Illustrated.   See "Reader: Ants are
       interesting" above for format.

962.   Reader: The robin's egg blue reading book.   1973,
           39 p.

       Folk tale about the Little Red Hen and the Sly   lit   int
       Fox retold.   Second portion of book consists of
       series of questions and answers about this story
       and others.

963.   Reader: The second reading book.   1973, 29 p.

       Short story about a visit to the zoo.   Major   lit   int
       portion of book consists of series of pairs of
       questions, followed by two paragraph stories
       which answer the questions.

964.   Reader: Signs and signals / Mass communication, Teacher's
           copy.   1974, 70 p.

       Factual discussion of various systems of communi-   lit   int
       cation from hand signals to television.   Illustra-
       ted.   See "Reader: Ants are interesting" above
       for format.

965.   Reader: The tangerine reading book.   1973, 43 p.

       Aesop's fables of the Hare and the Tortoise and   lit   int
       The Boy Who Cried Wolf.   Large portion of book
       consists of short series of questions and answers
       about these and other stories.

APPENDIX II cont'd

966.   Reader: The third reading book. 1973, 27 p.

Story about the unhappy fate of a rabbit's new hat.   lit   int
Major portion of book consists of series of pairs
of questions, each pair followed by a two para-
graph story answering these questions.

967.   Reader: Two fables. 1973, 16 p.

Aesop's fables of the Wind and the Sun and The   lit   int
Grasshopper and the Ant retold. Illustrated.

968.   Reader: The ugly duckling. 1973, 9 p.

Hans Christian Andersen's story retold. Illus-   lit   int
trated.

969.   Reader: What happened to Blossom Bunny's new hat?
       1973, 8 p.

Story about the unhappy fate of a rabbit's new hat.   lit   int
Illustrated.

970.   Reader: Why the country mouse went back home. 1973,
       5 p.

Shortened version of Aesop's fable about the City   lit   int
Mouse and the Country Mouse. Illustrated.

971.   Reader: The zoo book. 1973, 15 p.

Factual discussion of zoos and a story about a   lit   int
visit to a zoo. Illustrated.

972.   Reading strand, primer lessons, Vol. 1, 1a, 2. 1973
       199 p.

Fifteen detailed lesson plans intended as a bridge   meth   prim
between reading isolated words and/or simple   voc
sentences and reading texts. First grade level.

973.   Reading strand, level C, Vol. 1-11. 1973, 845 p.

Sixty-two detailed lesson plans centering around   meth   int
various reading materials. Second grade level.   voc

974.   Reading strand, Level C, Navajo Unit. 1974, 25 p.

Three detailed lesson plans centering around   meth   int
three traditional Navajo stories (in English).
Second grade level.

APPENDIX II cont'd

975. Reading strand, level C, Vol. 1-3 (second series).
          1974, 232 p.

          Twenty-seven detailed lesson plans centering around   meth int
          various reading texts. Second grade level.

976. Reading strand, level C, Teacher's guide and supplements.
          1973, 84 p.

          Explanation of the theory behind the CITE reading   meth self
          lessons and the methods used to implement these   theor col
          theories.

977. Reading test booklets: 1-4, 6-9, 11-14, 16-19 (some
          Teacher's editions). 1973, 300 p.

          Each page has one short paragraph from which readers   lit   prim
          are to extrapolate a question which the paragraph .
          answers. Teacher's editions have question printed
          below paragraph. First grade level.

978. Reading test booklets: lessons 1-4, 6-9, 11-16, 18-23,
          25-29, 31-34, 36-41, 50-54, 56-61 (Some Teacher's
          copies). 1973, 15 p. per lesson.

          Each page contains one short paragraph from which   lit   int
          readers are to extrapolate a question which the
          paragraph answers. Teacher's copies have question
          printed below text. Second grade level.

979. Rhetoric: oral interpretation, Vol. 1-3, 1973, 398 p.

          Twenty-five detailed lesson plans. Practice in   meth int
          reading comprehension and reading aloud with ex-   pron
          pression. Emphasis on English intonation and
          stress patterns. For second grade.

980. Sentence reading, Vol. 1-5. 1972, 1018 p.

          Ninety detailed lesson plans. Provides practice   meth prim
          in reading English sentences and in completing such   gram
          sentences which have missing words. Progresses to
          construction of sentences from given words. First
          grade level.

981. Sight and sound rhyme book. 1970, 77 p.

          Seven traditional rhymes including Baa Baa Black   lit   prim
          Sheep, Hey Diddle Diddle. Each story on different
          color paper. Illustrated.

APPENDIX II cont'd

982. Spelling, Vol. 1-13 (Vol. 10 missing). 1973, 786 p.

Ninety-three detailed lesson plans plus three
spelling games. Aim is to teach students the
basic rules of English orthography. Spelling
books accompany these lessons and are listed
alphabetically below. Second grade level.

    voc   int
    script

983. Spelling, Teacher's guide. 1973, 26 p.

Explanation of theory behind lesson plans described above, and methods for implementing theory.

    theor self
    meth col

984. Spelling book: exceptional verbs, Part I. 1974, 27 p.

Workbook providing practice in the recognition
and formation of past tense of English "irregu-
lar" verbs, such as to be, to buy, etc. Second
grade level. Answers provided at back of book.

    gram int

985. Spelling book: Fire engine red. 1974, 30 p.

Provides practice in forming English syllables,
recognizing correct syllable to begin a word,
recognizing correct word in a minimal pair,
writing English sentences. Concentrates on short
vowels. Illustrated. Second grade level.

    script int
    voc

986. Spelling book: Fire engine red, Teacher's copy. 1974,
     30 p.

Same as above, with correct answers filled in.

    script int
    voc

987. Spelling book: The homonym dictionary. 1974, 19 p.

Dictionary of words that have homonyms. Each word
of a homonym pair is listed alphabetically and
defined, then cross referenced to its homonym.
Second grade level.

    voc   int

988. Spelling book: Lemon yellow. 1974, 24 p.

Provides practice in forming English syllables,
recognizing correct syllable to complete a word,
recognizing correct word in minimal pair, writing
English words. Concentrates on long vowels.
Illustrated. Second grade level.

    script int
    voc

989. Spelling book: The past tense of verbs. 1974, 25 p.

Provides practice in forming past tense of 'reg-
ular' verbs. Answer sheets at back of book.
Illustrated. Second grade level.

    gram int

APPENDIX II cont'd

990. Spelling book: The plural of nouns. 1974, 24 p.

Workbook provides practice in formation and recog-   gram int
nition of plural forms of English nouns. Illustrated. Answers at back of book. Second grade
level.

991. Spelling book: The possessive of nouns. 1974, 34 p.

Workbook provides practice in formation of   gram int
possessive of English nouns, and differentiation
between possessive and plural forms. Answers at
back of book. Illustrated. Second grade level.

992. Spelling book: Present participle of verbs.

Workbook provides practice in recognizing and   gram int
forming present participle of English verbs.
Answer sheet at back of book. Illustrated.
Second grade level.

993. Spelling book: Sky blue. 1974, 29 p.

Workbook provides practice in distinguishing   voc int
between homonyms and supplying the missing word   script
of a homonym pair. Second grade level.

994. Spelling book: The superlative of adjectives. 1974,
12 p.

Workbook provides practice in choosing adjec-   gram int
tives and their superlatives and using them to   voc
complete sentences. Illustrated. Second grade
level.

995. Spelling book: Tangerine. 1974, 34 p.

Workbook provides practice in forming English   script int
syllables, recognizing correct syllable to com-   voc
plete a word, recognizing correct words in a
minimal pair, writing English sentences. Concentrates on long and short vowels followed by
'le/ll' and 'ke/ck'. Illustrated. Second grade
level.

996. Spelling book: Tangerine, Teacher's copy. 1974, 34 p.

Same as above, but with correct answers filled in.   script int
voc

APPENDIX II cont'd

997. Spelling book: The third person singular. 1974, 21 p.

Workbook provides practice in forming the third   gram   int
person singular of English verbs. Illustrated.
Answers provided in back of book. Second grade
level.

998. Syntax, units 1-39, 42, 45-53. 1972, 1816 p.

Three hundred and thirty-seven detailed lesson   voc   prim
plans introducing oral English vocabulary, sentence   gram
structure and sentence types, through group activities, games, etc. Ascending order of difficulty.
Kindergarten and first grade level.

999. Teaching for learning. 1974, 55 p.

Explanation and examples of basic teaching tech-   meth   col
niques used throughout CITE curriculum. Includes   theor   self
specific techniques for correction, verification,
etc.

1000. Visual strand, units 1-4, 8-14. 1971, 386 p.

Fifty-four detailed lesson plans. Aim is to   meth   prim
develop visual motor abilities and visual per-
ceptions to facilitate later reading and writing.
Kindergarten level.

1001. Vocabulary strand. 1974, 21 p.

Three dummy lesson plans to be filled in with   voc   int
details from vocabulary context sheets and out-
lines. Aim is to review known vocabulary and
introduce new words. Second grade level.

1002. Vocabulary strand, Vol. 3. 1973, 77 p.

Series of six detailed lesson plans. Aim is to   voc   int
familiarize students with various English words,
and to have them use these words in sentences.
Second grade level.

1003. Vocabulary book: The copper penny. 1974, 73 p.

Series of seven stories about children taking   voc   int
trips, hiking, horseback riding, etc. Vocabu-   lit
lary words are underlined in text. Illustrated.
Second grade level.

APPENDIX II   cont'd

1004.   Vocabulary context sheets and outlines. 1974, 151 p.

    Sixty short stories, each one featuring one vocab-   voc   int
    ulary word. To be used with lesson plans des-   lit
    cribed above. Some stories use anagram of word,
    rather than word itself, e.g., ozo for zoo.
    Second grade level.

1005.   Vocabulary, Teacher's guide. 1974, 13 p.

    Discussion of theory behind lessons described above   theor self
    and methodology for implementing this theory.   meth col

1006.   Word reading, series 1, Vol. 4-8 (1-3 missing). 1972,
    573 p.

    Seventy detailed lesson plans. Goal is to teach   voc   prim
    student to associate given 'words' with given
    symbols and to distinguish between minimal pairs of
    words. A preparation for reading. Not all words
    used are real English words. First grade level.

1007.   Word reading strand, series 2, Vol. 4. 1973, 62 p.

    Five detailed lesson plans to serve as a bridge   voc   int
    between earlier Word reading lessons and Spelling
    lessons. Reviews words already seen and has stu-
    dents break them into syllables and individual
    letters. Second grade level.

INDEX

Alakayak, Anecia - 795

Al'ankut qimugtait - 809

Al'aq's family's dogs - 809

Alaska Native Education
 Board - 697, 698

Alaska Native Language
 Center - 22-27, 140, 145,
 169, 205, 207-219, 221,
 222, 226, 229, 230, 239,
 240, 242, 248, 325, 327-
 331, 338-340, 649-660,
 662, 691-693, 700, 716

Alaska Native Language
 Center report 1973 - 140

Alaska State Language
 Center - 123-126, 227, 231,
 237, 238, 241, 244, 246,
 661, 663-669, 721

Alaska State-Operated School
 System - 4, 113-117, 138,
 146-149, 170-184, 243, 270,
 301-320, 324, 326, 332-337,
 341-343, 345, 707, 726, 727,
 731-738, 753

Áłástsii - 461

Alberta Native Communications
 Society - 88

Albert, Roy - 128

Alexander, J. T. -45

Alexie, Anna - 840

Alexie, Joe - 796

Ałk'idą́ą́ ádahóót iidii
 beeháníihígíí baa hane' - 480

Ałk'idą́ą́' bisóodi shiłįį' nít'éé'
 - 509

Ałk'idą́ą́' diné yee dahináanii
 baa hane' - 516

Ałk' idą́ą́' jiní - 468

Ałk'dą́ą́' 'oozéé'asdiid jiní -
 490

All about me - 812

Allagich igluŋich Inupiat - 165

Allagit allaniarit - 245

Allen, Shonnie - 364

Allen, T. D. - 867

Alphabet - 191

Alquux tutat - 4

Alrakum qupai - 773

Alvarez, Albert - 592,593,617

American Baptist Publication
 Society - 46

American Bible Society - 30,
 127, 454, 455, 797

American Indian culture and
 the reading program - 894

American Indian education, a
 selected bibliography, supplement no. 1 - 885

American Indians: an annotated
 bibliography of selected library resources - 868

Amirlucuar - 774

Amucalu - 599

Analgaam qikmii - 660

Analgaam qimmiŋi - 145

Aŋalgaam qimmini - 243

Analytical bibliography of Navajo reading materials - 437

Anatomical atlas of the Navajo - 441

Andersen, Hans Christian -
762

Anderson, Anne - 83

Anderson, Marjorie - 365

Anderson, Theodore - 857

Andrew, Annie - 798

Andrew, George - 799

Andrew, Helen - 800

Andrew, Maxie - 801

Angaginaagamagis tunumkaasaqangis - 5

Angaiak, John - 791, 802

Angalgaam qimugtai - 775

Angnilria asriq issuri-
yagaq - 813

Angulan kegeluneq-llu - 759

Animal book - 318

Animal book, duck - 198

Animal, fish and birds -
345

Animal stories of the Kobuk
River Eskimos - 261-263

Animals of our land-caribou
197

Annotated bibliography of
young people's books on
American Indians - 869,878

Annuǵaavut paŋmapak - 188

Annuǵarriugniq niǵrutit
amiŋiññiñ - 152

Annutit iqaluk tinmiat - 170

Antell, Lee - 868

Antell, Will - 868

Anuℓhuyuk - 218

Anuqlirtuq- 833

Aŋŋuttit qaluich tiŋmiuratlu - 171

Aŋun aŋuniaqtuaq taǵiumi - 189

Aoki, Haruo - 582

Apamitanoč natohosčič - 97

Apassingok - 649

Apatiki, E. - 658

Apayauq made a friend - 190

Apayauq paannaliuqtuq - 190

Appendix to a new perspective
on American Indian linguistics -
592

Aptitude, content and method of
teaching word recognition with
young American Indian children -
890

Apuyyaq - 153

Aqargig tulugaq ugrugnauraglu -
221, 237

Aragon, Claude - 525, 526

Arctic women's workshop - 160

Are you my mother - 185, 764

Arirqanek nuyalek pinga'un
tan'erlit-hlu - 23

Arithmetics - 12

Arnaq pingayun-llu angutet and
tutgara'urluq arnassagaq-llu-
823

Arts and crafts - 430

Aseriyagaq issuriyagaq - 814

Ashdla'go shibee ákohwiinidzinii-
520

Assumptions for bilingual instruction in the primary
grades of Navajo schools-581

At Colville: a story in the
Spokane language - 688

Ataataluqiik - 217

Atchagat - 191

Atcitty, Marlene - 456-458, 527

Atightughyuggaaghusit - 650

Atightumerg liinnaqellghet
I, II - 661

Atightumum liinnaqusit - 669

Atightuusim aallghi - 651

Atka Village, Alaska - 5-21

Atkan Aleut primer - 7

Atkan fishes - 11

Atkan plants - 16

Ats'iís - 466

Atuutit mumiksat - 258

Atx̂am hitnisangis - 16

Atx̂am kugan mataliin
angaĝiilazas - 10

Atx̂am qangis - 11

Atx̂ax̂ matal txin agunaa - 21

Auaqqanam quliaqtannik - 169

Austin, Martha - 364

Autiobiography - 228

Avelngayagaq kameksiigka-llu - 754

Avilaitqatigiik - 208

Avilaitqatigiik worksheets - 242

Awee chideeldlo - 513

Ayamitata ininimohin - 98

Ayaryaq, John - 228

Ayóo honishoi - 487

Ayugenerilenguut yuut - 842

Ayumiim ungipaghaatangi I -662,649

Ayumiim ungipaghaatangi II - 652

B

Baa' - 471

Baby's first laugh - 513

Badger, Herbert A. - 74

247

Bibliography on materials in the field of Indian education - 889

Bibliography; Seneca language - 642

Big Cove Band Council - 351, 352

Big-teeth - 811

Bik'ehgo nánidizídí - 396

Bilagáana bizaad bihoo'aah - 450

Bilingual/bicultural education - 866

Bilingual-bidialectal switching strand - 537

Bilingual education for American Indians - 865

Bilingual schooling in the United States, Vol. II - 857

Billy Aanda - 705

Bird book - 707

Birds and Animals of our land - 203

Birds, fish and animals - 170, 171, 182-184

Bits'áá dóó ho sé líí í gíí - 510

Black, Robert - 129

Black Mountain boy - 532

Blackbird, Elmer - 590

Blackhorse, Berneice - 370, 464

Blair, Robert W. - 369

Blanchett - 205, 229, 230

Blanchett, Marie - 759, 769, 771, 803-808, 812, 828, 831

Blinky - 778

Blueye, Esther - 638, 639

Boas, Franz - 269, 896, 897

Bodega Miwok dictionary - 353

Bonvillain, Nancy - 356, 357

Book of things you will never see - 142

Books about Indians - 880

Books for teachers and children - 873

Born to die - 398

Boy and the bird - 612

Boy and the seal - 22

Boy who ate too much - 850

Boyer, Mildred - 857

Bread is in the oven - 601

Breakthrough Navajo - 444

Breckman, Kathleen - 821

Breiby, John - 763

Bright, William - 348

Brisebois-Ward, Michele - 361

British Columbia Intercultural Curriculum Project - 882

Brow - 205

Brown, Harvey - 231

Brown Bear goes to school - 187

Bruce doo biⱢ hóóts'i idda - 366

Brugge, David M. - 544, 545

Buechel, Eugene - 675

Building of Atka Island - 21

Bureau of Indian Affairs - 58, 84, 101, 118, 453, 528-530, 548, 549, 595, 646, 676, 685, 739, 855, 858, 864, 865, 867, 869-871, 878, 887, 891-893

Burns, Wanda S. - 367

Bushotter, George - 676

But it can't wear glasses - 535

C

C and Sid - 566

Caarkat Goldilocksaamek - 844

Caarkat upsankunek - 845

Cacirkat - 706, 816

Cahuilla texts with an introduction - 44

Calendar for October 1974 - September 1975 - 396

Caliluta aquiluta-llu - 807

Callaghan, Catherine - 353, 354

Callaway, Sydney M. - 531

Can you read - 13

Can you read English? Then you can also read Eskimo - 249

Canada. Curriculum Division, Department of Education, Northwest Territories - 105-109, 139, 142-144, 166, 872

Canada. Department of Citizenship and Immigration, Education Division, Indian Affairs Branch - 875

Canada. Department of Indian Affairs and Northern Development - 95-98, 159-161, 163, 164, 206, 228, 234, 235, 247, 267, 588, 589, 872, 873

Canadian Arctic Producers - 160

Canek amllernek nallunritua -776

Carlson, Barry F. - 619, 688

Carlson, Vada - 532

Carnegie Corporation Cross-Cultural Education Project of the University of Chicago - 59

Caroll, Janet F. - 94

Cartel - 859, 860

Cat anerteqellriit; unguvalriit naunraat-llu - 761

Cat assikek'nganka - 777

Catalogue of linguistic manuscripts in the library of the Bureau of American ethnology - 900

Catching seal with a seal net -156

Cathey, Wallace - 525, 526, 533

Caucium piniun'llu - 792

Cree alphabet book - 84

Cree language - 87

Cree legends - 99

Crittenden, Carl - 63

Crowder, Jack L. - 373, 374

Crying on the beach - 296

Cufe horkopv - 629

Curious George - 843

Curious kid - 551

Curriculum guidelines for
  the skills of English - 565

Curriculum guide for beginning non-English speaking
  children - 547

Curriculum program for the
  Apache language - 38

D

Daałtł'idzee tok'eekaa - 295

Daan náhásdįį' - 496

Dah diniighaazh - 502

Da'iidą - 456

Dall, W. H. - 135

Damron, Rex - 684

Dan and his pets, Books one
  to five - 525

Dan and his pets, Teacher's
  manual - 526

Dart, Diane - 813, 814, 842

Dauenhauer, Nora -709, 713,714

Dauenhauer, Richard - 718,
  720, 721

Davis, Bertha M. - 546

Davis, Henry A. - 710, 711, 717,
  718

Davis, Ruth - 547

Day with Johnny - 305

Deel tsa aa dil-aa
  k'idogheełtaan - 299

Deestsin - 505

Deezbaa' - 457

Demientieff - 217

Demit, Fred - 703, 704

Dennis, Helen - 735, 736

Dennison, Johnson - 465

Denny, Annie - 696, 699

Densmore, Frances - 616, 677

Denunzio, Vincent - 548, 549

Descriptive grammar of Mississippi
  Choctaw - 74

Dialogue on the Navajo classifier - 386

DIAND - see Canada. Department
  of Indian Affairs & Northern
  Development

Dibaa asdlaan - 284

Dick, Galena - 466

Dick, Lynda - 375, 467

Dictionary of Mesa Grande
  Diegueño - 103

253

Downing, Todd - 76

Druck, Leah - 304-313

Duhtot'ił - 734

Dukt'ootł' - 714

Duncan, Homer - 376

Dzilth-Na-O-Dith-Hle Boarding
  School - 550

E

Eagle hunt - 130

Earth - 603, 793

Eastman, P. D. - 764

Eber, Dorothy - 111

Educational model for planned
  intervention in language development - 684

Edenso, Christine - 126

Egacuyiit kenurraita tanqiit -
  779

Ehanni ottunkakan - 680

Ehem - 600

Ehpit - 610

Ehtaste likotok - 609

Elementary education in the
  Northwest Territories - 872

Elementary Saulteaux - 624

Elements of Atkan Aleut - 8

Eli posonutekhotimok - 608

Elitnauram ayuqucia - 799

Ella iquilnguq - 751

Ellis, C. Douglas - 29, 85

Elluarlua auluklerkaga wangnek -
  824

Elluarrlua wangnek auluklerkaga -
  817

English as a second language
  on the Navajo reservation - 528

English-Dakota dictionary - 683

English for American Indians - 891

English-Mohawk dictionary,
  Parts I and II - 356

English-Wappo dictionary - 744

Enoch, Lincoln - 815

Enochs, J. B. - 470

Enrichment material for first
  and second year language laboratory program for "A course
  in spoken English for Navajos" - 529

Epistle of Paul the apostle to
  the Romans - 127

Erenerput - 780

Erkloo - 161

Ervin, Jessie - 707

Eskimo-Aleut - 120

Eskimo games - 267

Eskimo language course - 234

Eskimo Language Workshop - 751,
  752, 754-796, 798-831, 833-854

Eskimo reading course I-II
- 251

Eskimo's way of living -
852

Espons ali ehemuhke - 607

Estowen netty momen nere tek-
vpihoc vhvks - 625

Estrada, Beatrice - 876

Ethnological dictionary of
the Navajo language - 378

Every year - seasonal ac-
tivities - 609

Everyday Lakota; and English-
Sioux dictionary for be-
ginners - 679

Explanation of the sounds
used in Koyukon - 274

Eyeglasses - 611

F

Fairbanks Native Association -
136, 137, 271-273, 300, 694,
695, 725

Fasthorse, Rose - 377, 463

Feeling, Durbin - 54

Fickett, Joan - 723

Fields, Mary - 314-316

Fiitt, Nena - 317

First catch - 788

First reader - 650

First year Tlingit I-VI - 721

Fish that Pete could not
catch - 831, 839

Florendo, Nora - 721

Fluency first: instructor
training course - 883

Fly - 599

Following the crowd - 401

Football, Virginia - 106

For Christian boys and girls -
402

Forshaug, Jean - 820

Fort George Federal School
staff and students - 96

Foster - 233

Four food groups - 330

Four seasons - 773

Fox and the wolf - 580

Francis, Beatrice - 356

Francis, Gordon - 351

Franciscan fathers - 378

Frank, Jeanette - 368

Frantz, Donald G. - 41

Fredson - 338-340

Frog and the mouse and Why the
bear has a short tail - 737

From Cree to English, part one:
the sound system - 90

Fulton, Sylvia - 821

257

Grammar of Spokan - 619

Grammar of the Ojibwa language - 587

Grammar of the Serrano language - 643

Grammar of Tuscarora - 724

Grammar rules - 192

Grandfather stories of the Navajo - 531

Grant, Paul Warcloud - 678

Graustein, Jean McCarthy - 878

Gray, Arthur - 236

Gray, Minnie - 236

Greedy monkey - 405

Green, John - 739

Gregorio, Juan - 617

Grimes, J. Larry - 741

Guide to the spoken Blackfeet Indian language into English - 42

Guide to Title VII ESEA bilingual bicultural projects 1973-1974 - 862

Guide to understanding Chipewyan I - 67

Guide to understanding Chipewyan II - 70

Gunther, Erna - 719

Gwandaii Łuk neehiniidal - 345

Gwich'in "ABC" dehtŁy'aa - 328

Gwich'in ginjik dehtŁy'aa - 321

Gwich'in poems - 327

Gwich'in stories - 326

Gwich'in workbook - 329

H

Haa'isha'da 'iidiiltah - 506

Haa'ishá diné bizaad deiídiiltah - 379

Haalá wolyé - 479

Ha'at'iisha' shighi' hólǫ - 524

Hadohudigi-eeyah - 290

Hadohudigi-eeyah - 291

Hadohzil-eeyah - 279

Haida language workshop reader - 124

Haida noun dictionary - 123

Haida word lists, Vol. 1 - 125

Hail, Raven - 45, 46

Haile, Berard - 381, 382

Hale, Benny - 571

Hale, Horatio E. - 268

Hale, Kenneth - 351, 383, 384, 391, 392, 554, 593

Hall, Geraldine - 385

Hamaa hlax̂ aasal isugix̂ - 22

Hand chart book to accompany Bruce doo BiŁ hóóts 'íid da - 459

Hand chart book to accompany
the curious kid - 552

Handbook for teachers and
aides of the Choctaw bilingual education program - 77

Handbook for teachers of primary
reading of the Yup'ik language -
828

Hane' ya'át'éehii Jesus Christ
bee yisdá'iildéehii - 447

Harkins, Arthur M. - 879

Harvey, Frank - 472

Harvey, Judy - 473-477

Harvey, Pauline - 264-266

Has tįį ts'ó sí - 507

Haskie and the ye'ii bicheii
- 373

Haskie dóó yé'ii bicheii - 373

Hastiin ch'ahii - 473

Hastoí táá - 474

Have you ever seen a walrus -
166

Here's Jack - 806, 821

Here's Sailaq - 239

Hen - 600

Henderson, Jerry - 478

Henry, David - 274-293

Henry, Kay - 277-281

He died in our place -
406

He does it, Euna Rose - 101

Health unit - 824

Hedges, Betty Lou - 853

Hell: eternal suffering - 407

Hello, tree - 575

Helpful hints for new BIA
teachers - 530

Helps for bible study - 446

Higgins, Roger - 386

Hilaakax̂t ii - 13

Hilada - 18

Hilal aluĝil - 14

Hilaqulim adungizulax - 17

Hilda - 464

Hill, Faith - 387

Hill, Jane - 102

Hill, Kenneth - 643

Hindle, Lonnie - 121

Ho dee yáá dą́ą́' hane 'ii - 448

Hobsen, Dottie - 514

Hoffman, Virginia - 555, 556

Hofmann, T.R. - 110, 119

Hogan, Lawrence - 597

Hoijer, Harry - 388, 389, 431,
432, 722

Holder, Preston - 897

Iroquois book of rites - 268

It was told that the Hopi
tribe was extinct - 490

It's me - 834

It's windy - 833

J

Jack, Noah - 824

Jack and the beanstalk -
804

Jackson, E. - 207

Jaglinski, Carol L. - 878

Jamassee, Nicotye - 164

James, Susie - 713

Jasper - 503

Jesus Baahane' - 484

Jesus nankak gwaadaai vagnanaak
gwedhaa dai' - 322

Jesus-num inuuƚha - 260

Jesus-ŋum in̄uuƚhanik - 236

Jessen, Mariana - 864

Jicarilla Apache Cultural Awareness Program - 31-34, 39, 40

Jicarilla Apache legends - 31

Jidii aƚtsan - 333

Jidii dintth'ak - 301, 302, 334,
335

Jidii t'inchy'sa - 303

Jii nạạị t'ee shalak - 336

Jimerson, Shirley D. - 697, 698

Joe, Anna Rose - 766

Joe and his happy family, Book
one and two - 533

John, Alfred - 705, 706

Johnny - 304

Johnny at the "Bay" - 315

Johnny dóó Willie - 463

Johnny goes hunting - 107, 342

Johnny goes to Yellowknife - 108

Johnny N.C. co Noozhii - 315

Johnny nahaazhrii - 342

Johnny vagoodƚit drin - 337

Johnny's present - 337

Johnsen, Richard - 457

Johnson, Broderick H. - 556

Johnson, Frank - 714

Jóhonaa'éi dóó nahasdzáán - 523

Jok drin Johnny dee'ya' - 305

Jonathan, Mildred - 696

Jones, Eliza - 281, 296

Jones, Helen Bimmer - 642

Joseph and his cow - 613

K

K'adoants'idnee - 297

Kalifornsky, P. - 691, 692

Kameksagka - 782

Kanavurak, B. - 239

Kane, Katy - 559

Kanearakgtar - 797

Kaneshiro, V. - 652-657, 669-671

Kari, James - 393, 560, 691-693

Karol, J ɔph - 679

Kaschube, Dorothea - 100

Kaukaq naucetaarpak-llu - 804

Kaveolook, Harold - 165, 240

Kaviaq angniilnguq - 826

Kaviarem kavirillra - 848

Kavirelit kalikanka - 820

Kavirliq Nacacuar - 783

Kayak, Lily - 166

Kee's home; a beginning Navajo-English reader - 385

Kéet - 710

Kéet, teaching unit - 711

Kegguterpalek - 811

Keim, Geri - 767, 825, 826

K'eƚa sukdu - 692

Kenai Tanaina noun dictionary - 693

Ker esan texts, two volumes - 269

Kess, Joseph - 122

Key to the Cree syllabic characters - 84

Keys to reading Apache - 35

Kii - 469

Kilpatrick, Anna G. - 53

Kinalda - 571

Kindergarten curriculum guide for Indian children - 562, 858, 864

Kingfisher Indian day school students - 86

Kipnuk Bilingual Team - 827

Kisitchisa qulinuaglaan - 195

Kiyahtaƚha Jesus Christ-m - 672

Kluckhohn, Clyde - 561

Koolerk, Paul - 235

K'os - 521

Koyuk reader - 270

Koyukon Cultural Enrichment Program - 282-293

Krause, Aurel - 719

Krauss, Michael - 120, 140

Kruege, John R. - 620

Kudatan kahídee - 717

Kuipers, Aert Hendrik - 690

Kukec - 606

Kuk'uq - 849

Kuliaktuak inuusiagun Jesus -
252

Kul'tilakessaaq pingayun'llu
taqukaat - 784

Kulusiinkut - 665

Kulusiq - 666

Kumluc'kaq - 762

Kutchin "ABC" workbook - 328

Kutchin Bilingual Teachers -
319

Kutchin literacy workbook -
344

Kutiq - 155

L

Lahkota project - 682

Lake Miwok dictionary -
354

Lamb and the party - 365

Lancaster, Louise - 28

Lande, Winifred - 828

Langdon, Margaret - 104

Language acquisition, Vol. 1
- 439

Language and related characteristics of 1968 Haskell
Institute students - 877

Language arts curriculum -
558

Language arts portion of
the CITE curriculum - 559

Language in American
Indian education: a news-
letter of the Office of
Education Programs - 892, 893

Language of the Sioux - 685

Language variation among the
Duckwater Shoshoni - 644

Languages of the tribes of
the extreme Northwest - 135

Lataput - 653

Latugîng - 15

Laughter: the Navajo way - 443

Lawrence, Erma - 123-125

Lazy mouse - 216, 768

Learning English - 450

Learning Navajo, Vol. I
& II - 382

Learning to read Navajo -
409

Learning to write Navajo - 387

Leavitt, Marie - 229, 241

Leer, Jeffry - 26

Lesson plans for kindergarten through third grade,
Vol. 1-4 - 634

Lessons and games for Iñupiaq
as a second language - 209

LEREC: learning English as a
second language through
recreation - 141

Let us rise - Passamaquoddy
songs for dancing - 615

Mahtoqehs naka malson - 605

Ma'ii dóó náshdóí baa hane'
- 497

Main features of Malecite -
Passamaquoddy grammar - 350

Maketacuaraanka - 802

Making clothing from animal
skins - 152

Making rope from sealskin -
151

Malguk quliaqtuak: aahaaliglu,
aniqpaktuaq aviŋŋaq - 210

Malguk quliaqtuak: aahaalliglu
piayaaŋillu; aŋiqpaktuaq
aviŋŋaq - 240

Mali naka tahahsumol - 604

Mallard named "Splash" -
805

Man goes hunting on the ocean -
189

Mančata - 95

Manning, Allen - 364

Many Goats, Betty - 364

Manual of Navaho grammar -
381

Manual of sentence patterns for
teaching English as a second
language -876

Maqaruaq, tan'gerliq, usvituli-
llu - 830

Maring, Joel - 1

Marken, Jack Walter - 881

Marsh, Bruce D. - 21

Martin, Judy - 395, 479

Mary and her horse - 604

Mathematics worksheets - 819

Mather, Elsie - 216, 768

Mathiot, Madeleine - 594, 595

Matter and energy - 792

Medenildiy - 696

Meet Cree - 94

Meganack, Seraphim - 27

Meyoryuk students - 831, 839

Michelson, Gunther - 358

Mic-Mac alphabets and Mic-
Mac phonetics - 352

Migémeóeöögemg - 351

Milanowski, Paul G. - 701-707

Miller, Wick R. - 2, 645

Milliea, Mildred - 352

Minnerly, Carol - 28

Minnesota Historical Society -
73

Minnesota State Department of
Education - 585

Miscellanea Selica IV: an interim
Moses' Columbia (Wenatchee)
Salishan vocabulary - 620

Miscellaneous stories - 6

Mister Goat's new hogan - 568

Mitchell, Charlie - 480, 481

Mitchell, Marjorie - 882

Miyaoka, Osahito - 832

Modern Native Americans: a
  selective bibliography - 879

Mohawk morphology - 355

Mohawk Staff of Salmon River
  Central School - 359, 360

Mojave language notes - 363

Montour, Doris K. - 361

Moon and the sun - 796

Morack, Kathy - 833

Morgan, William - 371, 373,
  396, 397, 436, 453

Moses - 306

Moses khya t'ah'in ts'a'
  Łuk kee'in nilii - 307

Moses nahaazhrii - 308

Moses tsal nya' ohtsuu -
  309

Moses tsee keechee'yaa - 310

Moses va'ai - 343

Moses vats'at - 311

Moses vitr'ii' - 341

Moshinsky, Julius B. - 618

Mósiłgai - 458

Mosquito - 718

Mother Nature at work - 576

Mountain of thirst - 19

Mourning dove - 855

Mouse and the man - 815

Mouse saves his uncle - 299

Mouse story - 692

Mouse that went away - 798

Mueller, Richard - 320-324, 344

Mullen, Dana - 141

Mullen, Diana - 883, 884

Multi-media resource list; Indian and Eskimo culture in the
  North - 863

Mulu'wetam: the first people - 102

Munro, Pamela - 363

Murdock, John - 112

Murphy, Penny - 437

Mus naka wikuwossol - 603

My alphabet - 292, 293

My best friend - 39

My family - 146, 248, 847

My grandfather - 15

My little book - 802

My mukluks - 782

My red book - 820

My story about me - 853

My uncle - 577

N

Naabeehó ashkii bijei - 410

Naabeeho 'at' a a dadine'ii -
  493

Nisenan texts and dictionary - 583

Nishnawbe News - 586

Nistam hiyiyomasiniikan - 96

Noah, Beíbel baa hane' - 451

Nolasquez, Rosinda - 102

Nolte, Nancy - 840, 841

Noorvik reader - 147

Normie's moose hunt - 294, 316

Northern Arizona Supplementary
  Education Center - 128, 379

Norton, L. - 219

Nts'aa' duhdii' - 706

Nuk'ankut - 705, 733, 770

Nuk'aq - 771

Nuk'aq ilai-llu - 808

Nuk'aq ilai' llu caliarkaput - 827

Nuk'aq's family - 770, 808

Number readiness workbook I -
  633

Numbers book - 602

Nunamtni - 786

Nunarpak - 793

Nupahlkiaq kep'arkat ililihlrat -
  24

Nuvuk aŋuniaqti - 199

Nuvuk the hunter - 199

O

Oćipe tipaćimohin - 589

Octopus - 411

ʔOʔedham neʔoki ha-káidag - 593

Oglala Sioux Culture Center - 680

Oh'-Kwe-O-Weh-Kha - 638

Ohannessian, Sirarpi - 563, 886, 887

Ohhonvyetv cokv - 631

Ohhonvyetv cokv svtuteenat - 632

Ojebway language: a manual for
  missionaries and others employed
  among the Ojebway Indians - 588

Ojibwe language: a course for
  elementary schools - 585

Old Horn, Dale - 101

Old hunting equipment for hunting
  birds and ducks - 158

Old Testament bible stories from
  Genesis - 412

Old Testament stories, book 3 -
  451

Olmstead, D. L. - 3

Omaha-Ponca language in writing:
  suggestions for a practical
  orthography - 590

Omwari - 649

One thing God wants you to do - 413

Ontario Region, DIAND - 589

Oozeva, Elinor - 672

Phillip and his family - 574

Phone, Wilma - 34

Phonology and morphology of
the Navajo language - 432

Phonology of Tuscarora - 723

Physical education guide with
English language practice drills
for teachers of Navajo kindergarten and primary school children - 579

Pictures from my life - 111

Pietroforte, Alfred - 750

Pilling, James C. - 899, 900

Piman shamanism and staying sickness - 617

Pingayun qimugkauyaraat - 787

Pingayut kaviighhaat - 655

Piraksrat - 157

Pit'eqarraalria - 788

Pitseolak - 111

Plains Cree: a grammatical
study - 93

Plan for fluency first - 884

Platero, Dillon - 564

Platero, Paul - 427-429, 470,
487, 488

Playful little seal - 813

Pono, Filomena - 34

Pope, M. - 333-335

Powell, J. W. - 897

Powers, William K. - 685

Preparing reading materials
in Navajo - 527

Preston, Scott - 489, 490, 553

Primer V - 60

Primer V, teacher's edition - 50

Problems of Navajo speakers in
learning English - 543

Programmed guide to Navajo
transcription - 368

Psalms, Genesis, Isaiah - 233

Ptarmigan and the owl - 772

Ptarmigan, raven and shrew - 221

Pulte, William - 54-56

Pulu, T. - 332-335, 345

Q

Qaillun irniaruat piurtellrat - 795

Qanemcicuaraak angalgaam - 789

Qanemcika wangnek - 853

Qaneryarat ayagnerita nepait - 760

Qanganacuar - 767

Qanganaq meqsartulria - 835

Qangpiiyaaq tulukaruk angayyagaq-
llu - 854

Qangqiirenkuk iggiayuli-llu - 772

Qanuq kayuqtuq kavaiqsiruaq - 222

Qanuq kayuqtuq kaviqsiruaq - 246

Qanusimik naivik - 172

Qanusimik qinilguiñ - 173

Qanusiq naguaguiyn niġikhavgu - 174

Qepgh aghaqukut naghaaghaqukut - 668

Qessanquq avelngaq - 768

Qimalleq - 757

Qungluk liillghii pugimammeng - 656

Qunguturaq naruyayagaq - 791

Qugyucullrem kanaqlangellra - 801

Qungluk learns to swim - 656

R

Rabbit and wolf - 605

Rabbit, black bear and wise owl - 830

Race, language and culture - 896

Racoon goes chickening - 607

Radin, Paul - 745

Ramah Navajo School Board - 511

Raven and the little girl - 207

Raven flies for light - 298

Raven gets fooled - 735

Raven got fooled - 288, 289

Rawhide Press - 688, 689

Ray, Lieutenant P. H. - 112

Read - 18

Read and write - 14

Reader 1 - 729

Reader 2 - 730

Reader 3 - 731

Reading strand, level b - 541

Rebert, Robert J. - 865

Rebus reading book series - 687

Recommendations for language policy in Indian education - 874

Red Cloud Indian School - 675, 680

Redden, J. E. - 742

Redhorn, Peter - 42

Reed, Irene - 751, 752, 760, 761, 791-794, 842

Reindeer hunt on the South Side - 9

Report on Tewa portion of tri-lingual program at San Juan Elementary school 1971-1972 - 708

Reprints - 901

Research Center for Language Sciences - 594

Reulhlinger - 689

Rey, H. A. - 843

Reynolds, Margaret - 69, 70

Richardson, Marry - 71

Rides Horse, Dora - 101

Rigsby, Bruce - 121

River Times - 136, 137, 271-273, 300, 694, 695, 725

Robins, R. H. - 855

Shuswap grammatical structure - 648

Sikkuark, Nic - 142, 143

Silentman, Irene - 501-504

Simmons, Rev. Samuel - 232

Simon, Velma - 299

Simpson, Carol A. - 29

Singer, Linda - 367

Sioux Indian dictionary - 678

Sisco, Wilfred - 505, 576, 577

Sisqeyal - 611

Sit kaa kax Kana.aa - 713

Sivuqam neghyugnallghan yataaghqellghan igii - 658

Skinuhsis naka sipsis - 612

Slager, William R. - 891-893

Sloppy cowboy - 512

Slug woman - 134

Smelt fishing - 753

Smith, Adalene - 56, 57

Snigaroff, Sally - 13, 14, 22

Snowhouse - 153

Snuffy, Eye-patch and Tail - 755

Snyder, Warren A. - 621, 622

Some aspects of Navajo orthography - 557

Some helps for new Christians - 416

Some suggestions for a university program in Navajo linguistics - 560

Someday you will stand before God - 415

Son of Former Many Beads - 436

Songs in Gwich'in - 317

Songs of the Teton Sioux - 681

Songs of the Yokuts and Paiutes - 750

Sounds of Navajo: Part One - 392

Sounds of Papago - 593

Sounds that begin words - 760

South Central Regional Education Lab Corporation - 65

Southeastern Pomo grammar - 618

Southeastern State College - 82

Southern Baptist Convention - 506, 578

Southern Puget Sound Salish - 621, 622

Southwest Educational Development Laboratory - 857

Southwestern Cooperative Educational Laboratory - 866

Sovalik - 205, 231

Soveran, Marilylle - 90

Spade, Watt - 58

Spalding, Alec E. - 247

Speaking Micmac - 351

Speckle - 417

Tait, Joyce - 91

Talaswaima, Terrance - 130, 131

Talawepi, Charlie - 128

Talking Smoke - 641

Tan ktolomolsin - 614

Tan'erlinguasaaq pehlahleq - 25

Tan'gurraq nervallalleq - 850

Taqukaq ganganaq-llu - 763

Taylor, Allan R. - 43

Teacher-Aide for Navajo area -
550

Teacher's book - guide to workbook I and II - 154

Teacher's guide to accompany
Navajo music - 375, 452

Teaching English to speakers
of Choctaw, Navajo and Papago - 887

Teaching reading to the bilingual child; motivational
techniques - 546

Teaching the Eskimo syllabics -
119

Teaching the Navajo language -
397

Teeluk - 205, 229, 230

Teeluk, M. - 221, 222, 248, 762,
769-771, 791, 807, 808, 828,
834, 844-853

Teeter, Karl V. - 350

Tefft, Virginia J. - 579

Tekakwitha, Sister Catherine - 98

Telii yázhí - 465

Tell me a story - 598

Teller reader - 148

Ten-legged polar bear - 194

Ten things God wants you to know - 419

Tendi - 306

Tendi goes beaver hunting - 310

Tendi goes beaver snaring - 105

Tendi goes hunting - 308

Tendi goes trapping and fishing - 307

Tendi's blanket - 311

Tendi's canoe - 341, 738

Tendi's mossbag - 109

Tendi's snowshoes - 343

Terrapin race - 630

Tesqua and the chief's son - 106

Teton Sioux music - 677

There is only one - 420

These belong to me - 851

Thessalonians I-II - 264

Things I like - 777

Things to do - 157, 816

Things you can do - 734

This is my family - 336

Thoburn, Tina - 853

278

V

Vak'aandaii - 331

Valencia, Alilano - 866

Verwyst, Chrysostom - 72

Vicenti, Arnold - 34

Victorious Life - 376

Viers, Gerald - 511

Vocabulary of the Eskimos
of Point Barrow and Cape
Smythe - 112

Vowel and consonant charts
- 276

Vowels - 202

Vowels in Upper Tanana - 698

Vpuekv - 637

W

Wabnaki Bilingual Education
Program - 598-615

Walapai I: phonology - 742

Walker, Willard - 58-59

Wallace, Laura - 512-515

Wangnek tamalkurma - 812

Waniwa Cing'aq - 806

Waniwa cinglaq - 821

Wardie, Hazel - 740

Wascium ka Dakota riska
wowape - 683

Watchman, John - 516

Watkins, Ben - 81

Watson, Editha - 544, 545

Way of planning birth - 367

Ways I take care of myself - 817

We are reading - 279

We work and we play - 205, 807

Webster, Donald H. - 167, 168, 224,
225, 250-256

Webster, Loraine - 686-687

Werner, June - 441

Werner, Oswald - 364, 367, 368, 441

Western Apache dictionary - 36

Whale - 150

What a child does in a day - 319

What about the Eskimo - 255

What animals think - 143

What can you hear - 4, 113, 181, 301,
302, 726, 727

What can you see - 114, 115, 173

What can you smell - 116, 172, 175,
176, 333

What do you eat - 174, 177-180

What do you hear - 138, 334, 335

What do you like to eat - 117

What's the answer - 422

What is he doing - 286, 287

What is it doing - 212, 213

What is this - 303

Which church saves - 423

Which religion is right - 424

White, Emily - 362

White, Moses - 823

White Mountain Apache Culture
  Center - 35-37

Whiteriver Public Schools - 38

Whiteside, Don - 895

Who am I - 284, 285

Why he loved Christ - 425

Why the rabbit is a thief - 629

Wii makut pikanka - 851

Wiinguuq - 834

Williams, Marianne M. - 724

Wilson, Alan - 442-444

Wilson, Edward Francis - 588

Wilson, Paul - 517

Wilson, Robert D. - 581

Winnebago Tribe - 745

Winter, Werner - 743

Wishram texts - 746

Witherspoon, Gary - 531, 532

Wolfart, H. Christoph - 29, 92-94

Woman - 610

Woman and the three men and
  the grandson and the old woman - 823

Wonakine - 615

Woosh yáx̱ yaa datúwch - 712

Words of encouragement, memories
  and thoughts - 491

Words that have their true meaning - 472

Words to be matched - 204

Workbook - 673

Workbook for Goldilocks - 844

Workbook for Upsankut, 2 - 845

Workbook I - 211

Workbook Primer 1-4 - 61

Working for wages - 144

Working Indians Civil Association - 683

Worksheets - 810, 818

Worm, Elizabeth - 840

Write Navajo - 364

Writing - 846

Writing Apache - 37

Writing in the Eskimo classroom -110

Writing to create ourselves; a
  manual for teachers of English
  and creative writing in Bureau
  of Indian Affairs Secondary
  schools - 867

Wycliffe Bible Translators - 236,
  250, 321, 322, 344, 346, 347,
  445-451